Have a Little Faith

Have a Little Faith

Fixing Broken Childhoods in the Philippines

Lesley Gomez

MONARCH
BOOKS

Oxford, UK & Grand Rapids, Michigan, USA

Text copyright © 2014
Lesley Gomez
This edition copyright © 2014
Lion Hudson

The right of Lesley Gomez to be identified as the author of this work has been asserted by her in accordance with the Copyright, Designs and Patents Act 1988.

Published by Monarch Books
an imprint of
Lion Hudson plc
Wilkinson House, Jordan Hill Road,
Oxford OX2 8DR, England
Email: monarch@lionhudson.com
www.lionhudson.com/monarch

ISBN 978 0 85721 504 8
e-ISBN 978 0 85721 505 5

First edition 2014

Acknowledgments
Every effort has been made to trace the original copyright holders where required. In some cases this has proved impossible. We shall be happy to correct any such omissions in future editions.
Unless otherwise indicated, all Scripture quotations are taken from the *Holy Bible*, New Living Translation, copyright © 1996, used by permission of Tyndale House Publishers, Inc., Wheaton, Illinois 60189. All rights reserved.
Scripture quotations marked KJV are from The Authorized (King James) Version. Rights in the Authorized Version are vested in the Crown. Reproduced by permission of the Crown's patentee, Cambridge University Press.
Scripture quotation marked AMP is taken from the Amplified® Bible, Copyright © 1954, 1958, 1962, 1965, 1987 by The Lockman Foundation. Used by permission.
pp. 205, 229: *God on Mute*, by Pete Greig, p. 204, 205, 228, 229. Copyright 2007, Gospel Light/ Regal Books, Ventura, CA 93003. Used by permission.
p. 244: Lyrics from *You are Worthy of My Praise* by David Ruis. Used by permisson of Universal and Music Sales.
p. 250: Extract from a poem by Elizabeth Mary Ursula Caswell (Smith). Used by permission.
p. 305: Lyrics from *Still*, words and music by Reuben Morgan © 2002 Hillsong Music Publishing. Used by permission of Hillsong Music Publishing UK.

A catalogue record for this book is available from the British Library

Printed and bound in the UK, December 2013, LH26

DEDICATED TO MY PARENTS REVD LESLIE
AND MRS ETHEL KEENAN, WHO BY THEIR
EVERY-DAY, ALL MY LIFE EXAMPLE, HAVE
SHOWN ME SIMPLY HOW TO LIVE LIKE THIS –
IN, AND FOR, GOD'S KINGDOM.

Contents

Acknowledgments

I cannot begin to thank everyone who has had a part in the writing of this book, nor can I include everyone who played a part in the stories I have told. But heaven, I think, keeps a record.

Our friends and co-workers in the Philippines, who work with all their strength for the kingdom of God and never receive recognition but give it all to the white missionaries!

Churches and individuals in the United Kingdom and elsewhere, who have done what you could for many years with donations, letters of encouragement and effective, fervent prayers. Your loaves and fishes have been miraculous in the hands of Jesus!

John Pitt, who was the charity's invaluable "contact person" and financial advisor in England for several years.

Diane G. Paul, my tutor with The Writers Bureau, who cheered me on and taught me how to write properly!

Brendan Neiland, my dear Irish prayer partner who prodded me to keep writing when I felt like it was beyond me.

Noel Abejero, Filipino photographer, whose images of Philippine life, especially family life and childhood, I absolutely adore.

My husband Peter, and children Michael, Ana, and Simon, Michael's wife Jeli, and baby Nathan Rain.

And apologies and thanks to my staff and boys at LAMA House who felt my absence too many times.

Above and around all others, thank you to the author and finisher of my faith and yours, our utterly amazing God!

Foreword

I have known Lesley for over thirty years since she spent time with us in the very early days in one of our "new boy houses". It was there that she saw and walked through some of our best and worst moments.

The best times were the belief that Jesus could change anyone and that they were worth dying for and struggling for – whether they turn out well or not. There was always room for one more because we knew that God's heart was big enough for one more.

The worst times were when many came, saw a miracle of the Lord, were baptized with the Holy Spirit, and a few days later, or some months later, left. We were therefore tempted to think of ourselves as failures until we remembered that most of Jesus' disciples left Him, even after three years, on the eve of His crucifixion.

Lesley has carried this heart on into her amazing life in the Philippines. We've been thrilled to see and to hear of the stories of individual lives of orphans, the lost, the bereaved, the demonized changed through living in Jesus' family with her and her family. We have seen Lesley over the years grow in the Word of God in prayer and in perseverance. We've been privileged to meet from time to time and encourage one another in this wonderful adventure.

I know you will enjoy this account of what God has chosen to do through an ordinary but extraordinary girl. She was obedient and therefore found the treasures that were waiting for her. Those treasures were children many believed insignificant, even unwanted, who have changed into young men and even some future giants for the Lord. May this book inspire you to live in obedience and discover the miracles the Lord will do through you. It's His promise!

Jackie Pullinger

Preface

Many years ago, when we were both in our twenties, Lesley's dad, Leslie (always known as Bertie), and I lived in a Church Army caravan in County Durham in the north-east of England. We went around the local villages and towns preaching the wonderful gospel of what Jesus had done in our lives and what He could do in the lives of those who would accept Him as their personal Saviour.

These were days of great blessing and spiritual development, and Bertie and I became real brothers in Christ, almost to the point of knowing each other's thoughts and behaviour. I learned from Bertie of his deep love for the Saviour, and his compassion and understanding for his fellow men. His remarkable sense of humour was unique and, as our personalities bounced off each other, we both grew in grace and in our ability to present Jesus in any circumstance and situation.

God blessed us both with families who also want to serve the Saviour. So when Lesley invited me to write a preface for her book I felt deeply privileged and honoured. I have never met Lesley, or her husband, Peter, but I have followed their work through the regular prayer letters and I feel I know them both, as I have prayed for them, watching how the Master has led them in a remarkable ministry.

Lesley's call to work in the Philippines was a real step of faith for a young lady to take; such a step was truly mind-blowing. Over the years Lesley has weathered the storms of health, opposition, and the attacks of the enemy. Lesley and Peter, like the apostles, have suffered incredible hardships and difficulties but they have not allowed their suffering to lie to them. They have always sought the Truth from the Spirit of God and not from their circumstances. In their building of LAMA House and its wonderful ministry to needy young people and their families, they have developed the strength to stand up to adversity by focusing on how great is their God.

As I read of the remarkable experiences of Lesley and Peter, of their victories and defeats, their joy and their feelings of helplessness, I have been reminded of the 2012 Olympic Games in London and of St Paul's statement in 1 Corinthians 9:24, "Remember that in a race everyone runs, but only one person gets the prize. You also must run in such a way that you will win." The joy and ecstasy of winning a gold medal was the determined effort of every member who took part.

Have a Little Faith reads like the Acts of the Apostles where lives came into deep relationships with Jesus and, being set free by the indwelling power of the Holy Spirit, weathered every attack of Satan.

Lesley and Peter, with their team of workers, challenge us all to face every situation in the strength of the Lord and never to quit. Hebrews 12:1–2: "Run with endurance the race… keeping our eyes on Jesus, on whom our faith depends from start to finish."

Revd Canon Noel Proctor, MBE, MA
29 January 2013

Introduction

Shortly after my twenty-second birthday, in 1983, I left England to work as a volunteer nurse for six months in the Philippine Islands, at Miracle Bible College and Children's Home. Later, I founded Life And More Abundant Ministries (LAMA) and made the Philippines my home. I married Peter Gomez and we devoted our lives to helping the poor.

LAMA Ministries was registered in 1987 as a UK Charity, and in the Philippines as a non-governmental organization (NGO). The name LAMA is taken from the words of Jesus in John 10:10: "The thief cometh not, but for to steal, and to kill, and to destroy: I have come that they might have life, and that they might have it more abundantly" (KJV).

LAMA House provides long-term foster care and education for boys who have been abused or abandoned. We trace parents of lost boys and reunite them with family where possible, but most of "our boys" are alone and will remain a part of LAMA family as a lifetime commitment. We work closely with the Philippines Department of Social Welfare and Development (DSWD) to rescue boys from neglect, violence, prostitution, and child slave labour. We also minister in the regional jail. When funds allow we provide relief aid in crisis situations for families living in poverty, emergency medical fees, food, shelter, clothing, and basic needs.

All the people mentioned in this book are real, though some of the names have been changed. This is not a book of one-sided success stories – such a book wrongly assumes certain details would not glorify God. That would only make you feel that we have it all together, and question why you are struggling. The Bible clearly shows us that even our mistakes and failures will one day shout His praise. In every detail of our lives we can trace His wonderful, loving, and faithful ways!

Chapter 1

Dan-dan

**"What I want to do is to instil fear," he told
reporters earlier this year. "If you are doing an
illegal activity in my city, if you are a criminal
or part of a syndicate that preys on the innocent
people in the city, for as long as I am Mayor, you
are a legitimate target of assassination."**

"Tough justice: On the trail of Philippine death
squads", *The Independent*, Davao, 1 June 2009

At half past midnight we arrived in the drab city of
Dagupan, its topsy-turvy buildings grey with residue
from exhaust fumes. The roads, congested and chaotic
during the day, were eerily quiet as we made our way cautiously
past empty shops. We headed for the city Plaza, a sorry excuse
for a park where skate-boarding youngsters hung around late
into the night.

Peter and I had been married for less than a year and our
rented home was already bursting with an assortment of needy
people, but we couldn't ignore the desperate newspaper reports
about police brutality.

The influential people of the city denounced the street
children as trouble-makers; they wanted rid of them. The
children hung out at plazas, highways, shopping malls, tourist
attractions, and restaurants. But these were areas of the city
that wealthier residents wanted to claim as their own – and
keep beautiful. While walking along the streets or sitting in a
restaurant they were often approached by snotty-nosed street

children asking for food. Others tapped on tinted car windows, asking for money. Walking down the steps to the train station, mothers held out malnourished babies. They were considered rubbish on the street.

If we could befriend the street children, we thought, buy a few meals and pray with them, they might understand that God cares for them.

Watching from the sidelines we applauded their skateboard antics, conscious that we didn't really fit in. We discovered that some of them had parents and homes, but not the sort of parents who lie awake worrying where their children are late at night. For most of them going home was not an option because of the ugly things they had to endure there. The children were aware of the dangers that lurked on the street, but they were streetwise. In typical Filipino fashion they chose not to think about it, hoping it wouldn't happen to them.

We easily won their friendship, making friends with Noel first, who was high on solvents but fairly lucid compared with the others. He danced around us nervously, answering our queries with a raucous laugh, though nothing remotely funny had been said. His younger companions appeared brain-dead, powerless to even recall their names. They hid small solvent bottles under their grubby T-shirts knowing they would be beaten and taken into custody if found by the police. The police, of course, were not fooled by their pathetic attempts at cover up – the rancid smell was enough to give them away!

Noel confirmed the truth of the newspaper reports – sons abandoned to fend for themselves at too early an age, daughters sold into prostitution. They desperately needed someone to defend them. At the age of nine most already had a criminal career; they were old in crime.

I looked around at the dirty faces and bare feet of fourteen boys who had gathered to see what we had to offer. They gazed up at me, prodding with up-turned hands, begging for money or food. I saw no hope in their eyes. We were not in a hurry to leave. They seemed to understand that we were worried about them.

As Peter drove home in silence we were both lost in our own thoughts – what could we do? We wanted them to have a chance at a better life. The image of Noel's gaunt, sallow face haunted me for weeks. We decided to make monthly visits to scout the city. The children soon came to recognize our yellow jeep parked near the Plaza at night. We handed out our telephone number and address and told them they could turn up at our home any time and stay for as long as they wanted.

The bus journey from Dagupan to San Fernando City took two hours but was not expensive. A sign on the road clearly pointed the way to our bungalow, just off the main highway: "Victory House – a place for a new beginning! Peter and Lesley Gomez: Directors".

Before long, Noel took up our offer, conveniently arriving at lunchtime. We invited him to join us for a meal of rice, fried fish, and vegetables in fermented fish sauce. Not standing on ceremony, Noel sat down and helped himself. He attacked the food with such enthusiasm that everyone else paused to watch! Seeing our surprise, he explained between mouthfuls that he usually ate from garbage bins, whatever he could find.

The air-fan humming overhead did little to relieve us in the sweltering heat and when he took off his T-shirt to cool off I could see how desperately thin he was. Bits of glue were stuck to his skin, nose running and eyes glazed over, the telltale signs of a "Rugby boy". The powerful vapour that Rugby glue gave off was an addictive hallucinogenic; it did irreparable damage to brain cells. Noel shrugged off our concern.

"It makes me happy," he told us.

"Oh, Lord!" I sighed out loud.

"You all look so sad!" he said, laughing.

He jumped up from the table, having polished off all the fried fish, and proceeded outside to sit in the shade. The other boys hurriedly helped themselves to what was left of the vegetables while I made myself a cup of tea. I didn't feel like eating anyway.

Noel confided in Peter and Pastor Fred that when he was ten years old his parents split up. His mother's new partner kicked him out of his home, yelling, "I don't care if you live or die!" as Noel ran away into the city. He found company among the prostitutes and transvestites who hung around the city Plaza at night and soon learnt how to sniff glue and pick pockets.

He seemed quite an intelligent boy; it was a shame he didn't go to school. He liked to keep busy, helping me in the kitchen, running errands for Peter, or helping with repairs around the house. But a week later we woke as usual at 6 a.m. to find Noel was gone, and so was the money from Pastor Rogelio's wallet!

Noel was embarrassed when we caught up with him on one of our night visits, but it wasn't worth sacrificing the relationship so we didn't mention the missing money. We didn't realize all that hung in the balance of that gracious decision as he proceeded to take us to a play area near the Catholic monastery to introduce us to his friend.

Peering into the darkness, there didn't seem to be anyone there except us.

"Over here!" Noel hissed, kicking a bush.

Moving closer, I heard a groan and saw something move.

"He's in here!" he informed me in hushed tones, looking around nervously.

I crouched down to get a closer look and found a boy curled up, shivering feverishly. The boy stood to his feet uncomfortably. His appearance was made more wretched because his head was covered in infected sores and had been completely shaved. He was probably about nine years old.

"You take him home... or he might die!" Noel ordered.

"Poor little chap," I muttered. "What is your name?" I asked him. He stared back at me blankly and I noticed he was very cross-eyed.

"His name is Dan-dan," Noel answered for him, and with an air of his own importance proceeded to tell Peter the whole story. "Dan-dan ran away from home when his mother left them. He was afraid of his father. When his father found him on the street with me he offered to pay me 2,000 pesos to get rid of Dan-dan for him. I couldn't do that. It's a lot of money but I am not a killer," Noel said, wincing.

"Come home with us," I suggested.

They needed no persuasion. We bundled them both into our jeep and headed home. We quickly realized that solvent abuse at such a young age had caused Dan-dan to lose all ability to think intelligently. But as soon as the fever left so did they, craving the glue and the crowded streets above the security of a family and comfort of a clean home.

When we visited Dagupan again the park was strangely silent. We wandered the dimly lit streets until the early hours of the morning, but not a single street-child could be found. Only a lone vendor in the open-market was seen packing up his vegetable stall, leaving the rats scurrying to finish off a broken watermelon. Something was not right. "Let's go home; they're not here," Peter suggested wearily. But I was worried. *Where was Dad-dan? Was Noel in jail?*

We had heard that the police were "cleaning up" the streets. Street-boys would often disappear from their old haunts. Some would resurface in another town or city after trying to find their family; the unfortunate were thrown in jail. Worse still, some died from disease, drug abuse, or violence at the hands of those they stole from, or misguided policemen.

Spotting three youngsters chatting under a street light I suggested we go over and talk to them before going home. A young girl appeared to be anxiously waiting for someone, or anyone. She was too young. Her male companions were a little older, curiously dressed up like her in racy transvestite garb. They seemed pleased to see us, glad of the easy company of people who expected nothing from them.

As we chatted I asked them if they had heard about Jesus. Boyette, who was dressed in a tight pink vest, mini-skirt, and stiletto heels, looked like he had seen a ghost! "God sent you! I know I don't belong here – my family are Christians," he blurted out.

The truth is nobody belongs here, I thought.

We talked for a while then prayed together. It began to pour down with rain as we climbed into our jeep to go home. As Peter backed out of the parking space, he saw Noel running frantically towards us, dressed only in shorts. He jumped in the back of the jeep, shivering. He looked around nervously, as if expecting someone to jump out at him. Pointing to a ragged scar on his back, he told us he had been stabbed the week before in a fight. I cringed, tracing the ugly mark with my finger.

"You could have been killed Noel," I told him.

"I know. Can I stay with you?" he muttered, holding back the tears.

He arrived the next day with Butz, a tough eleven-year-old with eyes that said, "Leave me alone or I'll kill you!" A long scar ran down the right side of Butz's face where someone high on drugs had once slashed him.

I had never seen so much seething rage in a child. Whenever anyone upset Butz during his time with us, he would immediately look for a knife to defend himself. But when we eventually told him to leave because of his violent outbursts he cried like a baby and begged to stay, promising he would change. It seemed highly unlikely, but we gave him another chance.

Noel left instead, and then Dan-dan returned. He arrived barefoot, in rags, stinking of glue. We didn't know whether to laugh or cry. We were glad to see him and always enjoyed his mischievous company but he was in such a derelict state.

Fights frequently broke out as the boys competed for our attention. Arguing about a bamboo stick one day Butz snatched it from Dan-dan. When Dan-dan grabbed it back the razor-sharp edge sliced through the palm of Butz's hand. He shouted as blood spurted out on the ground.

Peter and I ran out of the house to find Dan-dan standing up straight, hands behind his back as if to say, "It wasn't me!" Butz held his hand out to show us, pulling the flesh apart to make it bleed some more. He enjoyed the sight of his own blood. Taking a clean cloth from the washing line, I held his hand in the air to stop the flow. He looked at me as if I were crazy as we marched him to the jeep, with Dan-dan following close behind.

In the emergency department we almost had to sit on him to prevent him from fighting the nurse. When I removed the blood-soaked cloth he tried again to re-open the wound. "He's going to need stitches," the doctor told me.

Butz was still squirming and making a fuss when, to everyone's relief, a little girl entered with a cut on her elbow. She was quite calm. Butz eyed her suspiciously, blushing with embarrassment when their eyes met. He instantly calmed down and put on a brave face to impress her, glancing in her direction at intervals to see if she was looking at him. Suppressing a smile, the doctor quickly sutured the wound.

Back at Victory House I somehow managed to prevent him from ripping out the stitches before the wound was healed. He and Dan-dan declared a cease-fire.

They would often sit on the floor like boys half their age playing marbles, or search for spiders in the garden to antagonize so that they would fight each other. They kept their prize-fighters in empty matchboxes, taking great care of them. Screams could be heard from the kitchen when, looking for a match, I found a spider instead. But it was good to hear their laughter and see them enjoying a lost childhood.

As soon as the stitches were out Butz was gone. When we bumped into him weeks later back on the street, he cried tears of joy and skipped around us like an excited puppy. When he was living with us his face had reflected only anger and the

HAVE A LITTLE FAITH

weight of a terrible sadness; now he seemed wiser, more settled, and a peace shone out of him. Nothing had changed in his desperate circumstances; he was still homeless – it seemed that prayer alone had made the difference.

After Noel left, we lost all contact with him for months. News on the street was that he was dead. When we did find him he was terrified. He hurriedly told us what had happened as if afraid he would not have enough time to spill it all out. "They grabbed us and took us outside the city... beat us up... I got away and kept running but my friend never came." He wiped his nose with the back of his hand and took a deep, sobbing breath. "I think they killed him," he concluded.

But this time Victory House was filled to capacity with boys in need. We had promised these boys we would help them but there were no places for them. It all seemed too much for me. I was learning that my ability to make a difference was very limited.

Noel, Dan-dan, and Butz held a special place in my heart. In an odd way I felt they were the reason for the fire that burned in my spirit and would not let me quit. I believed that seeds of faith sown in their lives would one day bring a good result.

Driving through Dagupan years later Peter spotted Noel. He pulled over to the side of the road and jumped out to talk to him. Noel laughed when Peter commented that it was good to see him fully clothed, for a change! He was doing alright, driving a tricycle for a living.

Four of the boys living with us were illiterate, so we asked a college student to come and teach them for a few hours each day. He would pin up the alphabet chart and go through it with them – they appeared to have it – but the next day it was back to square one. They got as far as A, B, C, D, and then became confused, with letters appearing randomly all over the place. He eventually threw his hands up in despair and gave up.

Without any pressure the boys attended church with us every Sunday. And each evening Peter told them stories from the Bible. They could understand the stories that Jesus told. When I returned from a trip to England I brought my big *Illustrated Children's Bible* back with me. I had treasured it as a child and wanted to share it with the boys. One evening Peter opened it to the story of the prodigal son, where a painting showed a father weeping, his arms wrapped around his wayward son's neck.

The boys sat cross-legged on the floor, transfixed by the story – it was familiar to them, having run away and got into all kinds of trouble themselves. I was aware that their own fathers might not be as welcoming as the father in the story, who had eagerly watched for his son's return. The boys nodded in agreement as Peter explained that the story was about our Father God, who will always welcome us back. There were tears in their eyes, and ours.

The following day Dan-dan asked if he could visit his father. Remembering what Noel had told us about him we were not sure a visit would be a good idea, and we had no way of contacting his father beforehand. Nevertheless Dan-dan insisted, so we agreed to take him.

Upon arrival in the city, Dan-dan led us off the highway and down an embankment, alongside a narrow polluted river that ran through the city. Tumble-down homes pieced together with bits of cardboard and old tin sheets stood shoulder-to-shoulder along the riverbank. Garbage floated in the water, breeding disease.

We came to a clearing where I could see a shack sitting apart from all the others. A man was cleaning up the yard. He watched nervously as we made our way towards his house. He said nothing as Dan-dan introduced us. I thought he was surprisingly short to own such a violent reputation – in the years that had separated them Dan-dan had overtaken his father in height.

Assuring him that we were not from the social services we explained our connection with his boy and after a while he relaxed. We sat together under a tree, talking and drinking the obligatory Coke. An hour passed and dusk began to settle around us so we offered to pray with him before we left. There was a pause, and then with tears in his eyes he finally made eye contact with his son.

"Please forgive me, son," he said, his voice shaking with emotion.

"Dad, it is done already!" Dan-dan said, smiling.

It was a holy moment.

Dan-dan decided to stay with his dad. Later they worked together as janitors in the City Hall before moving to a better house. It seemed like things would turn out well for him.

Chapter 2

Miracle!

**When God leads you to the edge of the cliff,
trust Him fully and let go. One of two things
will happen: either He will catch you when you
fall or He will teach you to fly.**

The man who had interviewed me paused and looked intently at me from the other side of his large desk.

"You have to promise me that you will be back. You might get to the Philippines and enjoy the sunshine so much that you won't want to leave. I am giving you this place – it could have gone to someone else," he said, seriously.

"Yes! I'll definitely be coming home to England. I really want to do my psychiatric training," I told him.

"Good! So I will see you at the start of term," he nodded.

"Thank you so much," I said, shaking his hand.

"One more thing… can I come with you?" he said, grinning.

Everything was going as planned. It was summer 1983 and I had recently resigned from my job as staff nurse on the eye ward at Gloucestershire Royal Hospital. It had been fascinating work. Now I was preparing to go to the Philippines for six months to work as a campus nurse for Miracle Bible College and Children's Home. After that, I would return to Gloucester and train for eighteen months as a registered mental health nurse. Psychiatry was complex and often seemed hopeless but that was what interested me – I wanted to be involved in finding answers for the hard things.

* * *

Having tied up all the loose ends I travelled to Cornwall to spend some time with my parents. At the end of August I celebrated my twenty-second birthday; two weeks later I was waving goodbye to my family at the airport. I was accompanied on the flight by a girl my age – Chrissy Hailes. I had met Chrissy at Hollybush Christian Camp earlier that summer. She was going to work as a missionary in Olongapo, near Manila. As she told me of her plans for prison ministry my own plans paled in comparison. At that time neither of us knew that we would be dedicating our lives to missionary work in the Philippine Islands. There was a lot then that we didn't know.

I was glad of Chrissy's company, especially when we arrived at chaotic Manila International Airport (or Ninoy Aquino International Airport as it is also known). People crowded around us and men shouted in our faces.

"I carry your bags!"

"Where you go?"

"You like taxi?"

I felt dizzy and tired after the long flight and it was a relief when Chrissy spotted her missionary friends Dorothy and Linda waving to us at the arrivals gate. We stayed overnight with them in the Village Hotel near the airport, parting company the following morning.

A hotel taxi was organized to take me to the nearby Domestic Airport. I was nervous, not being accustomed to big cities or even taxis. But the driver was helpful and spoke a little English. Operating half in survival mode and half in sleep mode I focused on my journey to Miracle, unaware of much that was going on around me in Metro Manila. It was only on later visits that I became uncomfortably aware of the degree of neglect in the vast human population; the dire mess of shanty homes and utter muddle of the filthy city.

At Domestic Airport I boarded a small plane for Baguio City in order to avoid an eight-hour journey by road to the province of La Union, on the west coast of the island of Luzon. Seated on the rickety plane as it pitched and soared over rice paddies and mountain ranges I wished I had taken the bus! There didn't seem to be very much in the way of in-flight comfort or safety procedures.

A thick blanket of humidity wrapped itself around me as I stepped off the plane and walked across the tarmac. Baguio City is situated high in the mountains and boasts a cooler climate than most of the rest of the Philippines, but it was still very hot compared to England.

At the arrival area I recognized Susanna straight away. She was just as I remembered her when she visited our home in England, as part of the Philippine Choir of Miracles – full of life and laughter. She chattered animatedly in English, then in Ilocano, as if I could understand every word. Of Chinese descent, her expressive features were quite different from those of her Filipino companions. "I would never have recognized you if you hadn't told me in your letter to look for a white girl carrying a banjo!" she laughed, as we hugged each other. It had been eight years since we first met in England, but it seemed like yesterday. As we set off for the capital city of La Union, San Fernando, she introduced me to the others in the group.

"This is our driver and pastor at Miracle Church, Abraham Duclayan. These young people are students at the college, and Maam Mercy… do you remember Mercy? She was also in the choir that visited England all those years ago," she shouted over the noise of the jeep engine.

"Of course I remember her! I couldn't forget any of you!" I replied.

I clung tightly to the handrail of the jeep as we rocked from side to side, hurtling down the winding mountain road, engine bellowing. All things considered, the journey in the small plane didn't seem quite so bad. An hour or so later, the vehicle came to a halt and Susanna announced our arrival. "Here we are Lesley... Mirac-el!" she said, with great dignity and a flourish of her hand.

Miracle Bible College was built on top of a hill, on the outskirts of the city of San Fernando. The steep road to the top was in poor shape but as the jeep struggled upwards I wasn't concerned; I was distracted by the beautiful fuchsia-coloured bougainvillea, the huge red hibiscus flowers, and the banana and mango trees. Climbing out of the jeep, dirty and sweaty, I caught sight of the view overlooking the South China Sea and the city beneath us with its jumble of rusty corrugated tin roofs. It was all so fascinating, my dream come true!

"Come! Let's go eat! Maam Severina has prepared something for us," Susanna suggested.

After lunch Susanna and Maam Severina gave me a tour of the Bible College. A two-storey building, the ground floor was made of cement painted white and the second floor built of timber. An apartment nestled at the top where Pastor Shields, the American missionary who had founded the Bible College in 1956, used to live. There were two classrooms, a kitchen area, and a chapel on the ground floor. In each class about forty students sat shoulder to shoulder in old-fashioned wooden chairs. They smiled at me and giggled as we passed by. My nurse's clinic was sandwiched between the two classrooms, clean and bright with cartoon characters painted on the door and cabinets. "Pastor Shields' daughter, Charlotte, designed all this. You will meet her later," Susanna informed me.

We walked through the kitchen; it was dark and not tiled, just rough cement surfaces and a broken sink. Susanna pointed to an area outside where an open fire blazed under a big wok, in a shed with a tin roof. "This is where we do most of the cooking," she said. As simple as it was, it seemed like a better idea than cooking inside. A student squatted near the fire, stirring the contents of the wok with a long-handled spoon. He grinned and waved at me. I looked up at the dormitories on the second floor. Rickety wooden stairways led up to the boy's dorm on one side and girls on the other. Most of the wood had been destroyed by termites.

Susanna walked with me back down the mountain to the "Mission House" where I would stay for the first few weeks, along with American missionaries from Oklahoma, Bert and Mary Brewster. A fairly new bungalow, I wasn't sure if I felt disappointed or pleasantly surprised, as I had half-expected to be in a mud hut in the middle of the jungle. The tiredness and excitement caught up with me as Mary showed me to my room and left me to unpack my bags. Thankful, but suddenly exhausted, I flopped onto the bed and fell asleep.

When I woke up it was night-time. An orchestra of crickets were chirping outside my window, dogs were barking, and cockerels crowing. For a moment I didn't know where I was. Then as the jet lag caught up with me I lay awake wondering what lay in store for me in the months ahead and thinking back to the events that had led me to the Philippine Islands.

* * *

It had all started in the Cumbrian Lake District at Keswick Convention in England. I was twelve years old, skinny and extremely shy, and had made my way to the front of a huge marquee packed with thousands of people in response to the appeal at a missionary meeting. I signed a pledge on a printed piece of paper that I later pasted in my Bible as a reminder of the event. It read: "On July 17, 1973, at the Missionary Meeting at Keswick, I made my personal response to God's challenge to whole time service at home or abroad. Signed: Lesley Keenan."

I had no idea where that strange courage came from that had me laying my life down, lock, stock, and barrel, to do anything no matter how difficult; go anywhere for as long as it took in service to God. It was so uncharacteristic it had to be a message from Him! Despite my young age I knew the commitment would cost me something and that it would entail service abroad, but I had no idea where exactly. I had a vague notion that perhaps God would call me to be a missionary to the American Indians, perhaps because having watched *The Lone Ranger* as a child I had always wanted to own a horse!

Then two years later I met Reverend Clyde Shields and The Philippine Choir of Miracles at Hollybush Christian Camp in Northallerton, Yorkshire. They were travelling around the world to raise funds for their Bible College. Sitting in the front pew of my father's church I was enthralled by their music and the emotional stories Pastor Shields told of missionary work in the Philippines. The tears streamed down my face from the beginning of their concert to the end and as they moved on to another venue our family followed them all over the north of England.

* * *

My eyes filled with tears again as I tossed and turned on my bed in the Mission house trying to rest. Since 1975 I had looked forward to visiting Pastor Shields and the choir in the Philippines, and now I was really here! But disappointment washed over me because Pastor Shields was not at Miracle, nor would he ever be again – he had died of a heart attack four months before my arrival. The awful sense of loss was felt by everyone who knew him for years after his death, and I grieved for him as if he were part of my own family. My pillow was wet with tears when I woke up at 6 a.m to the sound of Papa Bert calling me to breakfast.

After breakfast I hiked from the Brewsters' back uphill to Bible College, careful to avoid the many potholes in the road. The classrooms were already full of students at 7 a.m., one class studying the Old Testament prophets, and from the other room I could hear a guitar strumming and the lilting rhythm of the islands as they sang worship songs. I took a deep satisfied breath, feeling that everything was as it should be.

This is my destiny, I thought happily.

Checking out my clinic I found two showers and toilets at the back, a sink with running water and several cabinets, but no medical supplies. A wooden bed under the window could be used for examining patients. The only equipment was a blood pressure machine and a few thermometers. It didn't worry me as I had been assured that there were several nurses to help me.

There was a knock on the door and in walked a tiny Filipina lady wearing a white jacket. "Hi! I'm Liberty! Welcome to the Philippines!" she said, shaking my hand vigorously. Liberty was the campus nurse. After getting to know each other briefly she quietly informed me that she would be leaving in a few weeks to work in America and that I was the only replacement. "It really is an answer to prayer that you are here!" she smiled. I could hardly concentrate as she explained details of her patients, where to buy medicines, and other schedules. She obviously had a lot more faith in my ability than I did!

Those first two weeks were difficult and very lonely. Unaccustomed to the many night noises I lay awake most nights staring at the ceiling. My legs were a mess, having become infected by mosquito bites. Everyone was very friendly, but communication was a big problem as not many students could speak English.

I had decided before arriving in the Philippines that I was going to become as Filipino as possible. The food was strange, to say the least, but I knew that the basic law of travel was to eat what was offered. This made a good impression, but it also meant I had diarrhoea most of the time at the beginning. But in my third week I began to adjust, found some students who could interpret for me, and learned Ilocano phrases such as, "Where does it hurt?", "Do you have a fever?", and "How long have you been ill?"

Once they had overcome their bashfulness the children conversed with me, oblivious to my mistakes in pronunciation. With their help I began to learn the language. The students, on the other hand, would roll around laughing at my funny accent and try to catch me out by asking me to say silly things. I wasn't prepared for the awkward separation that comes with being in a foreign country and not understanding the language.

Several weeks later, as we all waved goodbye to Liberty and wished her well, I tried not to think about the fact that I was now responsible for the health of 120 people. A distant memory came to mind in which I was sitting next to my father in his old Humber car, complaining that I couldn't do something. His answer was always the same: "Never say, never! The Bible says you can do all things through Christ who strengthens you!"

"I can do all things through Christ who strengthens me," I repeated quietly to myself, as I walked back to the clinic alone.

As I prepared the medicines to distribute, a student appeared in the doorway, a look of panic on her face. "Maam Lesley, please come quickly!" she said. I followed her out of the clinic and up the wooden stairs into the girls' dormitory, a wide room full of wooden bunk beds and little else. She pointed to one of the bunks where a student was lying, almost lifeless. She had a dangerously high fever. I noticed her yellow eyes and skin. "Oh, no, it's hepatitis!" I groaned.

Nothing in my months as staff nurse on the eye ward back home could have prepared me for this, or any of what came next. Thankfully there were three hospitals in the city, so I set off for the regional hospital, known as "The Poor People's Hospital", where patients didn't have to pay to be examined or looked after. At the nurse's desk I was handed a dog-eared card with a number written on it and directed to join a crowd of people who were sitting outside waiting in the overflow of the outpatients' department. I glanced at my number – eighty-nine!

I sat there awkwardly for several hours with all eyes on me, the only white girl in a sea of curious brown faces. After what seemed like a hundred years number eighty-nine was called and I was ushered into the doctor's office. I explained who I was, which he found quite baffling. He couldn't understand why I would leave my country to work in his when most of his colleagues wished to leave the Philippines for work abroad. Having spent the best part of the day waiting I had no time for idle chit-chat so I got straight to the point.

"A student in the college has hepatitis," I told him, detailing her symptoms. Seeing the urgency of the situation he accepted my diagnosis and scribbled three prescriptions, telling me to isolate the girl and give her plenty of rest.

"She should have some blood tests – bring her in tomorrow for them. Recovery will be slow. Any complications just bring her back to the hospital," he said.

Back at the college I had to improvise as there was no isolation unit. I decided to move into the clinic and share it with patients, sleeping on a fold-away cot bed. Hepatitis was not the only problem. One contagious tropical disease after another reared its ugly head – typhoid, tuberculosis, dengue fever, as well as the inevitable chicken pox and mumps in the children's home. Realizing that the situation could very quickly get out of control I prayed with each patient when I gave them their medicines. I knew my own nursing skills were hopelessly inadequate, and that I would have to rely on divine intervention to do the real work.

I had been immunized against every imaginable disease before I left England, but I worried about my own health as there were very few times that I didn't have someone with an infectious disease living in close quarters with me. I took to washing my hands and wiping surfaces with disinfectant at every opportunity. It worked – for a while.

In addition, the clinic was over-run with cockroaches. At night they came out of hiding and the place became alive with them. They scurried over me as I lay in bed with the bed-sheet pulled tightly over my head. When I finally got rid of them the stench of disinfectant kept me awake instead. I tried unsuccessfully to teach good health and hygiene practices.

The male students could not be deterred from urinating in the garden, and it was common practice to spit all over the place. Worse than that, the septic tank, situated just outside the clinic, was emptied every month by pumping the contents on to the garden. There was never enough water to supply the needs of the college and this recycling effort saved watering the plants. The smell was nauseating until the sun dried everything out. How disease was not spread in epidemic proportions I will never know!

I eventually moved to the girls' dormitory, where the communal showers were a daily embarrassment! There was never enough water so I copied the girls by filling a tin can with cold water to throw over my noticeably white body, crouching down to avoid the curious stares and comments.

My working day started at 5.30 a.m. and I was on call throughout the night. As dusk settled us down after each busy day I sat outside with the students, chatting and getting to know them. The scent of the Kalachuchi and Dame de noche trees filled the evening air with heady perfume. As the sun set everything took on a softer golden hue. It never ceased to fill me with wonder.

In church services every one of the sixty-four children seemed lost in worship. I had never seen such devotion in little children and it was very moving. Spiritually they had so much more than the children in England. I recall looking up at the words painted in large blue letters on the front wall of the church: "Jesus said: Nothing shall be impossible to you." I thought I heard God's quiet voice in my spirit: "Do you really believe that Lesley?"

My father had often asked me to join him when he prayed for the sick. I vividly remembered a deaf girl receiving her hearing after a visiting evangelist prayed with her. I had often seen God do miracles. I thought of my initiation, thrown in the deep end, and I knew I did believe it, more than ever before.

Chapter 3

The Best Pathway

God will put in your heart something or someone that you will find precious. This all happens for a reason. It becomes your opportunity to make a difference.

Anyone who spent time with my father knew that with him laughter was as necessary as breathing! I suddenly found myself at a complete loss without his continual humour. In England my normal conversation was dotted with witty anecdotes and silly expressions, all of which had to be done away with now I was in the Philippines.

Pastor Bercero's family, however, were different. I often spent my free time at his home on campus. We both loved the old gospel songs and he laughed at my jokes when they were lost on almost everyone else. Pastor and Mrs Bercero had four children: two boys and two girls. His son Sammy was the same age as my brother Philip. He became my "little brother". His easy company saved me on days when I felt out of place and disjointed.

Sitting outside the main classroom drinking Sprite with a group of students, I watched curiously as two boys from the children's home shuffled past us awkwardly.

"Why are they walking like that?" I asked the girl next to me. She giggled and whispered to her friend.

"*Nakugit da*," her friend told me, in Ilocano. I didn't understand, so asked one of the boys to translate.

"They have been circumcised," he explained, grinning.

"What? When did they go to the hospital?" I quizzed him, annoyed that no one had informed me.

"Larry did it with his hunting knife," he said, as if it was the most natural thing in the world.

"WHAT!" I gasped.

A lot of chasing around ensued as I tried in vain to persuade the boys to "Let me have a look!" Only when the wounds became painfully infected did they relent. The students saw me get angry for the first time as I told Larry, in no uncertain terms, that there would be no more minor surgery attempts on campus. But they just laughed at me, mimicking my angry outburst.

* * *

I eventually decided to use my savings for bills at LORMA Medical Centre, a well-equipped, modern hospital where the doctors were courteous and helpful. With no salary or money from Miracle, my savings were soon gone. More often than not I had to rely on God's promise of healing as I prayed for the sick.

Perhaps the most outstanding healing I witnessed was in Theresa, a teenage girl admitted to the children's home. Rheumatic heart disease had caused havoc and she was close to death. Struggling to breathe, her heart could be seen beating wildly inside her barrelled out chest. All I could do was observe her, with the help of male nurse, Mario, who had joined me at Miracle in preparation for my return to England in April. There were times that we honestly thought she would not survive. But against the prognosis, she went on to attend Bible College then pastor a church in the mountains. When I saw her again years later, she was living a normal life, even trekking over mountain ranges to teach Bible studies in remote villages.

* * *

As Christmas approached, the students made colourful lanterns to hang in the trees and classrooms. It seemed that almost everyone was blessed with a natural talent for art and music. The campus was buzzing with activity and laughter. I ventured to the shops, to pursue the daunting task of finding gifts for sixty-four children. Taller than the average Filipino and conspicuous with my white skin, people stared at me and passed comments as I was pushed and shoved in the crowds from one shop to the next.

As I came out of the National Bazaar I was suddenly surrounded by a group of child beggars all looking up at me with forlorn eyes and outstretched hands. "Merry Christmas, Maam?" they chanted in unison. It wasn't a greeting, but a plea for money. The students had advised me not to give the street children anything for they said it encouraged them to beg, but I dropped a few coins in their hands. They soon forgot how forlorn they were supposed to look and ran away laughing excitedly to buy candy. *What sort of a Christmas will they have?* I wondered. Certainly, it would be nothing like I had known and loved as a child.

"I'm Dreaming of a White Christmas" blared out noisily from loudspeakers as people crushed around me. I retreated back to the college with little to show for my shopping spree. Looking in my bag to pay the tricycle driver, I couldn't find my purse. Gone, taking with it the money I had put aside for the children's gifts… along with much of my Christmas spirit!

Most of the students went home for the holidays and the children were invited to spend Christmas with friends or relatives, so I joined a team who were travelling into the mountains to minister in churches. American missionaries from Iowa, Homer and Barbara Hall had arrived at Miracle shortly after me and they joined Bert and Mary Brewster for ministry trips with a student singing group called "Miracle Sounds". I became close friends with the five boys Sammy, Condring,

Gideon, Peter, and Bhoy, and four girls Ditas, Lolit, Debbie, and Gina, as well as with Efren, a gifted interpreter. Efren's older brother Hulemio was the youngest member of the Choir of Miracles.

The Mountain Province enjoyed a cooler climate – it was just as Christmas should be! But I liked the warm climate and was glad to get back to the college when the tour was finished.

Peter Gomez was a singer in Miracle Sounds and a senior student at the college. He spoke English so it was easy to get to know him. He and his best friend Fred Laberinto were often assigned to help in the Children's Home. I was impressed with them as not many of the male students took time out with the children. More than that, I found myself becoming attracted to Peter!

He told me his parents had immigrated to Hawaii when he was fifteen and most of his family came to join them there. Now, at the age of twenty, he lived at Miracle with two sisters Myra and Debbie as his father, a minister, had founded Miracle Bible College with Pastor Shields.

In 1984 the strict rules at Miracle Bible College were like something from Victorian England and as a result the atmosphere could be a bit stifling at times. Girls were not allowed to have short hair or wear trousers or sleeveless tops. Boys and girls could not spend time alone together, and courting couples (restricted to seniors only) had to have a chaperone at all times. Peter usually got away with a lot more than the other students because Susanna, the college Dean, was his godmother – a role taken quite seriously in the Philippines.

"They have told me not to get too close to you," Peter said one day. I had no idea who "they" were and looked puzzled as he continued. "But I can't help it, because I love you!" Apparently blunt declarations like this were the way things were done in the Philippines. That was the slightly awkward beginning of our relationship; so much for my original plan to stay positively single!

* * *

By April, the time had come for me to return to England. I had been taking care of everyone else, but not looking after myself. As I stood at the top of the dangerously steep steps, preparing to make my descent for what I thought was going to be the last time, I could see Pastor Duclayan walking up the road to his classroom. I didn't feel at all well. Suddenly Pastor Abe (as he was affectionately called) charged up the steps and wrapped his arms around me, literally sweeping me off my feet. He lifted my limp body, carried me to his jeep and rushed me to the hospital.

My head was pounding and it seemed like the emergency room was moving in all directions. I could see the nurses and doctors but was unable to get my words out to answer their questions. It turned out that I had typhoid fever.

In the long days that followed a steady stream of students and teachers came to visit me in my hospital room. Miracle Sounds came one afternoon and sang for me, then told jokes to make me feel better. When Peter took hold of my hand the others looked at each other, giggling and whispering. But I was too weak to care anymore about other people's opinions. The word was out; we were officially courting!

Confined in the hospital I had time to reflect on my missionary experience. Without a doubt I had received as much on-the-job training as I needed at Miracle Bible College. Life had been a daily challenge, but I had learned to trust God and listen to His quiet instruction. I had learned to preach and pray for the sick, and had seen God answer prayer in incredible ways. And I had learned to eat all manner of strange foods and embrace the Filipino culture. Before I left England, six months seemed like half a lifetime – but it had come and gone far too quickly.

I slowly recovered from the typhoid fever and realized I would have to be more careful about what I ate and drank in future. I never wanted to have that horrendous illness again. Peter's friend Fred became our trusty chaperone.

Understandably, not everyone on campus was pleased about our relationship. I was preparing to return to England with Susanna, and Peter was going to tour America with Miracle Sounds, the Brewsters, and the Halls. Anyway, we would have plenty of time to think seriously about our relationship during the six months apart.

* * *

Pastor Bercero's son Sammy was graduating from high school. He asked me to attend his graduation. I felt honoured to be included in their family celebration. At the close of the very long ceremony we took lots of photographs together. The students and staff pleaded with me to stay for Miracle graduation – the highlight of the year and a grand affair. Several American guests were already arriving as guest speakers. In the end I relented, and changed my airline ticket. I returned to England a month later than originally planned.

I wrote an apologetic letter to the college in Gloucester, explaining that I would not be accepting the place for psychiatric nurse training after all. I felt bad, having promised the man I would definitely be back. But living with the poor had changed me. The things that were important to me before I left England seemed trivial now. A home of my own, a career, a salary – none of it seemed to matter somehow.

The long flight from Manila to London took almost twenty-four hours. After arriving at Heathrow Airport there was another five hours on the road to endure before Susanna and I reached Cornwall. My parents had moved to North Cornwall six years before, when I was sixteen. I had stayed in Yorkshire to live with the family of my best friend Jayne in order to finish sixth form. The move had been particularly difficult as our family had loved the Old Vicarage in the village of Pollington with its acres of gardens. But the sleepy village of Poughill, just outside Bude, was charming enough in its own way, with tall hedges and picturesque thatched cottages.

It felt good to be home, even though it was never really my home! As I roamed the rugged cliffs and sandy beaches I realized how much I had missed it all – the seasons, the English countryside, birdsong, the discipline of British society, and effortless conversation. England was wrapped up in a restrained hush. I had to admit I constantly yearned for quiet.

On the other hand "reverse culture-shock" unsettled me more than expected. Sitting in the bathroom one day I began to cry because it was so nice and clean, with a carpeted floor and pink toilet tissue, of all things! The shops in England were full of everything imaginable and the homes so comfortable, and yet most people could still find something to complain about. And there was so much waste – I couldn't bring it all together.

Susanna and I visited churches all over the country, raising funds for Miracle Bible College. She was a fiery speaker and congregations were hungry for her particular brand of passionate spirituality. The slides she showed of little children worshiping God moved many to ask us to pray with them at the close of each meeting. At one of the churches I noticed Revd Trevor Dearing who had ministered at my father's church when I was a child. He was like a hero to me because of wonderful healings that took place through his ministry. I felt I should be asking him to pray for me, not the other way around. But God was teaching me; it is His power at work in ordinary people that makes them extraordinary – nothing else.

I loved my life at Miracle Bible College with its many challenges, but in my heart I was constantly reminded of the young people who were desperately lost in life. As a teenager I had read David Wilkerson's book *The Cross and the Switchblade*. The best-selling account of his work among gangs in New York deeply moved me. I longed to do something like that, with God's help. The Bible College felt too safe, too religious, and too comfortable. I wanted to reach those outside the churches – the dirty, dangerous, unreachable youngsters.

So when Susanna moved on to visit friends in Scotland, I went home to Cornwall to rest and seek direction. Leafing through my Bible, I found one of my favourite verses – in Psalm 32:8: "The Lord says, 'I will guide you along the best pathway for your life. I will advise you and watch over you." I needed God to do that for me.

I felt sure God had more for me to do; that He was calling me to reach out to prisoners, prostitutes, drug addicts, and street-children. Why He would choose someone from such a sheltered upbringing for such a difficult task, I didn't know. My usual response to a challenge was to turn tail and run! But during my time at Miracle a surprising strength had developed in me and I became quietly confident that somehow He would equip me for the task at hand.

Cally and Pammy Pickard were among the first people to welcome my parents to St Olaf's Church when my father became vicar of Poughill parish. My sister Esther and brothers Andrew, Philip, and David (whom my parents had adopted as a baby) would often wander around the corner to their flat for coffee and biscuits. Cally could talk about her love for Jesus for hours, apparently hardly stopping for a breath. One evening at her flat I shared with her what I thought God was asking me to do in the Philippines. She told me that she had just read a book called *Chasing the Dragon* by Jackie Pullinger.

"It's an incredible story about God's work among drug addicts and the poor in Hong Kong. She was a single girl in her twenties when God called her... just like you," Cally told me. She took the book from her bookshelf and handed it to me. "What God did for her, He can do for you," she said.

I lay in bed that night reading *Chasing the Dragon*. I couldn't put it down. Finishing it in the early hours of the morning, I closed my eyes and prayed that one day God would make a way for me to meet Jackie Pullinger. I woke in the morning thinking how silly I was to make such a request. I couldn't expect to meet someone like Jackie Pullinger – she was famous; she had written a book!

Not long afterwards, one Sunday morning, I joined the choir at St Olaf's, dressed in blue robes and cap. Since childhood I had sung in the choir and I enjoyed the camaraderie of the choir ladies – even though they were much older than me. After the service, as the congregation filed out of church, I noticed a group of people looking at photos and talking excitedly. I joined them and was introduced to Reg Bryan, who explained he was visiting his sister Joan, one of the choir ladies.

"I have just returned from a trip to Hong Kong! Here, have a look. They are photographs of Jackie Pullinger and the people she works with. Have you heard of Jackie Pullinger?" he asked.

I laughed, surprised, and told Reg about my recent prayer.

He smiled, knowingly. "That's how God works! Leave it to me, I'll arrange a visit to Hong Kong for you, so you can meet her," he promised.

I could hardly believe it! God had answered that prayer!

* * *

In the last week of August, 1984, I travelled back to the Philippines with friends from England. Andy and Tracey Newlove were expecting their first baby, but felt God was calling them to be missionaries in the Philippines. I had known Andy since childhood. This time round I felt more comfortable with English companions close at hand.

At that time, it was the middle of the rainy season and torrential rain poured down relentlessly, causing floods and making life very difficult for everyone. Typhoid and dengue fever were rampant. I thought Tracey was very brave to arrive in a foreign country in the final months of her first pregnancy.

Peter and Miracle Sounds arrived back at Miracle weeks later, but soon he went to pastor a church in the province of Isabela, a ten-hour drive east from San Fernando. Peter visited me once a month but despite not having much time together I managed to get to know him better and began to understand why I was so drawn to him. Peter was a people person. He delighted in the stories told by an elderly couple in church and the way in which the wisdom of age was etched in the lines on their faces. He couldn't resist holding new babies, and he joined in the mischief and fun with the children. He welcomed the not-so-bright and the not-so-beautiful and celebrated their uniqueness. That was the common ground that strengthened our relationship.

Chapter 4

Chasing the Dragon

P astor Julius was a teacher at Miracle Bible College. He had lived on the street for much of his childhood, and polio had left him frail. When he married Imelda he asked me to be a sponsor – a sort of godparent for newly-weds.

Like most of the women in their village, his wife Imelda didn't consult a doctor during her pregnancy, expecting to give birth at home with her mother's help. But it was a difficult labour. With no midwife for miles around she was rushed to hospital in the local ambulance. It came as a complete surprise when she delivered twins.

I had never seen such tiny babies. The joy of seeing them make their way into the world was overshadowed by a sense of foreboding because of their being so underweight. But Pastor Julius had proved God many times. Besides, he really didn't like hospitals. "We'll take them home," he insisted. I tried to persuade him otherwise, but it was no use. He signed the "Discharge Against Doctor's Advice" form and packed up the family's belongings.

"I'll come with you, if that's OK?" I blurted out, anxious to help in some way.

Imelda made room for me in their bamboo home. To begin with they wouldn't hold the twins, afraid they might break, so I helped them bathe and feed the miniature newborns. They were just a little bigger than the size of my hand. Too weak to suck, we fed them by painstakingly dripping milk into their mouths from a teaspoon.

Life in a rural barrio was truly minimalist. We usually ate beans and rice three times a day, occasionally supplemented with a sweet potato from the backyard garden. The toilet was a hole in the ground, surrounded by a waist-high fence of bamboo. The people in the surrounding homes could easily look down from their upstairs windows and see me there. We bathed in the nearby river fully clothed − a new custom I had to learn. Once again it was easier for the men, who bathed naked. Every morning the women did their laundry down at the river, spreading the clean clothes out on the boulders on the riverbank to dry in the sun. Because there was no electricity everyone went to bed as soon as it got dark at 7 p.m. Then we awoke with the dawn at 5 a.m., I in considerably worse shape than they as I wasn't used to the wooden bed with no mattress. Whenever I walked through the barrio people stared at me and children giggled, covering their mouths with their hands, as if they had never seen a white girl before.

After a week or so, Pastor Julius held the little ones for the first time and he asked God for a miracle. It became his daily ritual. And God answered him, as the babies began feeding normally and then began to thrive. I felt that I had very little to do with their success; I simply observed what God had done.

Towards the end of the monsoon season I resigned from my nursing job at Miracle to much disapproval. I was convinced that God was moving me on. Alejandra, a graduating student, volunteered to work with me. Together we began to search the city for a place to rent. Weeks went by and we couldn't find anywhere suitable. If it had been England, the houses we had seen would have been demolished as they were in such bad shape. It was disheartening.

One day, after a day of house-hunting, we arrived back at the college hot and tired and longing for a shower and rest, but a student had been waiting for my arrival. "Maam Lesley, Pastor Julius is at the hospital − he has been trying to contact you!" she told me. The twins, now three months old, were seriously ill in hospital. Pastor Bercero had already donated blood for the hospital to use for the babies. Fortunately, the doctor was there when I arrived at the obstetrics ward.

"The older twin has pneumonia and is responding to antibiotics, but I'm concerned about the other one; he has liver failure and is having convulsions. I can operate, but there is only a 50 per cent chance of survival. Yet without it, he will die," he told me.

He looked at Julius and Imelda and then back at me, waiting for further instructions as to whether I would pay for the operation. I closed my eyes and sighed. Why would God take them now after answering our prayers when they were first born?

"Mum, it's me!" I said when my mother answered the phone.

"Lesley! Is everything OK?"

"It's Pastor Julius's twins – they're in hospital and they might not make it," I said, my voice shaking.

She told me that she would call all our friends and ask them to pray. My father prayed with me over the phone. Perhaps the situation was not as hopeless as it had seemed after all.

The operation did not go ahead, and then a couple of days later Pastor Julius came to Miracle. "Maam Lesley! Maam Lesley! They are fine! Both twins are completely healed! They can be discharged right away! The doctor can't understand it!" he said, wiping away tears.

I was so happy I could have hugged him, but Pastor Julius was a very traditional, straight-laced pastor – so I just shook his hand excitedly.

"God is good!" he said. "God is so good!"

I really admired Pastor Julius's unshakeable faith.

Meanwhile Alejandra and I continued our search for a place to rent. Again we turned back along the highway towards Miracle Bible College, frustrated. Then, out of the corner of my eye, I caught sight of a bungalow at the end of a dimly lit alleyway. It was easily accessible but hidden away at the back of a four-storey business block.

"That is the sort of thing we need," I told Alejandra.

"Let's ask!" she said, with her usual optimism.

We enquired at Asiatic Trading but the young Chinese woman told us bluntly that the house was not for rent. Undeterred, we asked her if we could come back later and talk to the landlord. She shrugged and nodded her head.

Mr Sia was sitting in his shop doorway when we returned to enquire again. "No, I am sorry. The house is not for rent. It needs repairs. No good for you!" he told us. He was a dignified man with a kind face. I felt at ease with him and told him our plan to help people in need. He listened intently as I talked about drug addicts and prisons. I searched his face for a reaction as I spoke, but he didn't appear to be bothered by any of it.

Then, as if he had just received orders, he jumped up from his seat. "Let me show you around the place," he said. Stepping inside, neither Alejandra nor I noticed the broken-down kitchen or the dirty windows. We both just felt sure that it was the right place for us. Mr Sia looked at us in a fatherly way and conceded with a smile, asking for a reasonable monthly rent. "Just give me some time to fix a few things before you move in," he said, as we left.

It felt like we had known him for years.

* * *

In December 1984, shortly after signing the contract to rent the bungalow I received a cheque in the mail. Some friends in England had donated the money for me to fly to Hong Kong as I had arranged to work with Jackie Pullinger for a month at St Stephen's Society (a Christian charity providing rehabilitation homes for drug addicts, prostitutes, and gang members). Eagerly, I booked my flight, ready to go.

In my excitement I completely forgot about needing further money to take with me, so when I landed in Hong Kong I had the equivalent of ten pence in my pocket. I was also dressed for the Philippine climate, not realizing that Hong Kong could be quite cold in February. I was totally unprepared but the "brothers" in the home gave me some of their over-sized clothes to wear.

I felt very privileged to meet Jackie and to learn from her. She was always very busy and I had been clothed, fed, introduced to everyone, and oriented to the work schedules when she arrived to greet me. She talked to me as if I was the one to be honoured. With everyone she reversed the order of honour, no matter who they were. When she found out that I was penniless she gave me some money. "I'll pay you back when I get back to the Philippines," I promised, but she wouldn't hear of it.

In many ways life was more comfortable in Hong Kong than in the Philippines. In the modern, high-rise apartment where I stayed with other British helpers, I enjoyed the luxury of hot showers, a flush toilet, a washing machine, a soft settee, and no mosquito bites.

Hong Kong is a shoppers' paradise with its glitzy malls and captivating street markets. At night the streets come alive like a circus, with rows and rows of brightly lit stalls. But I wasn't there to shop. I was there to learn how to reach people with God's love, and to find the courage to put it all into practice. However, I did treat myself to a Mars bar or two from the 7-Eleven store on the corner!

There was an order to Hong Kong society that was sadly lacking in the Philippines. It was refreshingly British. But I felt like a fish out of water. More than once I got lost in the bustling mega-city. Hardly anyone spoke English. On several occasions I don't know how I ever found my way back to Babington to the apartment, but somehow I managed to get there without anyone noticing my prolonged absence.

Jackie put me to work straight away, watching over a group of men who were withdrawing from years of heroin abuse. They lived in a flat in another high-rise building, a mere walking distance from where I was staying. The main doors of all the apartment blocks had security codes and steel grid safety doors. The sweet smell of incense sticks greeted us upon our arrival. Another security door had to be negotiated before we could go inside the flat that Jackie was renting. It all seemed very complicated.

The men were all sitting in the lounge when Jackie and I came through the door. Almost lunchtime, I could smell the rice steaming in the kitchen. I noticed some were still wearing their pyjamas. "So they cannot run away! They live in their pyjamas to begin with," Jackie whispered, explaining that it would be easy to find them on the streets and bring them back. She introduced me, and the men told me their names with a polite nod. John To, Ah Yin, Henry, Raymond, Jonathon, and Timothy immediately appointed themselves as my interpreters. Siu Leung, Ah Keung, Fai, Ah Ping, Ah Lo, and Ah Kam grinned shyly, also introducing themselves.

"We don speak Englis," Ah Ping said, apologetically.

"You just did!" I replied, giggling.

After lunch we sang worship songs together that had been translated into Cantonese. I tried my best to pronounce the Chinese words. John handed me the guitar and asked me to sing for them. In the Philippines I was often asked to sing and had written the lyrics of my favourite songs in a notebook, but I forgot to bring it with me. So I sang the only song I could memorize.

Just a closer walk with thee,
Grant it Jesus this my plea,
Daily walking close to thee,
Let it be, dear Lord, let it be.

They enthusiastically applauded my efforts and every day thereafter handed me the guitar, asking me to sing it again. It became the theme song for what was to become my first trip of several to Hong Kong.

I helped with the day-to-day running of the place, cooking noodles for those who didn't feel like eating anything else, and spending time praying, singing, and studying the Bible with the men. I found myself overlooking the fact that most of them had served time in prison as members of the notorious Triad gangs (gangs responsible for trafficking drugs around the world, and who are also often involved in illegal gambling, money laundering, contract killings, arms trafficking, prostitution, and people smuggling). The men I met had all been heroin addicts for most of their lives. But the scarred track marks on their arms brought back the reality of how desperate they really were, and when the laughter stopped I saw the weariness in their faces.

We spent a few minutes every day being quiet: listening and waiting for God to speak to us in our spirits. We gave Him our cares and received His strength and confidence. "It makes everything easier," Ah Yin told me. I could see it was true. Jackie taught me, and everyone else, to rely on God's Spirit to do the work. "The fragrance of having spent time with Jesus will go with you and spread to others," she told us.

At St Stephen's Society I saw lives that were on the brink of destruction transformed by the power of "praying in tongues". It wasn't strange to me: when I was a teenager back home our family attended a meeting at a Salvation Army Hall in Newark in the Midlands to find out more about the gift of tongues. During a time of charismatic renewal in the 1970s, churches of all denominations were being swept up in a new awareness of God through the baptism of the Holy Spirit. My parents were very interested in it and so was I. The experience that Jesus' disciples had at Pentecost promised to help me overcome my shyness. I longed to share my faith with others, but up to that point I hardly dared speak to anyone about my relationship with God.

After the meeting I joined a group of people who wanted to receive the baptism of the Holy Spirit. We went upstairs to the "Upper Room" and sat on cushions on the floor. A Salvation Army officer approached me. "Why are you here?" he asked gently. Perhaps he thought I was too young.

"I want to be filled with the Holy Spirit," I told him.

He prayed with me and we waited for something to happen. I was determined not to pretend. I wanted the real thing. We waited and waited as the other people started to move back downstairs and leave to go home.

I was beginning to feel like we should probably give up. And then it happened. It felt like a huge bucketful of God's love had been emptied over my head. Immense love poured over me and through me as tears of joy streamed down my face. I opened my mouth to say thank you to God, but instead started to speak in a foreign language. It was the gift of tongues. I stayed there, sort of suspended between heaven and earth for some time. Eventually the Salvation Army officer led me down the stairs, where my parents were waiting. With great delight he told them what had happened. I would never forget the experience. A new boldness became part of my still quiet personality. I began to use more opportunities to tell people about Jesus.

Back in Hong Kong I felt completely comfortable at St Stephen's, where Jackie and my new Chinese friends expected God to work in supernatural ways every day. It felt like the way things should always be.

Ah Yin had suffered a stroke after he withdrew from his heroin addiction. One of my duties was to assist him walking up and down the steep streets to the market every day. He leaned heavily on me and kept apologizing, but I didn't mind at all. The exercise strengthened his paralysed leg. I knew one day he would walk again, unaided. A lasting bond of friendship was formed between us in the time I was there.

One day there was a horrific accident in the workshop when one of the "brothers" completely sliced off the fingers on one of his hands with a circular saw. Surprisingly, his immediate reaction was not to curse in Chinese, but to speak in tongues. I raced to the hospital with him and another helper, the hand wrapped in a clean towel and the severed fingers in another.

In a delicate operation, the surgeon pinned them all back on and the hand was saved. The pins stuck out of his fingers in a kind of steel claw that gave people the creeps. I enjoyed accompanying him to the impressive hospital for his after-care, glad to be doing a little nursing in Hong Kong.

Jackie took me into the (now demolished) Kowloon Walled City one evening – a dark community of hundreds of squatter homes squashed together and built high on top of one another like a huge precarious monument. The place was overrun with Triad gangs, opium dens, gambling, and prostitution.

We carefully made our way down a grimy alleyway and arrived at the meeting room she had there. Several men were gathered waiting for us. I had met addicts before in my father's church in Cornwall, their teeth rotten and eyes glazed over. But I had never seen heroin addiction like this. This was not addiction that was supervised by doctors. The wasted bodies and sunken eyes of the men looked like something out of a horror movie. I had to make a conscious effort not to allow the alarm to show on my face.

Perhaps Jackie noticed, because she asked me to accompany one of them to a nearby noodle stand. My heart sank, but I nodded as he led the way out of the room. I had no idea where he was taking me in the maze of litter-strewn alleyways. He looked ghastly and was obviously uncomfortable because of the all-consuming need for a fix. We couldn't communicate but I smiled nervously at him as he ate his noodles. When the noodle bowl was empty we walked back to the meeting place. Lesson in trust learned, I looked around at the strange gathering and realized the nervousness had left me. After all, I was with people who wanted to know God, no matter what they looked like.

Later I joined a team led by missionaries Chris and Naomi Harrison, away from the big city, on one of the outlying islands. We prayed through the night with "new boys" – new admissions to the drug rehabilitation programme. It was a regular miracle at St Stephen's Society that those who were addicted to drugs hardly experienced any of the agonizing effects associated with withdrawal. I was on duty from 3 a.m. until 7 a.m. with a young man named Jonathon Lee. I liked his wacky sense of humour and we instantly became good friends. We prayed together through the night for a man who had tried several times to come off drugs. On a previous attempt, when the "new boys' house" had been situated in a high-rise apartment block, he had tried to escape through the window… on the twelfth floor. (A new house was found that was more suitable for those times when the urge to go back to the gang and drugs drove the boys and men to extreme escape attempts. With only two floors, surrounded by vegetable gardens in a quaint fishing village, this new accommodation was much safer.) At the end of our shift Jonathon insisted I join him for morning exercises, doing aerobics to Chinese music. This turned out to be more of an exercise in laughter than anything else.

The atmosphere of unconditional love, worship, and prayer brought life-changing results on an extraordinary scale at Jackie's place in Hong Kong. The lessons I learned are still with me today. Like all the men in the apartment, I gained weight during my time there – for the first time in my skinny life. Initially I struggled with chopsticks and John and Ah Yin kept re-filling my bowl with rice and delicious Chinese morsels so I could practise. I didn't want to offend anyone so just kept eating everything they handed to me!

At the end of the month, before I returned to the Philippines, the "brothers" gathered round to pray for me. John To looked very concerned. I could see he wanted to say something but wasn't sure if he should. "Are you sure about doing this work in the Philippines? It's very hard for an innocent young girl like you," he warned.

I didn't answer right away. I was thinking of something Jackie had said: "When you are working with the poor, the one who gave a testimony last month may be in prison this month. There will be times that you will have nothing to boast about but Christ," she had told me.

I knew I wasn't looking to make a name for myself. It did seem ridiculous but I believed God wanted me to reach into the worst situations with His love. Jesus asked us to lay our lives down for others and I was willing to do that even if people didn't thank me for it.

"I know, John, but I am sure. I will put myself in God's hands. All He needs is something to start with," I told him.

We sat looking at each other for a few moments and then John To nodded in agreement.

"I want to help. Is there anything I can send you there?" he asked.

I didn't hesitate for a second with my answer. "You can send me a Mars bar!" I said, laughing.

As I returned to Miracle I knew without a doubt that I could depend on God in every challenge. In Hong Kong I had learned first-hand that no one is so lost that Jesus can't restore them to a full and free life in Him.

For several months afterwards I would pick up a small package from John To at the post office – my Mars bar!

Chapter 5

Russian Roulette

On my return to the Philippines I began to feel restless, impatient to get started on the new path that God had shown me. In March 1985 the day finally arrived for me to move into the bungalow with Alejandra. "Victory House" was born and it felt like Christmas morning! As promised, our landlord had cleaned the place up for us and made sure the shower and toilet were functional. I was very grateful, knowing that not many landlords in the city would have gone to the trouble of doing this. A handful of students from Miracle came to help move our new refrigerator in place and arrange the furniture for me. They were excited to have a second home away from the college where they could hang out during free time, and where the regulations were not quite so strict!

At just the right time, God had provided everything we needed. When I gave Mr Sia the advance payment on the rent I only had enough left in my wallet for dinner that day. Visiting the post office later, I received a letter with a cheque from someone in England who wanted me to use the money for my own needs.

Alejandra and I were laughing, delighted at God's faithful provision, when Mr Sia's son-in-law came to fix the water pipes for us. Constan, quite a serious young man, asked a lot of questions about our mission. He was surprised that his father-in-law had changed his mind about the bungalow.

"This place has been empty for years, you know. I think it's not an accident that you are renting it. A lot of people have asked about it because it's in the middle of the city; they were all told it was not for rent," he said.

We agreed with him, and shared with him our plans for ministry. He paused in the conversation, searching my face to see if he could trust me with what he was about to disclose.

"Tatang Sia's eldest son, Mariano, is a drug addict. Last night I had to drag him off the roof [of the three-storey building in which the family lived]. He wanted to throw himself down onto the road. He has tried many times to kill himself," he told us quietly. A look of desperation crept across his face. "Perhaps you will be the ones to help him," he said.

Early the next morning Alejandra and I were eating our breakfast when Mariano knocked on our door. He put out his cigarette and meekly introduced himself. We invited him to come in and join us for coffee and bread rolls. He stepped cautiously inside. He was very thin and pale. I thought he looked like an empty shell of a man.

"Um... I need your help," he muttered, sitting hunched over in the chair.

"What is it?" I asked, hoping he would feel comfortable enough to open up to us, a couple of strangers.

With stark honesty the story of his life unfolded, like a dam bursting. "My family are successful business people, but I don't like the way I am. I'm hot-tempered, always feeling unhappy and inferior. I can't meet people's expectations, so whenever I am nervous I take drugs. I even drive under the influence of drugs. I took out life insurance because I know someday I will kill myself one way or another," he said.

He told us that he collected guns and usually carried one, loaded. He often played Russian roulette, placing a bullet in the chamber then spinning it and firing the gun against his head.

"When I was a child, my grandfather scolded me for not speaking in our Chinese language. He threatened to hang me if I spoke one word of Ilocano again," he said. He shuddered, the memory obviously still painful. "Since that day I don't care if I will die. Just the other day I argued with a man over a small amount of money and automatically reached for my gun to kill him... then changed my mind."

He stared at the floor, sinking deeper into the chair. Then he pulled a card out of his pocket to show me, explaining that he carried it with him at all times because it had a Ma-cho charm on it for protection. The Ma-cho Temple in San Fernando preached a mixture of Taoism and Roman Catholicism. The goddess Ma-cho was known as the "queen of the heavens and protector of the seas". Mariano told me he visited the temple often with his Chinese friends, to light a candle and ask Ma-cho to change him.

"My mother hates that I smoke after every meal, but I can't even quit that. Nothing works," he said dejectedly.

He sat in hopeless silence for a few seconds.

"I planned to kill myself last night. I was ready to jump from the roof, but Constan knew about it and pulled me down. He told me to come and talk to you," he said.

"God loves you so much, Mariano. Your life is very valuable to Him," I told him, leaning forward in my chair. He lifted his head and looked into my face, desperate.

Opening up her Bible, Alejandra read about Jesus, born as a human baby so that He could be the perfect sacrifice for our sin. Mariano listened closely as we told him that Jesus took all our guilt and shame on Himself when He died on the cross, so that we could live free and have a relationship with the God who created us. All new to him, he listened as if his life depended on it. Perhaps it did. Those who have no hope are ready to grab God's hand and take Him at His Word.

Then Mariano bowed his head and we prayed together quietly, asking Jesus to come and take over his life and set him free. When we had finished praying his face was radiant with a new peace and joy. He straightened up in his seat.

"When you put your hands on my head I could feel my hair stand on end!" he told us excitedly.

"But we didn't put our hands on your head! Perhaps it was an angel... or Jesus Himself! You see – you really are special to God," I told him, tears in my eyes.

He was trembling, his face wet with tears.

"Yes, it must have been Jesus!" he said, utterly convinced.

Mariano's life was changed instantly. The emptiness left him. Later that afternoon, he came back to see us. "It's funny, you know, after lunch I forgot to smoke! I always smoke after a meal," he told us.

Peter had finally arrived from Isabella, so Mariano introduced himself and told him what had happened. "I have quit smoking and I locked all my guns away. I won't be needing drugs anymore," he told him. He cried tears of happiness as he told Peter everything, going through the whole story again. And Peter cried with him.

"My life is changed around! I was so bad tempered before and my heart was like a stone; now it is more like cotton wool!" he said.

"There is a verse in the Bible like that. It says that though your sins are as scarlet, they shall be as white as wool," I told him.

"Really, that's in the Bible? I have to buy a Bible," he said, glowing.

His family didn't understand at first. His mother was worried that he would stop lighting the Chinese candle, afraid that bad luck would come on the family as a result. But he simply told her that there was no longer a need for that, and she had to agree – her prayers had all been answered!

In his enthusiasm he made an announcement over his two-way radio, to his Chinese friends in the volunteer fire brigade. "Tell everyone I am a Christian now!" he told them. Obviously Mariano was completely different, but they didn't expect it to last. They laughed at him, shouting, "Praise the Lord!" whenever they saw him. But they were nervous about coming inside our house, afraid of some magic power that might compel them to get saved.

When he stayed drug-free, however, all of his friends let their guard down and came to visit us. They wanted to know about Jesus too. The police department was situated right next to the fire station, just around the corner from Victory House. Soon policemen started visiting us during their coffee break, asking us to pray with them. Eager to know God and understand the Bible better, they were looking for answers to life's problems.

Months later, we organized a baptism in the sea and asked Loren, Pastor Shields' son, to officiate for us. Mariano was keen to get baptized; he wanted all his friends to see that he was a Christian. His companions in baptism were an unlikely pair. Edgar was formerly a drug pusher, and Tatang was a homeless man.

As Loren lowered them under the water they knew it symbolized the death of their old way of life. A brand new life had begun. Mariano shouted with joy and waved his arms in the air as he walked back to the beach, and Edgar and Tatang were smiling from ear to ear.

"Tatang" was an older man; his real name was Antonio. We had passed him every day, as he sat on the step outside Mr Sia's business block reading the newspaper, begging from passers-by and smoking a cigarette stub he had picked out of the gutter. He liked that we greeted him every morning, always calling him "Tatang", which means "father".

We became firm friends after we invited him to the nearby Chinese restaurant for a good meal. He looked grubby and didn't smell great as we seated ourselves around the table in the Crown Restaurant. The waiter looked at me as if I were mad.

"Order whatever you want," I told Tatang, as he scanned the menu, confused.

Perhaps we were as odd as others supposed, but Tatang felt normal for the first time in a very long while. I felt glad about that, believing he deserved a little respect. As we chatted I was surprised that he spoke English fluently and appeared very well educated. As he tucked into a steaming bowl of beef and noodles, he told us about his musical career. In his younger years he had played saxophone and piano in a band. His wrinkled, weather-worn face lit up with the memory of it. He didn't tell us how he ended up sleeping in shop doorways and eating out of garbage bins as a down-and-out. And we didn't ask.

During the monsoon season we found him curled up in a doorway, shivering uncontrollably. I asked him to come and live with us because I thought he would die if we left him sleeping on the street. When I took him to the hospital an X-ray confirmed that he had advanced tuberculosis.

His complete lack of personal hygiene and chain-smoking made him a very difficult boarder, but I couldn't tell him to leave. His tired old body was in desperate need of rest and kindness.

When the rainy season came to a close he returned to his step outside. We remained friends for years and eventually he went back to his family, resolving the problems that had pushed him away. We saw him one day as we were driving to Baguio, sitting outside a nice house on a rocking chair.

As more people expressed an interest in our mission, I had some business cards printed at the Printers' Press. On the back of each card was a simple map with directions to Victory House, and an invitation for people to come and see us if they needed prayer or counselling. As Alejandra and I went about our daily tasks every day in the city we gave out the cards to people we met. They often shared with us problems they were facing, glad of a listening ear, eager for advice. We were not trained counsellors but were certain that the Bible contained the answers to people's problems.

Once a week we invited people for Bible study and prayer, teaching practical lessons that addressed the problems they had told us about. Every week our small bungalow was packed with people from all walks of life – Chinese businessmen, the homeless, market vendors, policemen, firemen, and students from the colleges. It was nothing short of miraculous as broken marriages were fixed, financial problems sorted out, and lives generally changed for the better.

"After a while everything will calm down. You can't expect to always be on a spiritual high," Pastor Bercero cautioned me, after I excitedly related to him our latest answer to prayer. He didn't want me to get discouraged when the results were not so apparent, when answers to prayer seemed slow or out of reach.

But I wasn't looking far ahead, not even sure how long I would be allowed to stay in the country. There had been a lot of political unrest since 21 August 1983, when Ninoy Aquino was assassinated. He had been a key political figure and his untimely death gave President Marcos a bad image abroad. The economy was in decline, with sugar and coconut oil prices at an all-time low. Foreign debt had reached $26 billion.

When we had no money for food we practised what Pastor Shields taught his students − making it a day for fasting and prayer. Help would arrive before long, either by way of a cheque in the mail or a gift of groceries from someone.

I once heard a preacher say that we don't find God − He finds us. Like a shepherd He seeks out His lost sheep and brings them back to the fold. But the Bible also promises that we will find God if we search for Him with all our heart. Either way, there were times when God found people or they found Him, sometimes just before time ran out.

One day Alejandra went to buy paint and stayed to talk to Danny, the owner of the store. He was one of Mariano's friends in the fire service and had attended some of our Bible studies. "Will you tell me about heaven?" he asked Alejandra. She tried her best to answer all the questions that came pouring out of him. A few days later Mariano came to the house to tell us the sad news that Danny had died suddenly of a massive heart attack. We were stunned. More than ever before we realized the importance of listening for directions and seeing opportunities from God. So every day we asked Him to lead us to the people He knew needed our help.

Visiting Bethany Hospital one day, I noticed a flyer for Alcoholics Anonymous. "That sounds like our kind of place!" I joked with Alejandra. We decided to attend a meeting, trusting God to work through us. We arrived a bit late, so a thick cloud of cigarette smoke had already accumulated, smothering us as we entered the room. People began introducing themselves as we found a couple of seats in the circle of chairs.

"Hello, I am John and I'm an alcoholic," an Australian man said.

They went around the circle, each one saying their name and their status as an alcoholic. I thought it all sounded very final. All eyes were on us, the newcomers, when our turn came around.

"Er... hello, my name is Lesley and I am a Christian," I ventured.

I didn't know what else to say, and gave Alejandra a vague look. She was seated next to me and followed with the same refrain. Mostly Westerners, they humoured us and told us we were welcome as long as we did not "push our religion". Encouraged by the largely positive response I explained about Victory House, inviting anyone to visit us if they were interested in the power of prayer.

After the meeting, Bernie, the AA President, approached us. "I've been searching for years for something to fill the emptiness I feel inside. As soon as I saw you two girls enter the room I knew my search was over. I could see there was something very different about you. You have peace," he told us. Later he visited Victory House and prayed with us, handing his life over to Jesus as his saviour and helper. He immediately found the joy and peace that he was searching for. It transformed his business and his marriage. Sadly, a year later, Bernie died suddenly from a heart attack.

***

The Filipino people are deeply spiritual and almost everyone we talked to allowed us to pray with them, readily accepting Jesus as their Saviour. After seeing the change in Mariano's life, most of his family and friends wanted to hear about his new faith, including his Aunt Cathy and her family. When his younger brother Anson came to visit us with his girlfriend Beth, he wanted to know what had happened to everyone. Beth recognized that God had done something incredible and eagerly told us that she was a Christian, attending a church in Manila. Before they left, we offered to pray with Anson but he point-blank refused. "I am not ready!" he said resolutely.

This wasn't what we were accustomed to and his response took us by surprise.

Mariano's parents welcomed me as their own daughter and his sisters treated me as part of the family too. They wanted to know everything I could teach them about Jesus, and we prayed together often. I watched in wonder as God transformed their lives and families. He gave me a promise for them: "And I am certain that God, who began the good work within you, will continue his work until it is finally finished on that day when Christ Jesus returns" (Philippians 1:6).

Chapter 6

The Dungeon

If we were treated well and cared for by our parents, we would not have become like this. Just like you, you were well cared for by your parents – that explains what you are now. If we had been treated like you we would not have becomes thieves. Some tell us to stop stealing, but what can we do? We are poor. We don't understand why God chose us to be born poor. But when I grow up I will change.

Thommy, eleven years old,
speaking from inside a Philippine jail

Shortly after I had arrived at Miracle Bible College I joined a team of students on the prison ministry, which was led by "Mother Mabel". Mabel was an elderly American lady originally from New York and was a tough old character. What she lacked in size she made up for in personality.

The regional jail was located at the top of a hill in San Fernando, underneath the Capitol Building where the city council held office. Several church groups had been granted permission to conduct chapel services to contribute to the rehabilitation of the inmates. I had never been inside a prison before, but I was eager to experience as much of Philippine culture as I could. Walking into the regional jail was like stepping down into a dark and air-less dungeon, with only a small barred window allowing a shaft of light inside.

When my eyes had adjusted I could see three tall iron grid doors from ceiling to floor and behind each was a cell full of ashen-faced men. The men at the front peered out of the bars to see us, while others pushed their way to the front to get a look out. In the corner was a smaller, darker cell used for solitary confinement. A shudder crept down my spine as I took in the gruesome scene.

More than thirty men were crammed into each of the three cells, about 6 feet by 14 feet, with only one toilet. It smelled bad – of a concoction of stale bodies, urine, dried fish, and smouldering bamboo. I learned later that the inmates supplemented their meagre rations with dried fish and the smell of burning bamboo came from bamboo strips that were scorched to create different shades of brown and yellow, and which were used for various crafts including making pictures. They sold their finished artwork to visitors to make a bit of money. It appeared to be the only attempt to relieve the maddening boredom.

An armed guard had followed us into the prison, jangling a large ring of old iron keys. He opened the barred doors and most of the inmates filed out, as one of the students began to play the guitar. We sang some songs together, accompanied by Mabel who banged two coconut shells together to keep time. She didn't care what anyone thought of her, and the men had obviously grown fond of her wacky ways and outspoken manner. She preached a simple message of hope and then we prayed for the men as they stood with their heads bowed.

As the service ended, dinner arrived in the form of clear, grey soup in a plastic bucket. The men had a small plastic bowl each, with which they would scoop out of the bucket some of the unappetizing liquid to pour over their rice rations.

Conditions were seriously inhumane. On the way out we passed the cell for solitary confinement. Hearing groaning, I glanced inside but could see nothing in the pitch-blackness. The guard must have seen the concern on my face; I was never very good at hiding my emotions. I squinted at him, the sunshine outside stinging my eyes, as he explained that one of the prisoners had become argumentative. The guards had smashed his hands and thrown him in solitary confinement to cool off. The guard was showing off, but I was not at all impressed. I had nothing to say to him. I just wanted to leave.

The words of Jesus in Matthew 25:35–45 disturbed me after that first prison visit: "For I was hungry, and you fed me. I was thirsty, and you gave me a drink. I was a stranger, and you invited me into your home. I was naked, and you gave me clothing. I was sick, and you cared for me. I was in prison, and you visited me" (verses 35–36).

When Jesus was asked when they had done those things for him, he replied, "I assure you, when you refused to help the least of these my brothers and sisters, you were refusing to help me" (verse 45).

That challenge became the cornerstone of my life's work. But for some time, I dreaded ever going back to the prison. When we opened Victory House, Mother Mabel was preparing to teach in a Bible school in the Mountain Province, and we sensed God prompting us to return to the regional jail. We eventually found ourselves walking up the hill to the Capitol Building to speak to the warden about our plans to take on Mother Mabel's chapel services, with his permission. In those days security was lax and no permit was needed. He was eager for us to start right away. With no time for hesitation, we stepped down again into the putrid darkness and I found myself missing the formidable Mother Mabel.

We stood nervously facing the iron-grid doors that separated us from the tattooed inmates. The same colourless faces peered out. The guard turned the big old key in the lock and the sallow men looked us over as they filed out. About sixty men stood or squatted directly in front of us as we introduced ourselves. There wasn't a lot of breathing space between us.

I strummed my banjo as we sang a couple of songs, then I spoke to them about Jesus, with Alejandra interpreting. An armed guard standing at the entrance gestured at intervals for them to be quiet and listen, but, unlike during the time we were there with Mother Mabel, few paid any attention. They nudged each other and passed crude comments, trying to look up our skirts and flirt with us. A couple of feminine-looking men kissed and cuddled each other on the front row.

This was a mistake, I thought. It seemed they were doing their utmost to make us feel uncomfortable. Out of the corner of my eye I saw a rat run along the gutter and retreat into one of the cells. One of the men saw it too. "Dinner!" he grinned, raising his eyebrows. I had an awful feeling he might not have been joking.

We showered and changed our clothes as soon as we arrived home, but the smell of dried fish lingered. Worse still, we discovered we had brought bed bugs home with us. Even so, convinced that God wanted us to persevere, we set off again the following week. This time we both decided to wear trousers!

As soon as we started the service we could see that the atmosphere had changed. Everyone listened attentively as I spoke about God's love that covers every sin. When anyone did start to chatter, several others would look at them disapprovingly and tell them to hush. And I was conscious of a change in my own heart: in some measure I could feel the weight of love and forgiveness that God had for the dejected group of men in front of me.

At the end of our short service several men asked us to pray for them, mostly that their imminent court hearings would go well. My eyes welled up with tears as I placed my hands on their stooped shoulders and prayed a blessing on them. I knew God saw their hearts, not the crimes they now hated. They clearly sought forgiveness and redemption.

We shook hands wholeheartedly with each one of the men at the close of the service, stopping to greet those that had remained in their cells. The atmosphere was charged with a feeling that something extraordinary was about to happen.

They waved and smiled, and thanked us as the guard unlocked the iron grid door and we stepped out into the sunshine again. "No one expected you to come back. Looks like you have won their respect," he told me, grinning.

As the weeks went by, the inmates trusted us enough to tell us not only their names but also the crimes they were accused of committing. Sentencing was a very haphazard process, depending largely on how much money the family had for a decent lawyer. The scales of justice were often weighted by a corrupt legal system. Eager to blame someone, crimes were often blamed on the vulnerable. Stories of judges being bribed, innocent men being framed, and influential men cleared of blame were common.

But not every inmate claimed innocence. Many acknowledged their guilt and went on to trust in Jesus for forgiveness and a new life. This was true of Baltazzar who was nicknamed "Pastor" inside the prison. Baltazzar had been in jail for twelve years, waiting for his sentence. He had become a Christian inside the jail and spent every waking moment studying his Bible and praying. He soon had a following in Cell 4, where they had weekly prayer meetings and Bible studies. It became known as "The Christian Cell" as most of his cell-mates had also become believers.

The words from James 2:15–18, took on new meaning: "Suppose you see a brother or sister who needs food or clothing, and you say, 'Well, good-bye and God bless; stay warm and eat well' – but then you don't give that person any food or clothing. What good does that do? So you see, it isn't enough just to have faith. Faith that doesn't show itself by good deeds is no faith at all; it is dead and useless… I will show you my faith through my good deeds."

We prayed for God's will to be done in the court hearings, but these words challenged me to do more than just pray. We began attending as many hearings as we could, to offer moral support to the men on trial, and to pray then and there for God's mercy and favour. That is how we came to be at Baltazzar's final hearing, sitting in the back row, praying silently that God would intervene on his behalf. Dressed in orange prison uniforms, hands cuffed, three other inmates stood with him as the clerk read out the indictment.

"For possession and manufacture of illegal drugs…" she began.

At that time drugs offences received the death penalty. When Baltazzar was apprehended he was carrying a big sack full of marijuana on his back. My heart sank when the first man in the group was sentenced to life imprisonment at the maximum security prison in Manila. The judge read out Baltazzar's name and the names of the other two men. I held my breath as he continued.

"You are acquitted due to lack of evidence," he said.

Baltazzar threw his hands straight up in the air.

"Praise the Lord!" he shouted, as the judge looked up edgily.

"Hallelujah!" the guard shouted back.

Lack of evidence! He was the one carrying the evidence! I thought, but I wasn't about to put them right! It may seem strange that we would take the side of criminals and pray for their release. After all, most of them confessed to being guilty. But that is what is so amazing about God's grace: He freely forgives anyone who admits their wrongdoing and asks Him for cleansing. For some that means a second chance to try again and get it right.

With Baltazzar's release, Jessie took over the position of "pastor" in Cell 4. There was little hope of release for him as he was accused of plotting to kill a politician. With so much power and money against him he expected to spend the rest of his life behind bars. He had already been inside for nine years. But just before his final hearing a different judge was assigned to his case. As Jessie stood nervously in the courtroom waiting to hear his sentence, we were once again sitting at the back, praying silently. He stood up straight, with his shoulders back and eyes fixed on the judge as if to brace himself. The judge was quiet for several long minutes, scrutinizing the papers in front of him. Finally he looked up and concluded that, having spent nine years in prison, Jessie had over-stayed. The judge ordered Jessie's immediate release.

Jessie turned around to find me in the court room, tears in his eyes. Incredulous, we followed him back to the jail, where he would wait for release papers to be processed. Temporarily back in his cell, relief turned suddenly to stark fear. It seemed too good to be true. Maybe something was wrong. Maybe on his release a hired killer was waiting to get rid of him for good. "No Jessie, we prayed. God has answered. He is with you," I told him. And peace returned as we prayed together.

Upon his release, Baltazzar enrolled in the Pentecostal Bible College and we helped him with his tuition fees. After his graduation he married and became the pastor of a thriving church. We also enrolled Jessie at the Bible College, and later he became Baltazzar's assistant pastor. They devoted themselves to serving God with untiring enthusiasm. When they were not in church they would hike into surrounding barrios to tell the villagers about Jesus, often fasting as they prayed for God to work miracles and for wisdom to understand and share God's Word.

Soon, most of the inmates in Cell 2 and Cell 3 were eager to become Christians and it became fashionable to attend our services. But it was not, of course, a magic formula. Some inmates were transferred to the maximum security prison where they would serve long sentences.

Mike, for instance, was sentenced to life imprisonment for selling cocaine. He had become a Christian the week before his sentencing, kneeling tearfully on the prison floor in front of his cell-mates to ask Jesus into his life. Alejandra and I were visiting the regional jail when the van pulled up to take Mike away. His feet shackled in chains, he hugged his wife and children, afraid to let go of them. We watched helplessly.

"Physically I am broken, but spiritually I have so much peace, joy, and hope in Jesus," he told me, trying to smile. He pressed an envelope into my hand before climbing into the van to leave. I read his letter when I arrived home. "Grace, love and peace to you from God the Father and from our Lord Jesus Christ," it began, copied from his Bible.

I am deeply troubled knowing that I will be leaving, I would like to learn more from your preaching and the way that you explain the truth of the gospel. You taught us how to acknowledge and praise Him for His boundless love, grace and mercy to us which serves as a guiding light for me who was once lost in the dark. All the worries that lie ahead of me have turned into gladness and hope because I decided to surrender my whole being to Jesus Christ as my personal Saviour, Comforter and Redeemer.

Your pen is left behind here, so I entrusted it to Manny [a prisoner] so he can turn it over to you. As you read this I am on my way to Munti. Pray for me that the Lord will give me strength and courage to resist temptation. You are always in my prayers... Mike.

The change in the regional jail was so evident that on his day off the warden visited Victory House to learn more about Jesus. He asked for Bibles to distribute in his village, and asked us to pray that he would receive the baptism of the Holy Spirit so that he would fearlessly tell others God's Word.

The inmates were seldom allowed out of their cells; the only time they saw daylight and felt the warm sun on their skin was when they were required to fetch water for bathing. Although it was unlikely to be granted, I asked the warden if we could baptize the inmates who had become Christians. But without question he gave us permission to baptize them in the sea in groups of eight, with an armed guard present. Several of the guards who witnessed the baptisms also gave their lives to Christ. Families were rebuilt and lives changed in a way none of us could have dreamed.

***

Art was a small, stocky man in his forties with a big, bad reputation. His body bore the tattoos he had received in various jails across the island; he had been imprisoned for most of his life. After the prison service one week, he approached me. I noticed a tremor in his voice that was out of character for him.

"Maam... I am due to be released but I have nowhere to stay on the outside," he told me.

We had heard the stories of revenge killing and torture. They called it "salvaging" – a weird contradiction of terms. Art knew that as soon as he got out of jail he would find himself being a "suspect" again, or worse – he would be eliminated altogether. He had heard and seen things that made him a target and he didn't mind admitting that he was afraid for his life.

"Can I live with you and Maam Alejandra for a while?" he asked sheepishly.

A strange request... but there was something that endeared him to us. We had prayed that God would lead us to the people He wanted us to help, so we trusted that He was doing just that. He arrived at our door weeks later with a small bag containing his belongings, which he allowed us to search. I noticed both his arms were scarred with slash marks from his elbow to his wrist. "I slashed them to get a better high on drugs... I don't do drugs anymore... it was stupid," he explained uneasily.

Soon after his arrival, I came into the kitchen to make a cup of tea and found Art sitting at the table with a mirror and a lighted match. He was trying to burn the tattoos off his face! He was trembling as he tried to explain. "I can't hide these. If the police see them they might kill me – they are the marks of

75

a notorious prison gang," he said. He took off his T-shirt and I saw a huge tattoo on his back. "This one I can cover up if I don't take my shirt off," he told me.

He had been awake all night and was in a terrible state, as gruesome scenarios paraded through his mind. He told me he had been tortured in prison and that the threats had filled him with fear. Alejandra came into the kitchen and we sat around together praying, asking God to give him peace.

"This is a good Scripture for you to memorize," I suggested. Philippians 4:6–7: "Don't worry about anything; instead, pray about everything. Tell God what you need, and thank him for all he has done. Then you will experience God's peace, which exceeds anything we can understand. His peace will guard your hearts and minds as you live in Christ Jesus."

I believe that words in the Bible have so much power in them that they can go into a man's past and heal his wounds, and give hope in the worst despair. It was our instruction manual and our only treatment plan. For several nights we took turns to stay awake and pray with Art as he trembled in fear, unable to sleep.

He settled, but there were a couple of times in the middle of the night when I discovered he wasn't in his room. Venturing outside to look for him, I found him standing at the side of the road, waving a switchblade in the air at unseen enemies. I confiscated his knives whenever one reappeared but he was free to come and go and often brought another weapon home with him. I gathered quite an interesting collection. His violent past simmered just under the surface for some time. He always treated me with respect, but I was thankful for the security guard who stood watch outside the neighbouring bank at night. With the police station just around the corner, I felt God had truly directed us to the best location for our mission.

Over supper one evening, Art told us about a past incident when, under the influence of drugs, he had gouged out a piece of flesh on his forearm with a fork and ate it! He showed me the scar. "I came off drugs cold turkey inside the jail," he explained. But it was not effortless. One day he came home with a large bottle containing several small black bugs and stale bread buns.

"What on earth is that?" I asked.

"Korean bugs," he answered calmly, and went on to explain that they were a natural hallucinogenic when eaten. I think he supposed that because they had come from nature they were permitted. But they were confiscated. "I'm sorry," he said, meaning it.

He had been brought up with no clear concept of right and wrong, but he was willing to learn. In order to prove his good intentions he tried to quit smoking, buying handfuls of candy every day as a substitute for his cigarettes.

One Sunday evening he arrived at Miracle Church late. I could see that he was drunk. He grabbed one of the girls from behind. Seeing my disapproval he bolted down the stone steps and along the highway. I almost fell headlong down the steps as I ran after him. We laughed for a long time afterwards at the curious sight of Maam Lesley chasing an ex-convict down the national highway!

The pastors and teachers at Miracle Bible College thought I was out of my mind inviting such people into my home. In Christian circles it was considered highly improper for men to live with single girls. But, while I deeply respected them, I was not concerned about other people's opinions. That was the least of my worries!

After several months, Art began looking around for a job and seemed to be making progress. Sometimes when we turned on the tap at Victory House only mud sputtered out. Purified water was not available in the shops so we boiled our drinking water, but unsurprisingly, I eventually succumbed to typhoid again. I was ill in bed one day when Alejandra came into my bedroom. "There is a policeman at the door," she told me.

Painfully weak, I staggered out of bed. He was apologetic, explaining that Art had been arrested in the early hours of the morning. "He gave us your name as a point of contact," he said, sceptically.

I confirmed that, unlikely as it sounded, Art was indeed living with us.

"I'll come round to the police station right away," I told him.

Alejandra propped me up and we inched our way around the corner.

The policeman on duty at the station looked at me and smirked. "Art was walking in the Plaza last night when a *bacla* [homosexual] approached him and became 'overly affectionate' let's say! Art smacked him in the face. The *bacla*, a Filipino tourist from America, has threatened to sue," he told me, looking for my response.

I had a very high fever and was probably delirious when I scolded the officer for detaining Art. "What would you have done?" I challenged.

He glanced at Alejandra, questioningly. I could see he was wondering who was this crazy white woman dressed in pyjamas! My strength failing, I slumped down in a nearby chair.

"Why do you even care?" he asked me.

"He is going straight; I don't want him to go back to jail," I cried.

He shook his head in disbelief.

"Go back to bed… you look terrible!" he said, motioning for me to leave.

The case must have been dropped as Art was not detained for long. That was the last time he would sit inside a jail cell. He went on to find a place to live and worked his way up in the building trade.

Years later, about to cross the road to get a tricycle home, I heard someone shouting at me.

"Manang! Manang Les!"

I looked up and saw Art waving frantically from the other side of the road. His mates at the building site looked on in disbelief as he hurried across and grabbed my hand, a huge smile on his face! I'm sure his friends could see that I was not in fact his *manang* (older sister)! I was younger and a *puraw* (a white woman). Art had always called me "Manang".

"I am married now, you know! And my stepson is training to be a pastor! I work as the site manager at the building project over there!" he told me excitedly.

I was so happy to see him that I forgot about Filipino protocol and hugged him tightly. He looked over at his mates, as if to say, "You see!" as they jeered and applauded.

Chapter 7

Child Prostitute

**In a time and country where women were not
even considered "second-class citizens", Jesus
treated all the women he met with honour,
dignity, and respect – whether they deserved it
or not.**

Sitting at our kitchen table sipping tea in May 1985, an
article in *The Star* newspaper about the anti-child abuse
work of missionary Father Shay Cullen caught my
attention. A recent survey claimed that the Philippines had
the fourth largest number of child prostitutes in the world, an
estimated 20,000 in Manila alone. "Wherever there are coastal
resorts or American bases there are children of both sexes
selling themselves to local and foreign clients," it reported.

The youngest prostitute interviewed was seven years old
and the oldest sixteen. San Fernando City and neighbouring
Bauang were described as "a bastion for paedophiles". The
girls earned between 100 and 1,000 pesos (£1–£10) a day
in Manila, but in the provinces rates were as low as 20 pesos
(about 20 pence) a day.

At one tourist spot in Pagsanjan, renowned for its beautiful
waterfalls, there were at least 3,000 boys involved in the sex
trade. A paedophile ring was uncovered there, consisting
mostly of Caucasian teachers, who used a legitimate adoption
organization as a front.

It disturbed me that the city where we lived played a part
in such grim statistics. We had heard that terms existed between

the shady businesses and the authorities, who disregarded what happened behind the closed doors of "members-only" nightclubs. A conspiracy of silence surrounded the exploitation of children for sex. It seemed hopeless and yet I felt there must be something we could do, in our corner.

In the Philippines a prostitute was known as either a "hostess" or a "guest relations officer" as they sounded more respectable. Signs could be seen outside bars and nightclubs blatantly advertising vacancies: "Wanted: GRO – attractive with pleasing personality".

We really had no idea what we were getting into as neither Alejandra nor I had ever been to any of the clubs. We decided to make a start by visiting the red-light district late on Friday nights, until the early hours of the morning. There were about thirty small disco bars situated along the road, on the way to the American army base. There was nothing remotely inviting about them. Walking up and down the stretch of road, we stopped to talk to any of the girls who greeted us. They were happy to meet us. But we could never talk for long; the girls' bosses told us in no uncertain terms to move on and stop interrupting their work.

The "guests" at the disco bars objected to our intrusion into their world. A couple of times men grabbed us, mistaking us for working girls, but the girls quickly came to our rescue. When we stopped to chat with a group of girls around a drinks table one night an Australian man approached me angrily. "You can't change these whores!" he shouted in my face. I glanced apologetically at the girls. It seemed to me that the "white" men were particularly degenerate.

Prohibited from going out much during the day the girls usually slept instead, cooped up in run-down rooms behind the run-down bars. "No one else bothers to talk to us. People pass by but they look away, because we are dirty," a pretty sixteen-year-old told me.

None of the girls spoke Ilocano, the language in our region. They had come from other islands and adopted new identities, assuming names like Girly, Angel, and Kisses. Alejandra spoke Tagalog, but with 170 different languages in the Philippines conversation was limited. Still, we gave them our address and telephone number inviting them to visit us if they could.

We soon made a friend and ally in Delia, who spoke English fluently. We chatted under the flashing lights of Tropicana Bar. A girl straddled the narrow bench next to us; spaced out on drugs she writhed seductively to the throbbing music, trying to get noticed. Delia smiled at me and raised her eyebrows, trying to help me feel a little less uncomfortable. She genuinely wanted to help the younger girls escape the wasted life she had known. She had the beautiful face and hair of a classic Filipina beauty, yet at twenty-two she was worried that she would soon be too old to attract many customers.

"When I came here I forgot about falling in love. Now it's too late for me," she joked wryly. I had to admit she looked older than twenty-two, but I didn't tell her so. "My dream is to find a decent white man to marry me and take me to America," she told me. It always astounded me how many intelligent, beautiful Filipina girls shared Delia's dream. "When I am in the USA and have a lot of money I can divorce him or wait for him to die; if he is really old I won't have to wait very long!" she laughed.

I couldn't work out who was being taken advantage of. Poor Delia kept hoping as one after another of the indecent white men used and discarded her. Undeterred, she held on to her dream – it was how she survived.

One night she introduced us to Ninette who had arrived at the bar the previous day. Ninette looked out of place, still dressed modestly in her flower-print dress as if she were going to church. She claimed to be fifteen but looked younger. She sat with her knees pulled up under her chin, rocking to and fro, obviously in distress.

"She ran away from home and applied here to work as a waitress," Delia confided in hushed tones, afraid her boss would hear us talking. She shrugged and rolled her eyes as if unable to believe the girl's naivety. A child prostitute, Ninette's body had been sold quickly for the high price of 2,000 pesos (a month's wages in those days).

"She didn't see any of the money, of course. Look at her – it seems she will lose her mind," Delia whispered.

The next day, she brought Ninette to our house. She had smuggled the frightened girl out. "I only have thirty minutes; they think I'm at the market," she explained hurriedly.

"It's OK! You go… we will help her," I promised, hugging Ninette close to me. Ninette sat down and began to cry. Alejandra brought some juice and cookies and invited her to eat, but she declined. We sat in silence for a few minutes, not sure how to proceed. What could we possibly say to make things right? I told her about the young woman in the Bible who came to Jesus and worshipped Him by washing His feet with her tears. "The other people wanted the woman to leave the house, but Jesus welcomed her and honoured her," I explained.

She looked at me in disbelief.

"He can't forgive me," she murmured, shaking her head vigorously.

We helped her understand that she was not at fault and that God wanted to heal her brokenness. She returned to the bar that afternoon, but found the courage to escape the following week, jumping on a bus to Manila and then home. I had given her enough money for her fare.

Delia came to tell me the good news. She was excited as she made preparations to stay with a "white man" at a nice hotel. "He wants to marry me! I am also getting out of here!" she said, clapping her hands with glee. But when the week was over, Delia was back at work and he was gone.

* * *

Almost a year after we moved to Victory House, it was election time in the Philippines. Corazon, the widow of Senator Ninoy Aquino (who was assassinated in 1983), accused President Ferdinand Marcos of impoverishing the nation through illegal transactions. President Marcos countered that Senator Aquino was one of the founders of the Communist Party of the Philippines, the armed wing of which, The New People's Army, was responsible for killings, kidnapping, and terrorist activity throughout the country. A political time bomb, newspapers speculated that all missionaries other than those from the Catholic faith would be expelled from the country, along with the American army bases. Foreigners were advised to stay in their homes as much as possible. Suddenly, there was a lot of anti-American feeling, and everyone with white skin was considered to be American. Suspicious of America's ultimate intentions, the Filipinos were fiercely protective of their independence. Visiting the red-light district late at night was out of the question. Instead, we had to rely on the girls coming to visit us.

As expected, the election that took place on 7 February 1986 was hopelessly fraudulent – the only country that congratulated Marcos on his win was the Soviet Union. Chief of staff Fidel Ramos and the defence minister Juan Enrile called on Marcos to resign. Suddenly, decisively on 22 February, the EDSA Revolution (or People Power Revolution) broke out. The rebels received the backing of the powerful Catholic Church and consequently the support of the people in Manila.

But where we lived, in Northern Luzon, people remained staunch supporters of Marcos. He was born in Ilocos Norte, not far from us, and to the locals he forever remained a hero. When the Marcos family were forced to flee to Hawaii, Corazon Aquino was sworn in as president, despite apparently only ever having been a housewife. It seemed that Cardinal Sin, heading her advisors, would actually be running the country. It was such an amusing name for someone in his profession!

At this point, Peter and I were not sure where our future together would lead. I didn't want to put pressure on him to join us at Victory House but I couldn't see myself living in rural Isabella, where he was pastor of a small church, either. I didn't want to think about having to return to England. We lived one day at a time, never sure what would happen next in Manila.

Months went by and the rumours of a Communist take over came to nothing. Then, after loads of paperwork and hassled trips to and from Manila, I was granted a missionary visa that allowed me to remain in the country for three years. Things gradually became more stable and our outreaches to the streets and jail resumed.

Very late one night, Bhaby arrived at Victory House. When I opened the door she looked up at me with huge brown eyes, just like a lost puppy.

"Please, please let me stay with you. My boss kicked me out of the bar; I have a skin disease," she pleaded, showing me the dark spots all over her body.

Too tired for conversation, I invited her in and made a bed up for her. "We'll talk about it all in the morning," I mumbled, retreating back to bed.

I was drifting back to sleep when we were startled by someone hammering on the front door. The Sia's guard dog was barking frantically. "What on earth?" I muttered, following Alejandra down the stairs. She gingerly pulled the curtain back and peered out into the darkness. I could see a Filipino man with a shock of white hair like Albert Einstein. He was shouting angrily and pounding his fist on the door. "He has a gun!" Alejandra hissed. Before I could stop her, she had opened the door.

"Calm down and stop waving that gun around!" she ordered.

Alejandra always had a certain air of authority about her, and the man apologized as he stepped inside. He was obviously drunk, but he did at least calm down when he saw my frightened face. Bhaby was hiding underneath her bed, terrified. He asked us if she was in the house, accusing her of stealing 800 pesos from him before she left. We didn't reply to his question, not knowing what to do.

"Give her back! You can have her when she has returned the money. She is ugly and useless anyway!" he told us.

We thought we would never see her again if we let her go, but felt we were in no position to argue with him. I was praying as I went to Bhaby's room and brought her out. He grabbed her, dragged her to the door, and left. Shaken, Alejandra and I sat for some time, praying desperately for her safety. We didn't hear from Bhaby again. A week later the bar was closed down.

It was no longer safe for the girls to visit our house. Their refuge had been found out. The girls advised us to meet with them during siesta hour instead, between 1 p.m. and 2 p.m. While everyone else was snoozing in the hot afternoon, we sat outside in the shade, chatting and eating green mangoes dipped in chilli vinegar. For that hour at least, we could have been any normal group of girlfriends meeting together.

But the stories they told us exposed the horror of the sex trade, and so it was far from normal. Any romantic notion of bright lights and happily ever after was shattered. I didn't want to seem condescending so I tried desperately not to appear shocked, but my mind was in turmoil.

A missionary friend had recently shared with me her plan to start a home for abandoned babies. She asked me to find out about babies in the red-light district. Asking the girls about it one afternoon they told me that most of the newborns were sold. That was illegal, of course, but all life in the red-light district was outside the law and the authorities usually looked the other way, unwilling to get tangled up in the vast mess of it all. The girls looked at each other uncomfortably as Candi blurted out what really happened.

"Some babies are killed… as they are being born," she said, demonstrating the sudden twisting motion of strangulation as she spoke.

I couldn't believe what I was hearing. Maybe she was high on drugs and talking nonsense, or just trying to shock me.

"It can't be!" I objected.

"No, Maam. It's true," she insisted.

Seeing my obvious dismay, she tried to soften the impact of what she had just revealed. "It doesn't happen often," she said, looking around nervously for the others to back her up somehow.

A teenage girl, sitting on the step of one of the shanties, spoke up. "Usually we get abortions. We can buy medicine at the drugstore without a prescription. It's easy… and if that doesn't work the Mamas get rid of it by massaging our tummy until we miscarry," she told me.

I felt sick.

"You must know how dangerous that is!" I told them.

They nodded, and sighed. "I know. Two of my friends died; they were not taken to the hospital because abortion is illegal," the girl said.

"What choice do we have?" an older girl asked, looking away angrily.

I felt powerless to do anything about it. I looked into their lifeless eyes not knowing what else to say, afraid to ask any more questions.

I thought of all the children I had seen running around the area. A social worker had told me there were over 7,000 neglected children in this small area. Passed around from one "mama" to the next, many did not go to school and some grew up into the trade.

"What if you want to keep your baby – can you?" I eventually asked.

"Yes, especially if she has white skin," one of the girls replied. I assumed she meant that a pretty little girl with white skin would make an ideal child prostitute.

In the end, nothing came of our research except lost sleep on my part. My friend returned to America because her own children couldn't adjust to life in the Philippines and the planned home for babies was withdrawn.

We tried our best to support the girls who got pregnant. I referred them to the Reproductive Health Clinic, which was the "underground" name for a Family Planning Clinic. The Catholic Church taught that it was sinful to use contraception, and the girls were embarrassed to attend the clinic because of the questions asked.

When a girl named Jubilene learned she was pregnant, she insisted on keeping her baby. The news reached us that she had given birth early that morning, so Alejandra and I decided to visit her with a gift of baby clothes. The woman at the "sari-sari store" directed us down a narrow alleyway to a house built of scraps of plywood. We climbed up the bamboo steps to go inside.

"Jubilene! Are you home? We came to see your new baby!" Alejandra called out.

We both gasped as we peeked inside the open door. Every available space on the floor was taken up with a baby or toddler. A middle-aged woman made a quick retreat to the back of the room, trying to hide. She was holding a baby, feeding it from a bottle. I could see it was not milk – the greyish watery liquid was rice water, probably with sugar in it.

Jubilene was the only mother there, lying on the floor with her newborn. I handed her the gift, meekly explaining to the woman the purpose of our visit. She looked at us suspiciously, obviously displeased, and then disappeared through a back door.

"They are making me go back to work tonight," Jubilene whispered.

She was so grateful for our concern, desperately missing her own mother and unsure of her baby's future. We prayed together. But we left wishing we could have done more. That feeling never left me.

Chapter 8

Just Married!

... let us exalt his name together!

Psalm 34:3

I didn't tell many people in England about my relationship with Peter because I was nervous about their opinions, and a bit embarrassed at the speed with which I had fallen for him, having known him only for a short time. But when I received an invitation to my older brother, Andrew's, wedding, it seemed a good time to let everyone know. Peter and I made plans to visit England together so he could meet my family and friends. As I suspected, everyone did have their own ideas... the most extreme reaction among acquaintances and some friends being that it was completely against God's will for anyone to marry someone of a different cultural background.

After Andrew's wedding, Peter and I travelled around England together for four months, visiting churches that sponsored LAMA Ministries. As I suspected everyone had their own ideas about cross-cultural marriage and what missionary life should be like. It was confusing, but we believed that God was in our relationship and He would see us through any future difficulty. I was packing our suitcases to return to the Philippines before Peter found the courage to ask my father what he thought about our getting married. Dad hesitated with his answer, tormenting Peter for a few moments. Finally, Dad gave his consent, cautioning him to take good care of me. My parents could see that Peter was committed to serving

God and I think that calmed any fears that they must have quietly felt.

In December 1986, my family arrived in the Philippines for our wedding. There was much to do but I didn't cancel any ministry activities because I wanted them to experience it all during their brief stay. Just before the wedding day, we went for a boat ride along the coast. We passed a derelict hotel on one of the beaches, built in the old Spanish style.

"Look, Lesley! It must have been fantastic once upon a time. What a shame to leave it to go to ruin like that!" Dad said.

"I know, everywhere buildings are started and never finished. People run out of money," I explained.

Further along the coast, we saw a small village of grass-roofed shacks. I had never seen anything like it in the area in which I had been staying – it looked like a picture from an old missionary story. My parents wanted to go there, but the sun was already going down so we had to head home instead.

Finally 13 December came round – the day of our wedding day at Miracle Church. A lot of symbolism and superstition is wrapped up in a Filipino wedding, mostly from Spanish influences. The ceremony usually involves a great number of groomsmen, bridesmaids, and sponsors. The more sponsors that are chosen, the more prestigious the couple are thought to be, particularly if they include political figures and prominent people. But I wanted to keep things simple, so persuaded Peter to scale things down to just a few of the special people in our lives.

My sister, Esther, was maid of honour and Peter's nieces were bridesmaids. Peter's brother Ezekiel was the best man. His son was a groomsman with Sammy, and his two youngest children were the ring-bearer and flower girl. They stole the show.

My father conducted the ceremony, the only "British" part of the day, He also gave me away. "Who gives this woman to be married to this man?" he asked, looking around the church.

Then, after an awkward silence, he smiled and answered, "I do!" Everyone laughed and applauded.

The church was packed with a diverse crowd of friends – doctors, lawyers, street vendors, and businessmen, as well as our extended family of homeless people, call-girls, ex-convicts, and street-boys. Friends from England, Phillip and Sheila White, who had been working in Manila, recorded the event on video for us. Marrying Peter felt like everything was exactly as it should be – it was the same feeling of certainty I had experienced when I first walked onto the campus of Miracle Bible College.

At Filipino weddings *everyone* is unofficially invited to the reception. That means everyone within walking distance of the church. Peter's cousin, a professional chef, managed the kitchen, creating a delicious feast with plenty for all the guests.

We had marked two weeks off on our calendar for a honeymoon in Hong Kong. We stayed at Hang Fook Camp – a temporary housing area that Jackie was using for rehabilitating drug addicts. Not everyone's idea of a honeymoon destination but Peter and I loved it!

When we returned to the Philippines, Alejandra married a former student of Miracle Bible College, Johnny Manaol. After their wedding, they moved to pastor a church in Ilocos Norte, a six-hour journey north of San Fernando. Peter and I then decided to move Victory House to a bigger bungalow situated outside the city centre. A simple concrete house with six small bedrooms, it had previously been used as a dormitory for truck drivers. Our first impression of the place was that it was perfect for housing our large family, with a big kitchen and a garden area. I overlooked the fact, though, that there was only one toilet and shower, having given no thought to my own needs as the lone female!

But it was the start of a new adventure and I went straight to work to make it home. Pastors Fred (Peter's best friend) and Rogelio (Peter's uncle) moved in with us as staff. Our new life together was straight away shared with them and several young men who had the worst kind of problems; it was a time of adjustment for everyone!

Pastor and Mrs España were both teachers at the Pentecostal Bible College in San Fernando, where they were in charge of the prison ministry. When they heard about Victory House and our own prison ministry, they came to meet us. An older couple, they delighted in telling us the story of their romance and ministry together. They had lived and worked among the tribal people of the Philippines after they graduated from Bible College, and then dedicated their lives to serving the inmates at the regional jail. I deeply respected them for their devotion to God's calling and to each other. We joined forces. In later years, they became trustees of LAMA Ministries.

My dad was still curious about the old hotel he had seen on the boat ride before our wedding, and so were we, so Peter and I decided to investigate. The caretaker was sitting outside the entrance when Peter pulled the jeep up outside. We introduced ourselves and told him we were interested in the place. Filipinos tend to automatically assume that anyone who is white has plenty of money – he took one look at me and allowed us to go inside the property to explore.

"It was called 'The Seagull'," he told me, leading us up a grand staircase to the second floor. Peter and I played the part of prospective buyers and we made our way up to a separate apartment on the third floor.

"This is the penthouse," the caretaker said.

I peered out of a window across the sea, and caught sight of the grass roofs of the shanty village, at the furthest point along the coastline. Going back down the stairs, I noticed the swimming pool in the centre courtyard. We stood for a while in a large room with ornate woodwork and arched windows. With my overactive imagination, I could see the place restored and stately, full of people who were once homeless.

Afterwards we couldn't get The Seagull out of our thoughts. So a few weeks later we enquired about the building at the bank. But the manager told us a restraining order prevented its sale, since the owner had gone bankrupt. Someone had offered £35,000 but the bank wanted more. We smiled and thanked him. That was more money than we ever thought we could find.

I was content in our bungalow for the time being, anyway. At first, my new housemates were embarrassed to find me cleaning the toilet or scrubbing the floor. They had the notion that all Western women had servants. But I enjoyed housework − it was my relaxation! There are clear-cut male and female roles in Filipino society that I constantly transgressed, but I tried my best to match the stereotype of a Filipina wife − to begin with at least. That meant getting up at dawn to go to the market for our daily food, then washing our clothes by hand in cold water every day. After dinner the men retired to the bamboo shade in the garden to tell stories and relax for a while. Ignoring protocol, I usually joined them as it was the only chance I got for idle conversation. They eventually got used to me intruding on the "men-only" zone. Being a woman in the Philippines appeared to be much more difficult than being a man in the country.

I enjoyed the hum of the open market, setting off as early as I could before the meat started to smell bad in the heat. The market was a bustling community of noisy, happy people. To me it represented everything I loved about Filipino culture. It is customary to have favourite vendors or *suki*. I usually stopped at the coconut stall, as my favourite recipes included coconut milk. A coconut was selected from a pile on the ground, cracked open with a machete then grated with an old-fashioned machine that the vendor pumped with his foot! The gentleman selling coffee beans always grinned at me and beckoned me over to his stall. I didn't have a coffee percolator but I always stopped for a chat as it was one of the few places that smelled really good!

The meat market was not so appealing, with all manner of animal parts hanging from large hooks. The vendors flicked off flies as customers picked pieces up, poked them, sniffed them, and put them back down. When a pork chop slid off the table into the gutter it was simply rinsed off with some water and put back on display. With an abundance of fresh fruit and vegetables, I could easily have been persuaded to become a vegetarian (the Philippines, though, is a nation of meat-lovers and it is considered rude to not eat what is offered).

There was a huge variety of fresh fish, including octopus, shark, squid, tuna, blue marlin, and big tiger prawns. Peter liked to eat mudfish, which, to me, resembled a snake. Mudfish were sold alive then killed before cooking by administering a hefty blow to the hard shell of a head. Once or twice I purposed to buy some for him but the whole procedure gave me the creeps! They were handed to me in a plastic bag, still jumping. I walked home as quickly as I could with my arm extended outward so that the bag was as far away from me as possible! In the end I gave up, as it was all too stressful.

I enjoyed trying different foods and Peter and Uncle Rogelio taught me how to cook Filipino and Chinese food. "Eat what is set before you," my mother always told us. She probably hadn't envisioned pig intestines, cleaned and fried until they were crispy, or cow's stomach cooked in bile, or pig's ear cooked in its brain… Later I realized that it was perfectly acceptable to refuse the more unusual and distasteful recipes. It seemed that eating raw fish fingerlings, shrimps that were still moving, or dog meat were rituals of sorts to prove one's manhood!

On the whole we got along very well together. Living in community proved the best way for God to form His character in us. Much of the pastor's theological training was useless in our line of work. Basically, our daily challenge was to live as servants – with God-given, extraordinary grace and patience. Love your neighbour as yourself was the starting point of our Christian adventure and on-the-job training. In later years, Fred and Rogelio told me it was the most valuable training they had ever received.

***

Whenever we passed through the red-light district I felt uncomfortable; it didn't feel right that we were no longer helping the girls there. But I had no interpreter, as none of the men wanted to accompany me at night. Instead Peter agreed to start children's meetings in the red-light district every Saturday afternoon. We found a place to congregate behind the disco bars. But in the dry season there was no shade, so our time together was cut short to prevent sunstroke. In the monsoon season we parked the jeep in the clearing and crammed fifty or so grubby children in the back. We sat together like smelly sardines in a tin, telling Bible stories and singing songs. Despite the conditions, I loved every minute and so did Peter!

On one such visit I noticed the nearby Barrio Health Centre had been vandalized and graffiti had been scrawled on the walls. I wondered if there was any hope of really making a difference – it must have been so discouraging for the doctors and nurses who had hoped to help the community, as now, the place was being used for a public toilet. "I wonder if we could use that place as a children's church?" I asked Peter. We made enquiries and no one objected to our borrowing it once a week. The children pointed at the obscenities scrawled on the walls and laughed. But it was not funny. Like ancient hieroglyphics, the graffiti told the story of their young lives. They were children with tainted bodies and minds, a grossly distorted view of life.

On Boxing Day, 1987, we organized a Christmas party for the children. We were caught up in happy chaos with so many excited children screaming, shouting, and enjoying the fun. I was grateful that Pastor Lito and his wife Maureen, graduates of Miracle Bible College, were on our team – we needed all the help we could get! After yelling instructions for the party games at the top of his voice, Peter eventually got everyone organized into groups. There was an egg-throwing contest, eating-an-apple-on-a-rope game and "breaking the pot". The favourite game was always breaking the pot, where a clay pot was filled with candies and hung up high and the children took turns to hit it with a stick, blind-folded. The successful blow broke the pot and the winner got a prize, while everyone else scrambled in the dirt to find the fallen candy. During the pandemonium several adults who had gathered shouted misguided directions and laughed hilariously at the children beating the air, having wandered completely off course!

Sitting on a borrowed wooden bench with three bar-girls, I noticed a little girl wandering from house to house crying. She had no clothes on and her hair stood up in a matted mess. I couldn't understand why everyone ignored her cries, so went over to lift her up for a cuddle. She was so frail. As I carefully sat back down on the bench, bouncing her gently on my knee, I noticed scars on her legs and back that looked like cigarette burns. She was probably two or three years old.

Peter glanced at me and saw the anguish in my face. I could no longer enter into the spirit of the party. An awful sadness was tearing me up inside. *How could anyone do this to a child? And why does no one seem concerned?* I thought, fighting back the tears.

Suddenly a burly, stone-faced woman stomped towards me, grabbed the little girl's arm, and dragged her away crying. I recognized her as the woman Alejandra and I had seen when we went to visit Jubilene, in the house full of babies. She was not at all pleased to see me again but I followed her, regardless.

"Hello! What is the little girl's name?" I said, trying to sound friendly, but feeling far from it!

"Her name is Pekpek. You want her? I'll sell her to you for 10,000 pesos!" she responded angrily.

It was not a real name but a crude term for a girl's private parts. Everything in me wanted to pay the money and take the little girl away from the loathsome woman, but I knew it was illegal. Instead, we did the right thing and reported the abuse to a social worker at the DSWD. She appeared concerned to begin with, but hesitated when we told her that the child was living in the red-light district. She told us we would have to make an official complaint to the Barrio Council there, then the police department. After that we would have to find three witnesses who were willing to sign written statements. Only then could they send a social worker to examine the child and verify if she was being abused. The impossible red tape meant that the system procrastinated long enough to protect the abusers rather than the abused.

Determined to rescue the little girl, we pleaded with people in the barrio and the police department. As expected, they wanted to help but were afraid to get involved. Back at the DSWD office I insisted that the social worker come and take a look at the little girl. Reluctantly, she came with us but by this time the woman made sure that Pekpek appeared well taken care of. The resulting social worker's report stated that there were "no visible signs of abuse". I was livid!

"No visible signs? What about her bruised arms! You must have seen the scars from cigarette burns, and she is obviously malnourished!" My voice was shaking and face flushed with emotion. Peter had never seen me so angry.

"I could see no cigarette burns or bruises. Maybe she is too thin, but the woman promised to fatten her up," she replied calmly, avoiding any eye contact with me. There was nothing I could do to persuade the social worker otherwise.

The children loved it when we arranged outings to the beach. It was the only time they seemed free and happy, like birds let out of a cage. On Sundays, we brought them to Pastor Abe's church. He had also moved out of Miracle Bible College to start a church and children's ministry. They came as they were, dirty faces, spewing bad language and full of mischief. It pleased me that the congregation had the opportunity to consider what exactly a church should be. I wanted nothing to do with religiosity – I would much rather have a church full of trouble.

Sometimes we caught sight of little Pekpek, but she was quickly swept away and hidden inside the house. As the months went by I came to realize there was nothing more we could do. Nevertheless, whenever I visited the DSWD office I asked the social worker if there was any progress on the case, making it very clear that I was not going to forget about it.

More than a year later we received a telephone call from a different social worker who told Peter she had been assigned to Pekpek's case. "Please, can you meet me at the regional hospital immediately," she asked. Surprised by this sudden development, we left for the hospital right away. The social worker met us outside the children's ward. "I need you to confirm if this girl is the child you knew as Pekpek," she explained, as we went inside.

I looked around, anxiously searching the faces of the five children sitting on their beds, all of them looking malnourished. The social worker stood at the foot of one of the beds and pointed with her mouth at a little girl with pale skin and dark shadows under her eyes. My heart was beating wildly. I wasn't sure. I looked at Peter questioningly and noticed tears in his eyes.

"It's her," he whispered, hardly able to choke the words out.

We tried to talk to the little girl but the nurse told us she was mute and never spoke a word. She was obviously emotionally disturbed. I gripped Peter's hand as we left the hospital; a sharp pain stabbed at my chest as if my heart was literally breaking. The social worker updated us as we walked to the highway to go home.

"She was given to a childless couple. Her name has been changed to Faye. They plan to adopt her," she said.

"Was she given or sold?" I asked, pointedly.

"Well, they said she was given," she mumbled, looking at her feet.

She was sold... I knew it! I thought angrily.

"If the social workers don't prosecute, why didn't we just buy her a year ago?" I asked Peter when we were back at home, frustrated beyond words. But I didn't really expect an answer.

"It's out of our hands. We have to leave it," he told me.

"I can't leave it! I can't just give up and leave her like that," I told him, tears welling up in my eyes. For weeks after, I cried myself to sleep, reliving that hospital visit.

She was six years old when we saw her again. The social worker kindly invited us to attend the court hearing for final adoption proceedings. Perhaps she wanted us to have some closure, or perhaps she hoped I would stop pestering the DSWD about it. Either way, we were relieved to see Faye dressed up prettily with a ribbon in her wispy hair and looking healthier.

Her new parents told us that when they took custody of her she had worms coming out of her nose and ears. They did not seem to have much money or resources to help a disturbed child. I tried to talk to Faye but she just gazed at me with the same vacant, sad look in her eyes. We never saw her again.

***

One thing was certain: the children of the red-light district understood that Jesus loved them because we took the time to be with them. We were sowing seeds of change in their lives, giving them a glimpse of the better life God wanted for them; something cleaner and more beautiful.

As the years went by we often bumped into young people in the city who stopped to say hello, then realized they were the children we had ministered to in the 1980s. Now married, they had decent jobs and were raising their children in the right way. Most of them attended a new church that had been built by the Assemblies of God in the middle of the red-light district.

We laughed together when we met Riko, now a young man, who played the part of Herod in one of our Christmas nativity plays.

"We had some fun, didn't we?" Peter said, happily.

"Yeah! You will always be our Uncle Peter," he chuckled.

Chapter 9

Street-boys

**... Jesus, the champion who initiates and
perfects our faith.**

Hebrews 12:2

Y ou can recognize your calling in life as that which
makes you come alive inside; it stirs your soul and
energizes you. It is something that flows from you easily
and joyfully. Funnily enough, ministry to juvenile delinquents
was all of the above for me. It was hard for me to grasp that
the boys in the detention centre were capable of such serious
crimes. I just loved their company.

Alejandra and I had begun to visit young offenders at the
detention centre soon after we moved to Victory House, making
the journey by bus. The social worker in charge welcomed
our offer to teach Bible studies once a week. The wards were
under eighteen years old and all had criminal cases filed against
them. It was one of the few places in the Philippines that kept
youngsters out of the adult jail system. They responded well to
us because we took a genuine interest in them.

The law required that they be given a speedy trial because
of their age, but it hardly ever worked that way. A guard stood
watch at the entrance of the compound with a loaded gun, but
it was easy for boys to escape if the guard became distracted
by some commotion in the dormitory. Sometimes escapees
would turn up at our house where we welcomed them, gave
them something to eat, prayed with them, and subsequently

returned them to the detention centre. They could only come to live with us if they were acquitted. If they escaped custody they were treated as fugitives, despite their age.

Peter and I continued visiting the young offenders every week with a team of friends who had also graduated from Miracle Bible College. One of the boys, Big Michael, was seventeen. His father was African–American. His mother, a bar-girl, sold him as a baby to a tiny woman who unofficially adopted him. He had attempted suicide three times during his time at the detention centre.

At one of our meetings we asked the boys if they would like to share with us what God was doing in their lives. Big Michael hesitantly got to his feet. Surprised, the other boys encouraged him, whistling and clapping their hands. Obviously feeling very uncomfortable he put his hands inside his T-shirt and rolled it up as he was talking until it was rolled right up to his neck. With enormous effort he struggled to get his words out. "I just want to thank God for helping me in this place. The judge is letting me go home soon. Thank you Jesus!" he said.

Rowdy applause and more whistling echoed around the room; some even brushed tears from their eyes. Everyone liked Big Michael. He was like a cute toddler in a big man's body! But his hulk-like appearance gave the police the wrong impression. While he was celebrating his release with friends, the neighbours got nervous and called the police. He panicked, thinking they would put him back in the detention centre. When he wouldn't calm down the police beat him up. He tried to run away... so they shot him. One bullet took off the end of his nose and the other went through his cheek.

Big Michael lived in hope that his biological father would get in touch with him one day and arrange for him to live in America. The truth was the man had conveniently forgotten that he had a son. I suggested he stay at Victory House for a while, but he didn't want to leave his "Ma", with whom he had returned to live. Praying for his safety became the focus of our prayer time with the boys.

Romeo was a boy who turned up at Victory House and handed me his release papers, smiling triumphantly. He was tall, dark, and handsome – as you would imagine a Romeo to be. He lived with us for over a week, eventually persuading his parents to let him go home. After a month or so he returned with a friend. "I'm back in school and promised to stay away from my old gang. Now I'm worried about my friend Ton, here," he told me, pulling the other boy close in a brotherly hug.

We sat together on the low wall of the porch outside Victory House. Romeo did most of the talking. "Ton is seventeen," he told me. He looked older, as if he had lived a very hard life. "He cannot speak clearly, because of 'inborn'," Romeo explained. That was the word used to describe any abnormality at birth – Ton had been born with no palate in the roof of his mouth. In England such defects were corrected soon after birth, but in the Philippines it was only investigated when the parents could afford the operation. "He is an orphan and his older brother treats him badly. Can he stay with you? He needs a safe place," he said and looked at me longingly, while Ton stared at the floor in awkward silence.

I couldn't say no. It was almost time to eat so I invited them both inside and introduced them to Pastors Fred and Rogelio. Ton soon relaxed and joined in our conversation. His speech was rasping and difficult to understand. He had to eat very slowly. I guessed he had been taunted all his life, probably accounting, in part, for his tough exterior. When we woke the following morning Romeo had already left to go home. Over breakfast Ton opened up and told us the truth.

"I am not an orphan. The police have been watching me. They know that I was selling drugs and they threatened me. I have to get away from my home town," he confessed.

I was worried, but appreciated his honesty. Because of his honesty from the start I was prepared to give him all kinds of chances. Fortunately his father came to the house the next day – Romeo had informed him of Ton's whereabouts. He was a middle-aged man, dressed respectably in an old suit that had seen better days, his hair slicked back with hair-cream. He spoke politely, apologetically. I could see he was tired of trying to hold his family together. "We'll do what we can to help," I promised him. I was moved by the rare love he showed Ton, who had brought him nothing but trouble.

Ton had run out of options and he attached himself to us. He was accustomed to giving orders and throwing his weight around. I had to remind him every day that violence was not the solution. "That is not you anymore," I would tell him. And he would nod in agreement but promptly forget again.

After a few weeks we visited his home, at the invitation of his father. Built of bamboo, it was starting to sag and leant precariously at an angle. Ton's father apologized for everything – his drunken wife, his troublesome sons, and his rickety home. He felt indebted to us and desperately wanted to make a good impression. "Please don't give up on him. If he stays here the police will put him in jail, or worse. They will find something to pin on him," he told Peter. We assured him that Ton was doing fine; that he was respectful and hard working. Hearing those few words of encouragement, Ton went off to the store to buy us a snack. He walked with a swagger; it was that swagger that got him into a lot of fights.

Ton tried diligently to put everything we taught him about the Christian way of life into practice. He was baptized in the sea, completely handing over his messed-up life to God. The embarrassment he felt because of his speech impediment was gradually replaced with a new self-confidence and a keen sense of humour. He learned to pray out loud and it didn't matter that few could understand what he was saying, because God understood perfectly!

His gang mates were arrested for possession of drugs, including one friend who called himself Satan. Ton knew he had been rescued from that exact fate and had been given a second chance. Over time he told us about his life as a notorious street fighter, a frightening catalogue of violent crime, and his experiences drug pushing. Whenever Ton went home, even if it was only for a few weeks, he got into trouble because of rival gangs, drugs, and old gambling debts. He told me he was worthless. I would remind him of the verses in Lamentations: "The faithful love of the Lord never ends! His mercies never cease. Great is his faithfulness; his mercies begin afresh each morning" (3:22–23).

It was difficult to show Ton seemingly endless mercy, especially when he confessed to stealing money from my purse because his life had been threatened over an old debt. Learning to live in God's unrelenting love, Ton was our first test subject. I therefore insisted that we practised doing for him more than what was expected.

We planned to go to Manila to register our charity as a non-profit organization in the Philippines. Ton came with us, to avoid any further setbacks. Our legal advisor arranged for us to get cleaned up and sleep at her home for the night, and invited us to attend her church that evening. One of several large churches in Manila, the congregation numbered around 10,000.

When we arrived at the place, it was buzzing with excitement. The church was celebrating the Jewish Feast of Tabernacles, in a huge marquee in a supermarket car park. We were among the many people standing outside the marquee when, towards the end of the service, it began to rain. As rain descended in torrents the congregation continued to sing and dance, their fine clothes getting drenched. I glanced over at Ton, who had been standing next to me. He was on his knees in the rain, with his hands in the air, weeping. Something wonderful had happened in his heart. It was a real turning point for him.

Later that year we learned of a charity called Project Luke that funded medical procedures with the help of volunteer surgeons. They arranged for Ton's cleft palate to be fixed. This was the beginning of a successful partnership with them and we referred several patients over the years. Ton was still recovering from his operation, at home with us, when news reached him that his brother had been seriously injured in a knife fight and was in intensive care. For days Ton struggled with the old instinct for revenge. It would be years before he learned to let go of the violence completely and walk in the gentleness of Jesus. But he did... eventually.

In 1987 there were an estimated 75,000 street children in Manila, and their numbers were multiplied in every city. Around 70 per cent of them were boys. Peter, Ton, and I had begun to visit the cities at night and had made friends with several of the boys. Some of them, such as Dan-dan, Butz, and Noel, came to live with us temporarily.

I was trying to work my way through the paperwork to get a licence from the DSWD for Victory House to be a residential facility for boys, but I just wanted to get on with helping the street-boys, not filling out endless forms. The head social worker tried to frighten me into complying. "You could be accused of kidnapping by some unscrupulous parent," she warned. She was right, of course. I had been blissfully unaware of the "proper channels" we were supposed to go through.

My vision was to provide for boys who had nowhere else to go, for as long as it took. The DSWD guidelines were a two-year maximum stay. As a result, the children in government facilities were constantly running away, or were transferred for a further two years just to meet the standards. They felt unwanted. The way we at Victory House operated was completely different to "standard procedures", but it worked for us.

Eventually, the DSWD allowed us to continue under the provision of a foster parents' licence. That was a surprisingly easy process.

At that time, Miracle Children's Home was struggling, and some of the children were being discharged to relatives or foster parents. Ricky, fourteen, was an orphan. It seemed natural that he should come to live with us. We enrolled him at the Baptist School. He loved to study.

A concerned pastor brought Fred. "The boy's life is in danger," he told us. I had been watching the small boy as the pastor told Peter about his case. He had such a sunny disposition and easy smile. How could this cheeky little boy have a death threat hanging over him? He was only ten years old.

As I went through the questions with Fred on our "intake form" it became clear why he got into trouble – his father was out of work and usually drunk, while his mother worked in the market all day, every day. He and his siblings were left to fend for themselves. He started hanging out with gangs of older boys in the barrio when he was seven. They gave him a sense of belonging, especially when he began to smoke marijuana and sniff glue with them, most days getting through two bottles of gin. Things got worse when he started slipping into neighbours' homes undetected, pilfering whatever he could sell. He was caught several times but managed to sweet-talk his way out of it. Now someone had threatened to kill him. It was no idle threat; it was not uncommon for the men of that area to take matters into their own hands.

Fred nodded enthusiastically when we told him he would have to go to school and that there were rules he would have to keep. We began to see that he thrived when we gave him the attention he craved. He listened to us, did well in school, and was always polite and happy! But Fred and Ricky were two of the exceptions.

To begin with we had a list of rules that we strictly enforced, but we found that it just didn't work that way. I developed a less stringent code, allowing the boys more freedom. That met with resistance from the Filipino men who helped me for they preferred a more authoritarian approach. But when the boys felt appreciated, with less out-of-reach expectations, they accepted the structure and discipline.

I was relieved when Mama Adella came to live and work with us when Miracle Children's Home closed down. She and her five boys had been living there since her husband died. She was a very small, quiet woman from the mountain region of Balili, where tribal customs were still practised. It was good to have her female company and maternal influence in the home. Everyone loved her.

The worship songs of Don Moen and Ron Kenoly filled our house, and quiet times of devotion with the boys at the start and close of each day were like our lifeblood. Somehow the boys learned to pull together and allow for each other's disordered personalities.

But Daniel was different from the other boys. He was a recovering cocaine addict from a wealthy family in Manila. His desperate mother had not been able to find a drug rehabilitation unit for him. The only place we could recommend was the Teen Challenge Centre in Cebu, where we had recently spent a few weeks of training. But Cebu was another island and Daniel couldn't face being so far away from his family.

Everything had gone horribly wrong for him when he met a girl in his school with the same family name as his. He found out that they shared the same father. His dad secretly had another family and the other children were going to the same school as him. Terribly confused and offended he began to abuse alcohol and drugs. He became addicted to *shabu* – a methamphetamine drug that has a reputation of leading to violent crime and suicide.

He was twenty-three years old when we met him; a gentle, well-mannered boy. "I know only God can help me now," he told me. He stayed with us for two months. It was not long enough, but he felt duty-bound to support his mother. She kept in touch with us by phone, and said he was doing fairly well.

When he relapsed, he immediately took a bus and arrived back at Victory House high on drugs. He threw his arms around me and kissed me on the cheek. He clung to my neck, whimpering like an injured puppy. I tried to convince him to stay. If only he would give us more time…

"I just don't fit in here with the other boys," he explained.

"Why did you come back here if you were not intending to stay?" I asked.

He just smiled a distorted, high-on-drugs smile, said goodbye, and kissed me on the other cheek. Then he bolted, running clumsily towards the highway. Before Peter could catch up with him he had jumped on a passing bus going back to Manila.

Several months later, the regular telephone call from his mother was strained and dark. Daniel had been found hanging by his neck in his bedroom, under the influence of *shabu*.

I knew there would always be an element of failure in our work, but I felt terrible. What was I thinking? I was a nurse, not a psychiatrist. How foolish to think I could help these boys. It all felt too big for me – for all of us – at Victory House.

Where is the victory in Victory House now? I asked myself. Self-doubt haunted me for months.

Chapter 10

Archangel Michael

Most Filipino couples expect to have a baby in their first year of marriage, usually hoping for a boy to continue their family name. Almost every day in the market the vendors would ask loudly for a pregnancy progress report. It got to be quite embarrassing when I always replied in the negative. "So, what method are you using?" the woman at the vegetable stall asked. With a band of curious onlookers eavesdropping I tried to explain discreetly that we were not using any family planning methods. That only fuelled everyone's enthusiasm to offer all manner of strange advice on how to conceive. With our bizarre newly-wed lifestyle it was hardly surprising that I hadn't yet conceived.

My brother Philip came for a visit. He loved the Philippines and I had always wished he would come and move here. He and Toto, another boy who came to live with us, got on famously together. Toto called Philip "Budish". We had no idea what it meant, but it was clearly a term of endearment.

"*Mama! Tapos na to!*" ("Mama, I'm finished!"), Toto would shout from the bathroom. He was probably around the age of seventeen, but had the mental age of a toddler.

"OK! Good boy!" I would shout back.

Once, turning around to face him, I let out a shriek. There he stood, stark naked, leaning proudly against the bathroom door.

"Pastor Fred! He-elp!" I yelled, musically.

Pastor Fred ran into the kitchen, eyes searching the floor for a snake or a rat. I directed his concerned gaze to the bathroom. "Ay!" he shrieked, laughing, as he ushered Toto to his room to get dressed.

We had found Toto in the Municipal Jail. Because he couldn't speak clearly nobody knew his name, how old he was, or where he lived. Police had taken him into custody for throwing stones at passers-by.

He suffered from a severe form of epilepsy. His teeth were rotten and would often break during a seizure. There was a struggle every time he had to take his medicine or visit the doctor or dentist, or do anything he didn't feel like doing. We were sitting together around the kitchen table one morning enjoying fresh bread rolls and coffee when Pastor Fred announced that he had some bad news. Seeing the concern on his face we stopped chattering and waited for him to continue.

"You know how we leave our toothbrushes in the mug on the bathroom sink?" he began. We nodded, all eyes on him, wondering what could be so bad.

"This morning I noticed Toto was using yours, Maam Les," he said.

Pastor Fred got up from the table and danced around the kitchen, laughing at me. I think that was when we decided that anyone wanting to work with us would need a keen sense of humour.

We got the impression that Toto had grown up in a Videoke bar as he loved to grab the microphone in church and launch into song and dance. But we had to curtail his efforts as his erotic dancing was not appropriate for the Sunday morning congregation to witness. For a long time we couldn't decipher what he was singing. "Wah-wah titit… wah-wah titit… oooh," he bellowed. After much thought, Pastor Fred was finally able to name the tune. "One way ticket, one way ticket to the moon!" he sang triumphantly.

We may never have known his name if he hadn't tried to make conversation with a baby in church.

"*Pangalan mo?*" ("What is your name?"), he asked in his muddled language. Uncle Rogelio overheard him as he went on to introduce himself: "*Ako Toto*" ("I am Toto"). Like many who have suffered at the hands of abusive adults, he confided only in children, babies, and animals.

My brother Philip was a surfer – so we threw body boards and towels in the jeep and took the day off. As soon as we arrived Toto stripped off all his clothes and sprinted into the sea, naked. Philip ran after him with a towel, but Toto was heading straight for a group of girls. Philip stopped in his tracks, turned, and walked casually in the other direction pretending he didn't know him. On this occasion, someone else would have to sort that one out.

For several weeks after Philip returned to England Toto waved frantically at airplanes, shouting "*Sama ako Budish!*" ("Take me with you, Budish!").

My father came to visit for Christmas in 1987. He brought with him two young people from his church, Simon and Lesley. He wasn't his usual light-hearted self on arrival in Manila. "We had a good flight…," he began, but I could see he was worried. "Something terrible happened. Derek Martin, bless him – he drove us to the airport in London. When he went to get my suitcases out of the boot of his car, the car behind slammed into his legs." Dad began to cry. Derek was his close friend, and trustee for Childs Charitable Trust, one of our biggest supporters. "We just had to leave him there outside the airport; we had to go!" Dad continued.

Derek's legs were crushed badly, and they never fully recovered. He received compensation, and promptly wrote a cheque to LAMA Ministries. It was enough to build a church in Kalinga, where Alejandra and Johnny were pastors. He believed in overcoming "evil" with good.

Around the same time a young man named Mogens from Denmark arrived unexpectedly at the suggestion of a friend of his. He just turned up, having found his own way with very few directions. It was the first of several visits and he fitted in easily, helping the boys with housekeeping and playing games with them. He joined our street ministry teams, going into the red-light district and the prison.

At that time, visits to the detention centre came to a halt. One of the boys had asked us why the Santo Ninyo idol didn't answer his prayers. Santo Ninyo idols were in almost every shop, restaurant, and home. Incense smouldered and plates of food were offered to them at mealtimes. Alejandra, still a frequent visitor to us, explained that an idol couldn't possibly answer prayers. She told them that Jesus died so that we could talk to God as a man talks to his friend. It opened up a lively discussion. The boys wanted to understand; they needed a real faith to hold on to. Unfortunately, though, we had offended some of the older members of staff, and they no longer wanted us to teach Bible studies to the boys.

* * *

We had a chance to take a few months off, so in June 1988 we flew to Hawaii where I met Peter's mother and the rest of his family for the first time. I could hardly believe I was in Hawaii. It was everything the travel brochures claimed – a paradise on earth and unbelievably beautiful. We also travelled to mainland America, where Peter introduced me to friends he had met in 1984, when he was on tour with Miracle Sounds.

Time away always meant more work piled up on my desk. I enjoyed corresponding with the growing number of sponsors and I was managing to cope with the challenge of official paperwork, but maths had never been my strong point. As a student I had taken my CSE Maths exam three times before my teachers finally felt sorry for me and gave me a passing grade. At the end of each month I dreaded balancing income and expenditure as much as I had Mr Turner's maths class!

At the beginning of 1989 Pastors Fred and Rogelio left us to work elsewhere. Both were single men hoping to get married, and they needed to be in a place where it was easier to find a good woman. Mogens had done just that, having fallen in love with Nancy, Peter's classmate in Bible College, who had been helping me with translation work. She eventually settled in Denmark with him.

In August 1989 I discovered I was pregnant at last. There was jubilation in the market place! At the same time my permanent visa was approved, eliminating the hassle and expense of renewing visas. And we received a cheque with enough money for airfares. I hadn't been home to England for three years. All at once, my prayers were answered.

I spent a lot of time studying the *Book of Babies Names* that I had found in the Malayan bookstore in town. I liked Ishbel, Liah, or Vienne for a girl, but what if it was a boy? Reading *Daily Light* one day, I sensed God was trying to tell me something.

"Since the first day… your request has been heard in heaven. I have come in answer to your prayer. But for twenty-one days the spirit prince of the kingdom of Persia blocked my way. Then Michael, one of the archangels, came to help me" (Daniel 10:12–13).

We therefore decided the best name for a boy would be Michael. It would be a reminder to us that answers are on the way.

I was almost six months pregnant when we boarded the plane for Heathrow. Alejandra and Johnny had agreed to take care of the boys at Victory House in our absence. As soon as I arrived at the vicarage my mother insisted I rest, so I spent my time in front of the television. The "Iron Lady", Margaret Thatcher, was the prime minister at the time; East Germany's entire government had resigned; Communism was losing its grip and the Berlin Wall came down in November of that year. In Romania, Nicolae and Elena Ceauşescu were executed by firing squad, then in February the president of South Africa lifted a thirty-year ban on the African National Congress and Nelson Mandela was finally freed from prison – he had been there twenty years. Incredible changes were taking place in the world.

On 28 March I woke at 2 a.m., quite sure I was going into labour. It was a two-hour drive to the North Devon Hospital in Barnstaple. I prayed all the way that God would keep the baby in until I got there! It wasn't until 4 a.m. the next day that we heard the news: "It's a boy!" Weighing in at 7lb 3oz, Michael had arrived!

Watching the news in the patients' television room while recovering from giving birth, I could not believe my eyes. Noel Proctor, chaplain at Strangeways prison (now HMP Manchester) was being interviewed, and he had a glorious black eye! I recognized Noel from old photos my father had shown me. He and Dad had worked together on an evangelistic mission when they were in the Church Army. What on earth had happened? I hurried over to the phone to make a call. "Dad, have you seen the news? It's Noel Proctor! It looks like he has been beaten up!" I told him.

Around 1,000 prisoners had rioted in the prison, resulting in a violent siege that lasted twenty-five days. The prison was damaged so badly it cost £55,000,000 to rebuild it. In a Philippine prison, the guards would have opened fire and ended the riot immediately, regardless of the loss of life. It illustrated how extremely divided my world-view had become.

Back at the vicarage, my bedroom was filled to overflowing with flowers, presents, and cards from friends who welcomed Michael into the world like a little celebrity. But always in the back of my mind was the thought of how it would all work out with our communal lifestyle in the tropics. We lived in a dangerous environment.

My father dedicated Michael in the ancient St Olaf's parish church. We chose four godparents: Abigail, Chris, Keith, and Reynolds. The verse in each of their greeting cards was exactly the same – a prayer for me to hold on to:

Lord, take this child and make him Thine.
Let heavenly grace upon him shine,
Preserve from every evil thing,
Safe and secure beneath Thy wing.

As if to test that trust, news reports showed customs officers in Middlesbrough in the north-east of England seizing what they thought was the barrel of a massive gun on a ship bound for Iraq. Investigations revealed the gun, commissioned by Saddam Hussein, was part of "Project Babylon" and was the invention of a Canadian doctor who was assassinated shortly before the parts were discovered. Relations between Britain and Iraq became very strained and rumours spread around the churches that the end of the world was nigh.

Well, if the world ends we will leave it from the Philippines! I thought. By this time Michael was three months old and it was time for us to return. Saying our goodbyes at the airport was more difficult than ever. At the departure gate Dad tried his best to smile, but his face flushed and his shoulders started shaking, the tears rolling down his cheeks. It was excruciating. We waved until we could no longer see each other, then my parents walked to the car park and we joined the check-in line.

Chapter 11

A State of Calamity

**Although the world is full of suffering, it is full
also of the overcoming of it.**

Helen Keller

Michael would come first, I resolved. But I knew that would be difficult to put into practice with so many others clamouring for attention. Everyone was excited to meet Michael and couldn't wait to hold him. The only sad news that marred our arrival back in the Philippines was that Toto was missing again and that Ton had clashed with Alejandra and Johnny and had returned home.

I was getting used to my new routine a month later when Peter took a tricycle ride to the neighbouring town of Bauang, with two of the boys, Elmer and Johnny. He had found a lot for sale, where we could possibly build a bigger home for the boys. *Perhaps we can even have some space of our own,* I thought. Michael was asleep in his cot. I glanced at the clock – it was past 4 p.m.; Fred and Ricky would soon be coming home from school. It was 16 July 1990.

Suddenly the house shuddered. I had become accustomed to frequent tremors and expected it to be nothing to worry about. Sometimes the only evidence of a tremor was the door silently swinging on its hinges. But this was different. The house began to shake violently; this was no ordinary earthquake!

With my heart beating wildly in my chest, I snatched Michael up and staggered outside. Mama Adella ran out of the house at the same time. We sat in the middle of the garden, where nothing could fall on us. Frightened, we prayed aloud, not sure if we should stay put or start running somewhere – but where? We could hear people screaming. Then the Schofield family – missionaries from Ireland who were living in an apartment nearby – ran down our pathway to join us.

"They're saying there'll be a tsunami! People are running for higher ground, so they are!" Marie exclaimed, her voice high-pitched, urgent.

"What is a tsunami?" I asked.

"It's a tidal wave! What're we going to DO?!" Marie gasped.

All around us we could hear panic and confusion.

"What if the ground opens up and swallows us… or is that only in the movies?" I worried, clutching Michael.

"It's only in the movies," Mama Adella replied. But I wasn't convinced.

"Well, if we die we will go to heaven," she said, matter-of-factly. Her face looked drawn; for a moment I saw the resignation of too much hardship reflected there.

Fred and Ricky arrived home safely, followed by Peter, Elmer, and Johnny. They looked scared. Peter related what they had seen. "We were in the tricycle when it started to veer to the side of the road. I thought the driver must be drunk, but then I saw all the vehicles were going crazy! The telephone wires were swinging round like a giant skipping rope, and the road was moving up and down in waves. I thought it was the end of the world!"

"Well now, you should have heard Karen [my daughter] shouting at me! 'Mom, get oyt o the hoyse! Get oyt o the hoyse NUY!'" Marie said, in her broad Irish accent.

We were all distraught from the ordeal, but as the shaking passed, we looked at each other and laughed until we could laugh no more. Thank God! We were still alive! And thank God for the Irish knack of laughing in the face of adversity.

The next day we read the newspaper reports – the Island of Luzon was in a state of calamity like never before. The 7.7 magnitude earthquake had struck at 4.26 p.m. with the epicentre north of Manila, in Nueva Ecija. The worst damage was in Baguio, the principal trade and educational centre near us. A gold mine in the area lost thirty workers when it collapsed. A factory building collapsed and burned with workers trapped inside. Three hotels were totally destroyed. In one, at least eighty hotel employees and guests were killed.

Most of Baguio City's residents slept outdoors that night and during the following week, afraid to return to their homes because of frequent aftershocks. For the first forty-eight hours rescue efforts were hampered because the three main roads into the city were blocked by landslides and the airport was damaged. Hundreds of motorists were stranded and several buses had tumbled off the edge of the mountain, killing everyone inside. Relief efforts were further frustrated by heavy rain every day.

Local volunteers, mainly miners and cadets from the military school, worked with their hands and with picks and shovels to pull bodies from the demolished buildings. An estimated 1,000 bodies were eventually recovered in Baguio alone; they lay on the streets waiting to be loaded onto a truck and transported away from residential areas. Patients were relocated in tents set up in front of the damaged hospitals where the injured waited next to the corpses. There were not enough medical supplies.

Life was reduced right down to basic survival mode. Electricity and telephone lines were destroyed. Broken pipes completely disrupted water systems. The smell of death hung over many towns and cities. We heard helicopters flying overhead for weeks airlifting patients to hospitals and dropping supplies. When the main road leading to Baguio was eventually cleared, teams from the American army bases arrived with specialized equipment and rescue dogs, but most of the survivors had already been found by that time. Surgeons, anaesthesiologists, and supplies were despatched from Manila and Singapore.

Dagupan City, 68 km from Baguio, was almost completely destroyed, its buildings leaning at ridiculous angles. Department stores sank underground, leaving the first floor on ground level. There was talk of relocating the entire city, but residents stubbornly insisted they would rebuild on the same unstable site.

In La Union more than 2,000 families were evacuated when two coastal areas sank. Most of the buildings in Agoo, just 35 km from San Fernando, collapsed or were severely damaged. Strangely, San Fernando escaped any major damage. A gaping crack in the road, at the boundary into San Fernando, marked the end of the destruction.

We read the newspaper reports with a growing feeling of helplessness, thinking of those we knew in the disaster zones. We could only wait for news. *Were they dead or alive?* We went through the motions of living, in a blur of disbelief.

Weeks later, Ton came to tell us that his family were all safe, but their bamboo home was leaning even further at an angle and would have to be rebuilt. I was so glad to see him and even happier when he asked if he could come back to live with us for a while. "I joined a rescue team to help pull out survivors," he told me proudly.

When disaster strikes in the Philippines, people tend to quickly pick themselves up and they rise to the challenge of rebuilding the towns and cities. In order to do so, many Filipino families depend on pawn shops, or Indian money lenders, who loan five pesos and gain six in return. The "Bombay" or "5/6" rode around the city on motorbikes collecting debts every day. It was a crippling lifestyle for the borrowers.

Shortly after the earthquake Peter and I decided to go and have another look at The Seagull. If it had survived, perhaps the price would come down. But the answer was clear when we arrived at the front gate – it had suffered badly and was falling into the sea, its roof completely gone. It would never sell. It was time for that dream to die. Buying a piece of land and building a bigger place was obviously the better option. But we were giving what we had to help people in a worse mess than ourselves. At that point, it all seemed sadly unattainable.

I couldn't get Toto out of my thoughts. Had he survived the devastation all around us? Where was he? We searched for months, leaving our telephone number at police stations in the area. I had been reading a book about angels and wondered if we really could ask them to help us when all else had failed? We decided to put it to the test, praying together that angels would find Toto for us. A sense of anticipation filled my spirit. I fully expected to find him right away, imagining an angel like Superman… at the speed of light! But at the end of the day there was still no sign of him. It hadn't seemed to have worked.

Early the next morning we received a telephone call. It was the police chief from a town north of San Fernando. He told Peter that a boy named Toto was in his custody and that his colleagues had told him to contact Victory House. Peter could hardly believe what he was hearing.

"I tried to contact you yesterday, but couldn't find your number," the policeman told him.

That same afternoon we went to pick Toto up, but he didn't seem to know who we were. We talked with him for a while, reminding him of people and places in San Fernando. Gradually he remembered that we were his friends and consented to come home with us. The epilepsy had worsened, but as I helped him take his medicine every day, slowly the Toto we had come to love returned.

He had the habit of sitting on the porch reading the newspaper and commenting on the news for the day. It was hilarious listening to him, because he was holding the newspaper upside down, and he couldn't read. He loved to help me get Michael to sleep in the afternoon, swinging him in the rattan hammock, softly singing a lullaby – the words of which we could never understand. But I had to stay close by, as he tended to swing the hammock with too much enthusiasm. I could imagine Michael flying out of it and landing in the garden somewhere.

As the months went by, we realized we had saved about £19,000 in the charity bank account; it was something at least. The earthquake had caused the price of land to fall dramatically, especially as many people were selling their land in order to gain extra money for their rebuilding projects. Peter had begun talks with a colonel in the army who was selling the 1.5 hectares of farmland Peter had visited before the earthquake. It was a thirty-minute drive from San Fernando, in a small village near the sea called Pugo, in the next town of Bauang. Peter was convinced it was the right thing to do, and surprisingly he managed to bargain the price right down to what we had in the bank. We asked a lawyer to examine the papers and when he gave us the go-ahead Peter signed the deed of sale.

The day that we had prayed and dreamed about for years had finally come. We decided to model the building on the Spanish design of The Seagull, but on a smaller scale, and we hired Efren's architect brother Ruben to draw up plans for us.

Having lived with no salary for seven years, I knew God was faithful, but now we had to trust Him more fully. We never considered taking out a loan as it was too difficult to explain our financial situation to the bank – "living by faith" did not make sense to most people. We decided we would build with whatever we had, as funds came in.

Mariano, Tatang Sia's son from the early days of Victory House, had agreed to be a founding trustee for LAMA Ministries, so we dropped in at his restaurant to tell him of our latest plans. As soon as we sat down at one of the tables, we were surrounded by his family. His sister Bella couldn't wait to tell us that she had become a Christian, and Mariano's wife had recently been baptized in the Baptist church. Mariano's younger brother, Anson, nodded excitedly, eager for his turn to speak.

"Me too, I gave my life to Christ and I am in the church choir!" he told us.

"What... even Anson?" I teased.

The other people in the restaurant were staring at us, as we were making so much noise. They must have wondered if we were a little drunk. I looked over at Mariano and smiled, noticing that he had gained weight. His restaurant was a big success, and he looked so happy. *What a blessing*, I thought. *If this is the only reason I am here in the Philippines, it is worth it.*

But as Christmas 1990 approached, I was feeling defeated physically and emotionally. The charity account was overdrawn and the doctor had told me that Michael and I had tuberculosis. Twelve-year-old Dindo had lived with us a month before we got around to taking him to the hospital for a medical check. The chest X-ray revealed advanced tuberculosis. "Everyone in your house and in his class at school will need chest X-rays," the doctor informed me. Thirty X-rays! At least, only mine and Michael's showed possible signs of tuberculosis. I didn't want to accept it, but I knew the doctor was right to err on the safe side.

What exactly is this abundant life that Jesus offers and how can I lead the boys into it if I do not live it myself? I wondered.

I woke up after a restless night with a high fever and chills. At first I thought it was a reaction to the awful TB medicine, but the characteristic dizziness and thumping headache indicated that typhoid fever had returned to torment me. I was so weak I literally couldn't lift a finger. I lay in bed, wondering if I was going to die.

Peter wanted to rush me to the hospital, but having spent so much money already, I couldn't face it again. I asked him to call Pastor Abe, believing God would work through him. He had often helped me pray for sick students when I worked at the College. Peter phoned him and he came right away. I saw the concern in his face when he came into my bedroom. I must have looked terrible. Leaning close to my face he put his hand on my head.

"It will soon be Christmas – you can't go yet!" he whispered.

Go where? I thought, then realized he meant heaven.

"In the name of JESUS, I COMMAND the spirit of death to LEAVE this room! GO! In Jesus' name! I speak LIFE into Sister Lesley's body, and she will get out of this bed and BE HEALED! In Jesus' name, Amen and Amen!" he boomed.

I couldn't help but smile... He always said "Amen and Amen" at the close of his prayers. Then he left as quickly as he had come, confident his prayer would bring results.

An hour or so later, feeling stronger, I got out of bed and began to potter around the house doing some housework. Then I decided to put up the Christmas decorations. The typhoid had gone. I was healed!

Our celebrations were complete when Dan-dan returned to spend the Christmas holidays with us. He stayed through January, during which time he devoted his attention to impressing the girls in church with his polished appearance. With a little money my parents had sent for Christmas, we bought some inexpensive new clothes and shoes for him in the market, as well as cheap toiletries. I watched as he slicked his curly hair back with hair cream and splashed aftershave on his face every morning. He was every bit the handsome young man we had hoped to see emerge one day.

In August 1990 the Gulf War had broken out. As a result the price of building materials tripled, but we channelled every spare peso we had into the building fund. By March 1991, as summer approached, our finances picked up. I marvelled at the generosity of our supporters in England, as my recent newsletters had been either depressing or preachy, yet the supporters stood faithfully by me.

Excited to get on with the building, Peter employed workers from the barrio to help Ton and the boys dig the foundations. Tony and Pat Chamberlain, who were visiting the Philippines from England, officiated at the ground-breaking ceremony, and prayed for God's blessing on our mission. Things were moving slowly, but at least they were moving!

Now officially a non-government organization (NGO) in the Philippines, I was working on papers to register LAMA Ministries as a charity in the UK. I named our charity "Life And More Abundant Ministries" (LAMA Ministries) based on the Bible verse John 10:10: "The thief cometh not but for to steal, and to kill, and to destroy: I am come that they might have life, and that they might have it more abundantly" (KJV).

It followed that the new building would be called "LAMA House". As it was, we were often confused with Victory Bakery, Victory Boarding House, and Victory bus lines – all of which operated within San Fernando.

By now Michael was a year old and to everyone's delight began to walk. Mama Adella and the boys gathered around to applaud as he tottered from one side of the narrow living room to the other and into my outstretched arms. He chuckled and clapped his hands, then turned around and set off to the other side, where Oscar was waiting for him. I loved to see Oscar smile.

Oscar had been living with us for several months when we had an unexpected visit from Art – our very first resident at Victory House. He watched Oscar carefully. I could see he was deep in thought. He asked about him so I introduced them, pulling Oscar close to me in a hug. Oscar squirmed and giggled awkwardly.

"Hello, po!" he said to Art, nodding his head in the customary greeting.

Art was struggling. I had never seen him so emotional. He smiled weakly.

"*Manang*! When I was arrested my girlfriend was pregnant. We lived in the red-light district. Her name was Rosa. When I got out of prison I couldn't find her. Oscar... his mother's name is Rosa, right? He is eleven?... I think he is my son!" he explained shakily.

"Art! Yes, her name is Rosa. Oscar's mother died, you know – that's why he is with us," I explained.

I could see the painful regret in his face. Oscar's mother, a bar-girl, had died after a bungled abortion. A sister and two brothers were living with their grandma in the red-light district.

"You should go and talk to him," I suggested.

It seemed too far-fetched to be true. But Art and Oscar sat down together and talked all afternoon. Art was sure at the end of his impromptu visit that God had done something amazing for him – he had found his son!

Soon after that, Toto insisted on accompanying Peter to town. Peter told him to wait in the jeep while he went inside the store to buy something. When he returned, Toto was gone again. He disappeared without a trace, probably having jumped on a passing bus going who-knows-where?

We tried asking angels to intervene for a second time but we never found him. We sometimes wondered if perhaps he was an angel himself. After all, the Bible says that when we welcome strangers into our home we may be entertaining angels unawares. We sat outside in the cool evening with Ton and Pastor Fred (who often returned to visit us), trying to figure it all out and retelling stories of his funny ways. We concluded it was very doubtful. What we imagined celestial beings to look like just didn't match the mental image of Angel Toto running around naked, or gyrating like Elvis while singing the theme tune of the Batman cartoons, "Batman, ding-ding-ding". We looked at each other, quite confused, and burst out laughing uncontrollably.

Chapter 12

Life

**In order to bless you, God will sometimes move
in ways that are hard to understand or explain.**

Michael, Dindo, and I persevered with the TB medicine for six months. At our follow-up check-up the doctor seemed unconvinced as he looked at the X-rays. He suggested I seek a second opinion at the specialist Lung Centre in Manila. The thought of travelling as far as Manila to see a doctor had not occurred to me, but he convinced me that the facilities there were better than in La Union. We set off for Manila at midnight so that we would arrive before the outpatients' clinic opened. After a long wait and more X-rays the doctor arrived. He looked puzzled.

"I think my doctor in La Union felt it was best to prescribe the treatment because we foster street-boys and one of them has advanced tuberculosis. We're not coughing," I told him.

"Yes, I see," he said, studying my face.

"I don't believe you have ever had tuberculosis. We can't see any sign of it. There is haziness on your X-ray, Mrs Gomez, but I suspect that is more likely due to a bad case of pneumonia," he explained.

Michael's results were the same. I could have hugged him – I was so relieved! Instead, I stood and shook his hand vigorously, thanking him too many times!

"Have a safe trip back to La Union! Perhaps think about living separately from the street-boys you have to think of your baby, you know," he advised.

Hugging Michael tightly as we journeyed home, the doctor's final words troubled me. I certainly didn't want to put Michael at risk. But I was sure we should also be parents to the boys, not remote figureheads who had no real relationship with them.

The homeward journey from Manila to La Union seemed to take forever, but Peter wanted to keep going. I had learned to use the silence of travel time to think and pray. If I was honest with myself I sometimes struggled with the phrase "Life And More Abundant". That morning, I had been reading about Abram, who after winning a battle refused to accept the spoils of war. He left with nothing much to show for his victory. God told Abram that He was his "abundant compensation".

As Peter drove over the bridge into La Union I understood. Inevitably, there would be battles, but Jesus promised, "I am with you *always*" (Matthew 28:20, my italics). His strength in weakness, joy in pain, peace in anxiety, healing in sickness, and His companionship in loneliness – if that is not "life and more abundantly" nothing is!

On our return, I found that the TB medication had left me feeling drained and I had lost weight. All the fight had gone out of me. I wanted to run away from all the disease, poverty, and immense need to hide in a safe place. I thought back to the doctor's advice and wondered if we were right to continue living with the street-boys. What about Michael? At times I found myself crying for no apparent reason as intense homesickness surged over me without warning. But whenever I talked to God about it fear was replaced with His peace. He is, after all, that safe place. Even so, in May 1991 I decided to take Michael home to England for five months.

While I was away, another calamity was unleashed on the Filipinos. The "Great Quake", as it was called, had reawakened a dormant volcano on the island of Luzon: Mount Pinatubo. Aetas or Negritos were the tribal people who lived on the flanks of the volcano and initially they refused to move off their ancestral lands. but when small explosions dusted the surrounding villages with ash, the first evacuations of 5,000 people were ordered, though some resisted this order. On 9 June a Level 5 alert indicated an eruption in progress and another 25,000 people were evacuated. At Clark Air Base, a US military installation near the volcano, 18,000 personnel and their families quickly left their homes and were transported to Subic Bay Naval Station to return to the United States.

Then on 12 June the danger radius was extended to 30 km from the volcano, resulting in the total evacuation of 58,000 people. The massive eruption began at 1.42 p.m. on 15 June 1991. It lasted for nine hours and caused numerous large earthquakes. The mountain lost 300 metres in height. A pillar of ash and rock extended 40 km into the sky. It was the largest eruption the world had seen in more than half a decade.

To make things worse, Typhoon Yunya was passing at the same time and carried with it a large amount of rainfall. The ash mixed with the water vapour in the air causing a substance called "tephra" to cover the entire island of Luzon. Ash fall was recorded as far away as Vietnam, Cambodia, and Malaysia. Had Typhoon Yunya not passed by at the same time, the death toll from the volcano would have been much lower. Most of the 800 fatalities died due to the weight of the ash causing roofs to collapse. Between 15 and 30 million tons of sulphur dioxide gas was also ejected, and the ash cloud from the volcano covered an area of 125,000 square km, bringing total darkness to central Luzon.

Safe at my parents' home in Cornwall, we watched it all unfold on the World News. Worried, I telephoned Peter to find out if they were all safe.

"Don't worry, we're all OK. It's really weird though – we are in darkness and everything is covered in ash. I tried to wipe it off the jeep and wiped the paint off with it," he told me.

Dad called us together and we prayed, especially for Chrissy, who travelled with me to the Philippines in 1983. She was living very near Mount Pinatubo.

The ongoing news reports showed the gruesome reality for hundreds of people in the nearest city of Olongapo as they escaped, covered from head to toe in the toxic dust. In desperation, they clutched their statues of Jesus, Mary, or one of the saints for protection. Some of the idols were as big as the average four-year-old child. The Aetas worship a god named Apo Mallari. They call him "the Almighty" and believe he lived at the peak of the mountain. According to them, he caused the eruption because of his displeasure toward illegal loggers and the Philippine National Oil Company executives, who had drilled into the mountain searching for geothermal heat. After the eruption the Aetas felt that their god had betrayed them. They had dispersed and were scattered; their way of life became a thing of the past. They became nomads, begging in the cities all over Luzon.

Most of the Filipino people thought that God was punishing the nation. First the Great Quake, now this. As always, there were those who took refuge in God, and those who blamed Him and turned away, though churches of all denominations were full.

Around 364 communities and 2.1 million people were affected by the eruption. The US military never returned to Clark Air Base; it was instead turned over to the Philippine government on 26 November 1991.

Meanwhile, I had accepted a lot of speaking engagements around England and, although I longed to return to the Philippines, I continued with my schedule. I dreaded public speaking. When I noticed someone sleepily nodding their head, I brought my talk to an abrupt close, feeling that my audience were not interested. Never much of a talker, I spoke too quietly and had a lot to learn about conveying my message to others.

When I gained more experience in telling my stories, though, I realized that some people are just sleepy; the majority of listeners were hanging on my every word!

In my bedroom at the vicarage, with its matching lilac wallpaper, flowered duvet, and frilly pillowcases, I sat on my bed trying to put some thoughts down on paper to present to the churches. But my mind drifted far away to the Philippines, the all-encompassing sulphur dust, and the desperation.

One day my mother came in the room, interrupting my wanderings with a cup of English tea.

"Lesley, you look terrible! I am going to call Dr Clarke and see if he can arrange for you to get seen. Look at you, you're skin and bone! You're no good to anyone dead, you know!" she told me, frankly.

Dr Clarke was a friend of my parents who had a clinic in Cornwall for girls suffering from eating disorders, and a hospital in Buckinghamshire. "I'll be fine, Mum. I'm not anorexic!" I argued, reaching for a slice of her homemade chocolate cake. I was tired of seeing doctors every time I came back to England. Instead, I struggled on with the itinerary until Peter joined us in August.

The truth was I had been weak since Michael was born. There were only a few days in every month when I felt strong physically, but I pushed through regardless to get all the work done. My doctor ordered tests, including one for HIV as my immune system appeared to be failing. But in the end no light was shed on what was wrong. I decided my best option was simply to rest more, eat better, and trust God to restore my health. Of course, that was easier said than done when we arrived back in the Philippines in October 1991.

It was exciting to see the work progressing with LAMA House. Clearly, we were undertaking a huge venture as the building was like a hotel. But we honestly believed God was directing us in its design. The workers we employed from the village turned out to be some of the best around, and they appreciated Peter's eye for detail. He supervised all the work, inspecting the quality of workmanship to make sure it complied with the local building regulations. Local construction work rarely complied with any standards, but with the horror of the big quake still fresh in our memory we didn't want to take any risks.

They finished digging the footings, which had to be at least 1 metre below ground level, then began positioning steel bars. Since the earthquake all new buildings were required to increase the amount and thickness of steel reinforcing bars. It was expensive but made the building earthquake-proof. Work stopped and started as funds were made available. It was a long, drawn-out process, but one that Peter thoroughly enjoyed.

"I want to show you something. Let's go to the beach," Peter told me one day.

He drove down the barrio road, a short distance to the coast. I couldn't believe my eyes. The beach was wide and secluded, unlike any other beaches in our area, and there, beyond the tall palm trees, was the grass-roofed village I had seen from The Seagull!

"It's my village!" I whispered. Peter and I both had tears in our eyes.

We agreed that as soon as everything was up and running we would make that place a part of our ministry – we wanted to help the families get out of poverty. It felt good to be home and watch our dream taking shape.

However, my weight had dropped even further and the promise I made to do less and take care of myself had come to nothing. In November, my parents insisted I return to England, having arranged for me to check in at Dr Clarke's clinic. This time, I had to leave Peter and Michael behind in the Philippines.

As soon as I arrived in England I was taken to the clinic. Leah, the cook, was a friendly Maltese lady who, in an effort to pile the weight back on me, served up a hefty breakfast every day, and then two meals on one plate for lunch and supper.

They were delicious English meals like roast chicken, mashed potatoes, and vegetables as well as beef stew and rice, or tasty Mediterranean meals with coriander and chickpeas. All of that was followed by dessert and then fresh fruit!

The other girls in the centre couldn't be persuaded to eat even a biscuit with their cup of tea, but I downed the whole lot every day, with gusto. I soon became aware of hushed conversations around me as the staff questioned why I was there. All the tests came back with nothing unusual to report. In the end Dr Clarke discharged me from the clinic, with a supply of weight gain powdered drink. It had a picture on the front of each container of a handsome man with bulging muscles. I looked at it doubtfully.

"When you are 9.5 stone [60 kg], the correct weight for your height, then, and only then, can you go home to the Philippines," he ordered.

I had never reached 9.5 stone in my life! *I'd like to see you stop me*, I thought cheekily, but didn't dare say anything! Determinedly I forced the drink down every day. Weeks later I had managed to reach 9 stone and Dr Clarke relented. Before he could change his mind, I quickly booked a flight to Manila. I couldn't wait to see Michael and Peter again and be back at LAMA House.

In January 1992 I arrived back home. I had missed out on a lot. Pastor Fred had married Catherine, and was working as assistant pastor of a church in Bauang, situated among the beach resorts. It felt good to have him nearby – since our days at Miracle Bible College, Peter, Fred, and I had been practically inseparable.

Much of the ground floor of LAMA House had been completed by now, with five rooms that would eventually accommodate two boys each. One bathroom complete with two toilets and showers, a large kitchen, and a television room were now useable. At the front of the building was a spacious entrance where a grand staircase would eventually lead to the second floor. The home was built in a square, with empty space in the centre for a courtyard. It was amazing!

We decided we could live in what was finished. Mama Adella, Ton, Ricky, Fred, Dindo, and Oscar moved in with us. In March, my friends from England, Hugh and Julie Dowling, bravely committed to join us for a year with their son Jonathon, who was Michael's age. We lived together on the building site with the building work going on all around us.

I was conscious that Jesus had told His followers to invite the poor to parties; poor people who couldn't repay the favour (Luke 14:13). This seemed like a good idea to me, so on 29 March 1992, we invited all the children from the squatter village on the beach to Michael's second birthday party. There were over 200 children! We had balloons and chocolate cake and party food. The children had hardly ever tasted cake and forgot their shyness as adults and children alike clamoured to get a piece. Somehow we managed to divide it up into enough for everyone. It became something of a tradition. Jesus really knew the offbeat ways to have fun and make great memories!

Chapter 13

Twins!

Sweeping the floor of our building-site home in a vain attempt to keep the place clean, I became aware of someone standing quietly in the doorway. At first I didn't recognize him. Then I caught my breath in horror!

"Dan-dan! What happened?" I shrieked.

He didn't respond. I pulled up a chair and beckoned for him to sit down, grimacing as I got a closer look at him. His face was blue and swollen to twice its normal size and there was an ugly rope burn around his neck. What on earth had he done? Peter clasped his hand over his mouth in horror when he saw him.

"I thought you were with your dad?" I asked.

"I was sleeping… on the street in Baguio… five men… on motorbikes… grabbed me… tied a rope… around my neck… attached it… to the back… of one of the bikes… they dragged me… along the road… until I was… unconscious," he told us in gasps, finding it difficult to breathe.

He carefully lifted his T-shirt to show us infected slash wounds in both armpits. "They stabbed me… in my armpits… left me to die… on the side of the road… in the morning… a policeman… found me… took me to hospital… they stitched me up… then I ran away… came here," he said, his voice breaking when he saw the tears rolling down my face.

We sat together in blank silence. My heart was breaking as Peter prayed that God would turn things around for Dan-dan. If only the boys could know how much God really loved them, but they felt so utterly undeserving of any affection, and so incapable of meeting anyone's expectations. Extreme poverty of the soul calls for a supernatural transfusion of love – I believe that is what we call "the baptism in the Holy Spirit". I longed for that supernatural power to keep Dan-dan off the streets where he was self-destructing. But as soon as he felt better he was gone again. That was to be the last time we saw him.

Peter and I were at the hospital visiting a patient in the surgical ward soon after Dan-dan's disappearance. There were forty beds crammed into the ward, with barely room to walk between them. In the Philippines, the sick are fed, bathed, and watched by a member of their family, or a friend. They are called a "watcher". When medicine or supplies are needed the watcher buys them at a nearby pharmacy. If they have no money, the patient can receive no treatment.

As Peter quietly prayed for this particular patient, I noticed that her catheter was draining into an empty jam jar bottle. I had long since abandoned the practice of closing my eyes to pray – always watching either Michael or the boys. I stepped backward quickly, as a scrawny cat ran under the bed, followed closely by several kittens.

"Good grief!" I muttered, unable to suppress my concern as Peter said, "Amen!"

Across the ward I saw a teenage boy. He was completely naked because of the third-degree burns that were all over his body. The bed sheet was covered in dried blood stains. No one was sitting next to his bed so I went over to him, hoping it would not embarrass him. I remembered nursing a lady in a similar condition in England. Eighty per cent of her body was badly burned, but she was nursed in a pristine isolation room with strict, sterile procedures. Eventually she died from her injuries. What hope was there for this boy to survive?

Peter joined me and we introduced ourselves.

"My name is Jeffrey," he said, clearly pleased to have some company.

"What happened?" I asked.

"I was playing with my friend near a parked truck. The drivers were cooking their meal over an open fire. There was gasoline on the road. My friend and I had no time to get away," he told us. A single tear escaped from his eye. I looked around the ward for another boy with burns. *Maybe he has been transferred to a better hospital*, I thought.

"Where is your friend?" I asked.

"He died last night," he said. "No one wants to stay with me. I am going to die soon."

The floor looked like it hadn't been mopped for days and the fan blowing cool air overhead was covered in sticky black dust. *I could never work in this place*, I thought. My mind was racing, trying to figure out what we could possibly do. Julie, who was helping us for the year, was a registered nurse, and so was I. One of the rooms at LAMA House would be cleaner, more private. I signed the paperwork discharging Jeffrey against the doctor's advice, and we brought him home with us… to the building site!

Julie and I nursed him for several weeks and hope returned to him. Mama Adella cooked nutritious soups for him. Doctor Clarke sent parcels of bandages and treatments from England. We meticulously cleaned away the charred skin and applied the medicine, keeping everything sterile. Eventually, though, it seemed there was no more we could do as Jeffrey needed skin grafts. To begin with I admitted him to LORMA Medical Centre, but it was so expensive that I reluctantly returned him to the regional hospital.

Shortly afterwards a group of Catholic nuns visited the hospital and found Jeffrey. They were linked to a private hospital in Manila, which had its own burns unit. They quickly arranged for his transfer, paying all his fees, including for skin grafts. God had answered our prayers!

In October, after a visit to Hawaii to see Peter's family (during which time Hugh and Julie held the fort), my brother

David, then seventeen, came to visit us and stayed for two months. My sister, Esther, came a little later with Caroline Bickersteth, from Ashburnham Place, in England. The first of several visits, Caroline later brought her young friends Pippa, Simon, Richard, Giles, and others to help out at LAMA House or at Pastor Abe's place on short-term mission trips. Then Thelma arrived, Julie's mother, to help Julie and Hugh prepare to return to England. Their little boy Jonathon was not doing well physically and they needed to go home sooner than they had originally planned.

At the Post Office, after all the comings and goings, a small, lilac-coloured envelope from Hong Kong had been waiting for me. "Pete! It's Jackie Pullinger! She is getting married – to John!" I shrieked. At the beginning of October 1992 we flew to Hong Kong for their wedding. I was thrilled to be invited.

"The first time I met John I had a feeling that you two would one day be together!" I told them.

"Why didn't you tell us before? We could have got started a lot sooner!" Jackie laughed. She looked radiant, and so did John.

When we arrived home, we felt strengthened. Peter needed to resume work on the second floor as the rain was seeping into the rooms. We had funds available but the builders couldn't work in the torrential rain. So we prayed that it would stop during the day. To everyone's surprise, it did just that! For several months we only had rain at night-time, and we were able to carry on building during the day.

* * *

Sadly, due to lack of funding, Miracle Children's Home closed. Paula, Pastor Shields' eldest daughter, had done a good job of trying to accredit the home with the DSWD and raise funds, but now the family needed to go back to the USA, where her three children would go to high school. It was a huge step for her and her family to relocate in the Philippines after her father's death. Three of Pastor Shields' own children had tried valiantly to direct the mission, but Pastor Shields had not left any clear Filipino leadership to carry on his vision after he was gone. Before returning to America, Paula referred three boys to us who had nowhere else to go. They were Lito, Joey, and Almo.

I remembered Lito arriving at Miracle in 1984, escorted by two policemen who had found him wandering along the highway. His uncle had brought him from the Island of Iloilo a year earlier to live with an auntie after his parents separated. But his auntie mistreated him, so he ran away. At that time, he could not, or would not, give us any further information, making it impossible to trace his relatives. He was only eight years old then; now he was sixteen.

Joey, aged fifteen, was also a runaway. A man found him on the street when he was eight and took him in. He trained Joey to burgle homes. When the police caught Joey climbing out of a window with stolen goods they brought him to Miracle Children's Home. Joey was left with a distorted image of himself as a result of the sexual abuse that the man had inflicted upon him. Joey worked out with home-made weights and strutted around showing off his physique. But he had a soft, teachable nature.

Almo was found begging with his father in Manila when he was only three years old. He was covered in sores and malnourished. He was sold to an American man who claimed to be a missionary. After a while the man handed him over to a children's home in Baguio. When that home closed, Almo was transferred to Miracle Children's Home where I first met him at age seven.

He seemed like any lively mischievous boy when he was playing with friends his own age or younger, and loved to sneak into the neighbours' house to watch their television. Whenever there was a birthday celebration in the home he was the party clown, making everyone laugh. But if one of the staff tried to talk to him they were met with a wall of silence; he didn't speak to adults.

When we arrived at Miracle to collect Almo, we wondered what his reaction would be to yet another upheaval. "What do you think, Almo? Do you want to come and live with us?" Peter asked him, kneeling down to his level. He didn't say anything, as usual, but was obviously thinking about it. Then he looked right into Peter's face and then over to me and grinned from ear to ear.

When 25 December came around we had a Christmas party at the beach village and fed around 600 people. Just after the New Year celebrations, we had a surprise visit from Jeffrey. He even ran around with the children from the barrio, playing tag. I had often doubted my decision to take him out of the hospital, but now I knew it was worth it. When I saw him again in San Fernando, years later, he told me he was married and had a little boy.

Then, towards the end of January 1993, I discovered I was pregnant again. Peter and I were excited about having another baby and both wanted a girl, but with a house full of boys I wondered how that would work out. "If it is a girl she will have to be tough to grow up with LAMA boys," I joked with Peter.

We laughed, imagining what she would be like. But it was a very real concern; we were inviting some awful problems into our new family – problems I was constantly handing over to God for His wisdom and grace.

Easter-time in the Philippines is dark and oppressive, with bizarre rituals and ancient Catholic rites. In Agoo, a statue of the Virgin Mary "miraculously" began to weep tears of blood. Thousands of people flocked there hoping to receive a miracle, as stories surfaced of supernatural visions, prophecies, and even visitations from UFOs. In Manila, a class of high-school children were said to be possessed by demons having been found burning sticks under a sacred tree. The school priest arrived and forced them to kiss a crucifix, but it failed to help them as they were still considered to be possessed.

A man claiming to be gifted by Mary healed and exorcised "patients" in the Manila streets, by putting a crucifix in their mouth and praying over them. In Pampanga, Catholic penitents flogged themselves with whips that had razors in them, stripping the flesh from their backs. One thirty-five-year-old man was crucified, his hands and feet nailed to a cross, in appreciation of God having saved his brother in a plane crash. A man who claimed to be gifted by God cut the backs of the penitents with a razor. "Every drop of blood washes away your sin," he chanted as they walked for miles in the hot sun, imitating Jesus carrying a cross. It was like mockery.

The boys wanted to go to the beach with their school friends for Sábado de Gloria (Holy Saturday). The hottest time of year at over 39°C and 90 per cent humidity, it had to be the worst time to be out in the scorching sun. I armed myself with sun lotion and a hat and joined the rest of the village on the stretch of beach near LAMA House.

I parked myself in the shade with Mama Adella and watched the boys doing cartwheels on the sand. Peter took Michael and ran to join the other boys in the sea. Suddenly I felt cramps in my legs. When I tried to stand up, I saw blood on the beach towel where I had been sitting.

"Mama!" I cried. "Get Peter quick!"

She jumped up, waving and shouting at the boys.

"I have to go to the hospital, Pete, I'm bleeding!" I told him, trembling.

He carried me to the jeep and put me in the front seat, the boys clamouring to come with us.

"No, no, you stay here. It will be OK, it will be OK!" he shouted. But everyone could see it wasn't OK. He scooped Michael up in his arms, sat him next to me at the front, and drove at full speed down the rough barrio road to the highway.

"Pete, I think it's better if you slow down. We'll have an accident!" I told him, clinging onto Michael as we careened through traffic, horn blaring.

In the emergency department I began to cry. Nurses rushed around taking my blood pressure, putting an intravenous line in and taking blood samples. The doctor gave me an injection.

"This is a threatened miscarriage. You need to stay in the hospital for a few days," he told me, gravely.

I was scared. More than anything, I wanted to be in England. "Lord, please keep my baby safe," I pleaded as I drifted into drug-induced sleep.

The next day I was rested, and the bleeding had stopped. Dr Alviar ordered an ultrasound. The nurse studied the screen over and over again. She asked Dr Alviar to come and have a look. I could see Peter was nervous; he didn't like hospitals.

"Do you have any twins in your family?" the nurse asked Peter.

"No, not as far as I know. Twins… no! Why?" he asked.

She didn't answer him but went back to studying the screen again silently. Peter began to pace around the ultrasound office.

"There!" she announced to Dr Alviar, pointing at the picture.

"Ah, yes! Er… Lesley, you have twins!" he announced.

"What? No way!" Peter exclaimed.

"It is!" he insisted, grinning happily.

Twins! I lay on the bed speechless, worried that my husband was going to faint! Now what was I going to do?!

Chapter 14

Calm

When you go through deep waters and great trouble, I will be with you. When you go through rivers of difficulty, you will not drown... Do not be afraid for I am with you.

Isaiah 43:2, 5

"You have to stay on bed-rest for the remainder of your pregnancy," Dr Alviar told me.

"But that's another six months!" I argued.

"I know! I don't want you to put your feet on the floor except to walk a short distance to the toilet. And stay calm. Someone else will have to handle the workload," he insisted.

Dr Alviar had grown used to me arguing with his medical opinion. I smiled apologetically and promised I would do everything he told me. He, in turn, promised to come to LAMA House for my follow-up checks.

I wondered if Pastor Lito and his wife Maureen would come back and help us and when Peter mentioned it to them they readily agreed. They had three children now, and with no regular income it was an answer to prayer for them as they would now receive a salary. Reluctantly I resigned myself to staying in bed. I wrote letters, read books, and prepared Bible lessons. Michael often kept me company; we read his story books so many times I could say them off by heart.

Michael's favourite book was one that told the story of Lazarus being brought back to life. It was a beautifully illustrated book about Jesus and his best friends, Mary, Martha, and

Lazarus. When we got to the part where Jesus stood weeping at the tomb, Michael shouted with me, "Lazarus! Come out!" He clapped his hands when I finished the story, satisfied that Lazarus was alive and his family were celebrating with Jesus. I pointed to a picture of a little boy carrying a tray of drinks to give out to the guests. "Look, there you are, Michael, helping with the party!" I told him.

When he ran off to play outside I turned the pages back to a picture that had grabbed my attention, sensing God wanted to show me something. It portrayed Martha looking into Jesus' face, searching for answers. His strong hands gripped her shoulders as He looked into her eyes. Next to the picture, it read, "Don't be sad, Martha, just believe me." I studied it for some time, with tears in my eyes. "Don't be afraid, Lesley, just believe me."

It was another random holy moment.

Life at LAMA House went on busily around me. Construction firms were selling bags of ash from Pinatubo to mix with the cement, having discovered it made better bricks. So Peter hauled sand and gravel from the nearby river in our jeep and trained the boys to make bricks, drying them in the sun. The ladies from the village, seeing a business opportunity, arrived at the site mid-morning with homemade snacks and ice-cold drinks for sale. I made friends with Jeanette who was about my age and also pregnant. Her husband Ben was one of our builders. They had three very handsome boys and were hoping for a girl this time.

The children that I had nursed in Miracle Children's Home were all grown up by now and several came to help us. We appointed Teddy as pastor of our church. His brother Robert did all the electrical work, and Lazaro helped with building. Frustrated with slow progress and frequent delays, we sometimes questioned why we didn't have funds to keep working. According to "prosperity" teaching popular in American churches it was a sign that we were either out of God's will or had too little faith. It was confusing, but we persevered anyway and tried to see the bigger picture.

Mario, Arnold, Ben, and Leo, who lived with their families in Pugo, were excellent carpenters and joiners. We formed close friendships and they all became Christians. LAMA House became a permanent reminder to us of His higher ways. It was about much more than the building. And my confinement was a reminder that the work was *His*, not mine. He was God, not me!

When one of our labourers didn't come to work for several weeks, Peter asked the others about it. They told him that Jose had been coughing up blood and was diagnosed with advanced tuberculosis. He was confined to bed, unable to work. He lived nearby, so Peter went to pray for him. Jose was instantly healed. He got out of bed the following day and reported for work as normal. The weakness had vanished and every symptom had disappeared. Jose knew he had received a miracle. He dedicated his life to serving God at LAMA House as a house-father.

I woke up one morning to find a large white mouse running around my room. The boys had bought three mice in the market and were keeping them as pets. Peter promised to confiscate them, but they kept re-appearing to torment me. This was just the start of our troubles.

Then in April 1993 an official letter in a brown envelope was delivered to our door. Peter came into our room solemn-faced. I braced myself for bad news. It was a subpoena from the Municipal Trial Court in Bauang. The sale of our land was being questioned by the court, in a dispute over who had the authority to sell it to us. The letter informed us of court proceedings to annul the sale.

"I don't understand, Pete, we checked and double-checked all the land papers and we had an attorney helping us. How could we have missed this?" I asked.

"All the papers are legal. This woman obviously saw our big building and my white wife…" he explained.

We found out that the woman who filed the case was a gambler. When the colonel bailed her out of a large debt she gave him the right to sell her land. In a state of shock, we stopped the building work at once. It looked like we would lose everything.

I learned that things are never as they seem in the Philippines. We hired a keen young lawyer, who assured us that everything would turn out in our favour because we bought the land in good faith. "Let's trust God to settle it with no bribes, no lies, and no threats," I told Peter. He agreed and so did our lawyer. Most of the older lawyers we knew seemed crooked but he was different. We felt that God had directed us to him.

As the months went by court proceedings were continually postponed for one reason or another. We grew weary and faint-hearted. I went over the sale in my mind a hundred times. I remembered that the colonel and his wife had been in a hurry to have the papers signed. I felt uneasy about it then, and said as much to Peter, but he dismissed my doubts. *If only he had listened to me*, I thought miserably. But it was no good looking for someone to blame – I had to trust God to work everything out for good. One thing I could do, in my restricted position, was pray and listen for God's instructions in my spirit. I found encouragement in Isaiah 41:10–13:

> *Don't be afraid, for I am with you. Do not be dismayed, for I am your God. I will strengthen you. I will help you. I will uphold you with my victorious right hand. See, all your angry enemies lie there, confused and ashamed. Anyone who opposes you will die. You will look for them in vain. They will all be gone! I am holding you by your right hand – I, the Lord your God. And I say to you "Do not be afraid. I am here to help you."*

Then, some days later, after Peter had attended a particularly gruelling court hearing, I found Isaiah 54:17: "But in that coming day, no weapon turned against you will succeed. And everyone who tells lies in court will be brought to justice. These benefits are enjoyed by the servants of the Lord; their vindication will come from me. I, the Lord, have spoken!"

The Old Testament is full of stories about people who attempted great things for God and met with opposition. God always kept His promises and brought them into a place of victory. I knew that our God would fight for us.

At least the white mice had disappeared at last, and I thought I was doing a fairly good job of rising above the circumstances. My pregnancy was progressing normally, until one morning in late July... I woke to find a lot of blood in the bed. Peter raced me to the hospital again, straight to the emergency department. I began to panic as the same frantic scene replayed around me. Dr Alviar came right away and confirmed my worst fear.

"You have gone into premature labour, Lesley. I'm giving you some drugs to stop it," he said.

"No! My babies! I don't want any drugs," I argued feebly.

"I have to," he said, squeezing my hand. "I'm giving you something to calm you down."

I was trembling with fear.

As the tranquilizer began to take effect, everything became a blur of busyness around my bed. Then the porters came and took me upstairs to a quiet room, where Peter and Michael stayed with me. I fell into a deep sleep.

Early the next day, Dr Alviar came to my room with another doctor.

"We stopped the contractions and the twins are fine. But I have to catheterize you – you have gone into urine retention. I don't understand this so I have asked Dr Valdez to help me – he is the consultant urologist," he explained.

Peter and Michael stayed with me as Dr Valdez inserted the catheter.

"Just relax," they kept saying. *Yeah, right!* I thought.

The catheter went in without too much trouble and urine starting flowing out. But something was very wrong. Everyone in the room looked at the catheter bag and then at me – it was filling up with frank blood! I sank back in the bed.

"What is it? What's wrong with me?" I asked, but no answer came back as the doctors talked among themselves. More drugs were injected into my IV line and I became drowsy again. "I don't want any more drugs," I desperately muttered.

When I opened my eyes again, blood was still pouring out of my bladder. Dr Alviar was still there at my bedside. He looked worried.

"We have to give you a blood transfusion," he told me and handed me a consent form to sign. I hesitated, not sure if the hospitals had equipment to screen for HIV/Aids. I had read of cases in England and America where Aids had been transmitted through transfusions. I doubted that the Philippines could be any more advanced in that area.

Dr Alviar looked at me and frowned. "You have to stop arguing with me girl; you are haemorrhaging. Trust me with this," he said.

I smiled weakly, apologetically, and signed the paper. After searching through all the hospitals in the city, enough AB+ blood was found. The nurses assured me it was screened for Aids, but I wasn't convinced. Peter and I had been at the jail on a couple of occasions when prisoners had been taken to the hospital to donate their much-needed blood. It was a good source of income for inmates. I wondered, uneasily, whose blood was now running through my veins.

Bouts of terrible pain and panic came over me when the catheter repeatedly got blocked and I went into retention again. Dr Valdez wanted to change it for a three-way catheter so he could irrigate my bladder with ice water, hoping to stop the bleeding. The nurse went to find one.

"I think the twins are pressing on your bladder and have caused some problem there. I don't understand why that would cause retention but we will get to the bottom of it," Dr Alviar explained.

He smiled and we all giggled at his attempt to lighten up the situation. I had known him since 1984 when I began referring patients to him. He and his wife Grace had become good friends. She was a paediatrician and took care of Michael whenever he was sick. Despite my protests, I was glad he was my doctor. The nurse came back in the room, but she couldn't find a three-way catheter.

"Don't be ridiculous – of course you can find one!" Dr Alviar protested.

But in fact there were none in the hospital. They tried the other hospitals in the city and eventually found one, but it was much too big. I was getting more and more uncomfortable and starting to panic again.

Dr Alviar looked at me resolutely.

"There is nothing else for it, Lesley! Brace yourself girl: we have to get this oversized one in somehow!" he told me.

Exhausted, I gripped Peter's hand, closed my eyes and prayed that God would help him.

"I'm so sorry," he kept saying, and after the fifth attempt it was in place.

Another nurse came into the room.

"You are not going to believe this," she said sheepishly. "We don't have any ice water!" And so another search began.

We struggled for five days with the catheter and ice water until the bleeding subsided, then I absolutely insisted that it be taken out. Dr Alviar gave in to me this time.

"Can you count to three?" he asked me.

"Er, yes, of course I can," I replied.

"So… count," he ordered.

"One, two…" I began.

"Three!" he joined me. "That's it! It's out!" he cried victoriously.

I have never been so relieved in all my life! They never found out had what caused the bleeding. Another scan showed the twins were doing fine, despite all the IV drugs I had been given. Peter and Michael had stayed at the hospital with me the whole time. We were all tired and glad to be going home after a week or more of being away.

Back on bed-rest, missionary friends from Miracle Bible College came to visit me at LAMA House. Americans Terry and Leah Pinnick sat on my bed and prayed for me as I started to cry again. Leah hugged me.

"I just want to go home to England!" I cried, feeling sorry for myself.

"You will soon," she said. "You will soon."

Peter booked our airline tickets and got to work on his visa. He had to make several trips to the embassy in Manila. Two days before our flight, the airline informed us that there was a problem. I was not allowed to fly without consent from my doctor stating that I was well enough to travel. There wasn't enough time to do that so the airline postponed our flights for a few more days.

With no fax machine, Peter set off at 3 a.m. again for Manila to pick up the necessary form, arriving back home at midnight; a sixteen-hour round trip. He went to the hospital the next day, got the form signed, then travelled back to Manila at 4 a.m. the following morning to give it to the airline office. A powerful typhoon was entering the Philippines that morning, so when he came home shortly after leaving I assumed he couldn't get a bus because of the heavy rain. He looked completely dejected.

"I got on the bus and couldn't find the bag with all our documents inside. It's all gone – our passports, my visa, and the tickets – all gone!" he told me.

I couldn't take it all in. The rain buffeted the building in an almighty onslaught, symbolizing the difficulties coming down on us. We both felt utterly defeated.

But there was no time for wallowing in self-pity as the nearby river threatened to burst its banks. The boys were already busy filling empty rice sacks with sand and positioning them outside the rooms. Goats and animals were brought inside our building and people from all around evacuated their homes, carrying their babies and children on their shoulders through the floods. They took up residence on our second floor. During the night, Jose's sister, who was heavily pregnant, went into labour. With no way of getting her to the hospital she gave birth to her baby right there in LAMA House, surrounded by hundreds of evacuees.

Early the next morning, from my bedroom window on the ground floor, I could see the murky flood water rising as the rain continued to pour down. Mama Adella was busy preparing breakfast for more than 200 hungry people. Nobody had much sleep. We were all tired and afraid.

"I can't swim, Pete! What are we going to do if it gets worse?" I asked.

"We'll just have to slide you onto a piece of plywood; there is plenty around – we can float you out!" he offered, forcing a smile.

I didn't know whether to laugh or cry, but I nervously prayed that the rain would stop before the floods got higher than our bedroom window – just another few inches. Suddenly the rain did stop, and as quickly as it had rushed in, the water subsided. The boys ran outside to see if they could catch any fish that had washed ashore. They picked up dozens, struggling in the mud, and Mama Adella filled the freezer with enough for several meals. Our temporary residents gathered their few possessions together and returned to their homes, anxious to find out what was left and begin the clean-up operation.

The bridge in Bauang had collapsed, so the road to Manila was now closed. The bus that Peter had boarded previously was stranded on the other side of that bridge. When Peter went again to look for the bag, the driver handed it to Peter, with everything still inside it. He had found it lodged behind the seats!

Meanwhile, I had resigned myself to delivering the twins in the Philippines, but it troubled me to think about it. The deliveries I had witnessed were old-fashioned and often dangerous; maternity care seemed at least forty years behind that in England.

I was fed up of everything going wrong, but had to laugh when I read Isaiah 43:2: "When you go through deep waters and great trouble, I will be with you. When you go through rivers of difficulty, you will not drown!" We had certainly proved that verse in recent days. God also promised to be my midwife – Isaiah 46:4 reads, "I have made, and I will bear; even I will carry, and will deliver you" (KJV). That didn't leave very much for me to do! I was still smiling when Peter came home with the good news that our tickets and passports were back in his possession.

Chapter 15

Ana and Simon

**You made all the delicate, inner parts of my
body and knit me together in my mother's
womb. Thank you for making me so wonderfully
complex! Your workmanship is marvellous –
and how well I know it. You watched me as I
was being formed in utter seclusion, as I was
woven together in the dark of the womb.**

Psalm 139:13–15 – words given to me
during my pregnancy

The stewardess wheeled me off the plane, and straight through immigration. The wheelchair was designed to fit down the narrow aisle of the airplane, so it was a tight squeeze with my massive belly! I could see my parents waving excitedly as we approached the arrivals gate. I was so glad to be back on British soil, especially as it was summertime.

At the end of September 1993 I was admitted into the maternity wing of Barnstaple Hospital. Right away, the nurse brought me a cup of tea and a Rich Tea biscuit. *How nice*, I thought, grinning. She handed me a menu and instructed me to choose what I wanted to eat.

Mr Boyle, the obstetrician who had taken care of me when Michael was born, had asked me to come into the hospital early. He was planning to induce labour, which was normal for pregnancies with twins. The nurses probably thought I was strange as I was so appreciative of the hospital food, and thanked them for everything they did to and for me.

Safe at last, I thought. But a few days later I was going crazy with a very itchy rash all over my body. The situation worsened, until patches of my skin looked almost transparent and grey – it was very weird. One doctor after another filed into my room and silently peered and poked at the unusual display etched on my entire body. They had no answers other than that my hormones had gone berserk!

Mr Boyle suggested we get on with labour to relieve the situation, assuring me it would all go away as soon as the twins were born. With the weird rash and the history of my pregnancy I had become quite a spectacle in the maternity wing and the delivery room began to fill up with onlookers. Four more doctors lined up against the wall. The epidural injection hadn't worked at all. But after five attempts I couldn't bear to have him try again. When the midwife told me to push, I pushed with all my might – and so did each of the doctors lined up along the wall! They continued to offer their moral support, grimacing with me and bearing down, until we heard the words, "You have a little girl!"

A girl! I looked over at Peter and smiled.

"No time for relaxing! We have another one now!" Mr Boyle told me as he took the midwife's place at the foot of the bed. He felt around my tummy and looked concerned.

"I'm afraid this one is lying the wrong way up. I might need to do a caesarean section," he said.

The nurse began to prepare for an operation as they didn't seem confident that the baby would get in the head-down position by itself. First, though, Mr Boyle attempted to manipulate the baby around in my womb – it was extremely uncomfortable. After what seemed far too long he announced to the waiting audience that he had done it. Everyone applauded and the midwife kissed my forehead. "Hallelujah!" she said.

Thirty minutes after Ana, Simon emerged, the cord wrapped around his neck. The midwife quickly unravelled it and held him up for all to see,

"And this one is… a boy!" she said, exultantly.

"Are they both alright?" I asked Peter as the midwife checked them.

"They are beautiful and everything is fine," Mr Boyle told me, and added that he was very proud of me.

It seemed that everyone was. One by one the doctors excused themselves, with big smiles, and left the room. They all looked quite worn out.

Twins! What an accomplishment!

Ana was 5lb 8oz and Simon 5lb 12oz. They didn't need to go to the special baby unit, which apparently was unusual for twins. After a couple of days we were on our way home to Poughill with our two precious bundles. They weren't identical; they looked and acted completely different from each other. Ana had dainty features and no hair, and Simon had huge brown eyes. They were absolutely gorgeous. And we began to see that Ana was assertive and Simon was laid-back.

It seemed I was breast-feeding twenty-four hours a day for the next few months. I tried to synchronize feeds but the babies were on different timetables. Michael was fascinated with them both and thrilled to be a big brother. On the morning of our follow-up check-up he must have overheard Peter complaining of lack of sleep because as we left to drive to the hospital he looked worried. "Mummy, no!" he pleaded. "Don't take them back!"

In November, Peter returned to the Philippines with Michael as he was not allowed to extend his visa. Just before they left, my father dedicated the twins in his church. Then in February 1994 it was time for me to join Peter. Caroline Bickersteth, godmother of the twins, offered to come with me and help take care of them on the airplane.

After spending seven months in comfortable England I struggled with being back in our half-finished room on the building site. But I just had to get on with it. I found that I could still do what I did before; the only difference was that I had to do it in quick time. The days whizzed by in a frenzy of multi-tasking.

After church one Sunday, our builder, Ben, and his wife Jeanette rushed over to see me and show me their new baby girl, Catherine. Their prayers had been answered. She was gorgeous, like her brothers, with very dark eyes and a cute dimple in her cheek. Jeanette and I compared notes about our labour and smiled about Ana's shortage of hair compared with Catherine. "They will be good friends when they grow up," I said, imagining them playing with dolls together. Ana would need a girlfriend with all the boys around.

Our precious Mama Adella was a great help. She wrapped Simon snugly in a cotton blanket and fastened him to her back. He was content to stay there for hours while she cooked and cleaned. She had done the same with Michael when he was a baby. Ana was not so easy to please. But we discovered we could all get a good night's sleep if she slept on top of Daddy's chest, listening to his heart beating!

Our foster son Ricky married Marcy, and went to live with her parents in Ifugao, 300 km north of our home in La Union, and home of the famous rice terraces. Fred also left us to work as a taxi driver in Baguio. In his place he sent his younger brother Danny.

Don Bell, a friend from back home in Devon, came to help Peter with the building. He had recently become a Christian, and had abandoned himself completely to God's plans for his life. He was a plumber and got straight to work putting all the pipes in. It was a great advantage. Several years later, he became a missionary himself, in Kenya.

There was still a lot of building work to do but Peter concentrated on getting our apartment finished, situated on the third floor of the building. We moved in at the end of 1994, just before my parents came for a visit. To begin with it felt like we were staying in a hotel. The timing was perfect as the twins decided they would learn to walk – Mum and Dad were pleased to witness such an important milestone. Michael was noticeably more relaxed once we moved into our own place. I hadn't realized how much he had been absorbing. Nonetheless, he was a confident and sociable little boy.

My father loved being in the Philippines – it reminded him of his younger days growing up in Ireland where he had lived simply. And when we took them to visit the squatter village on the beach, they cried – just as Peter and I had. "If I was younger I would build a little house and live right here with these folk," Dad said. I knew exactly how he felt.

But it was difficult for my parents to get accustomed to all the noise at night-time. I didn't notice it anymore at that point, but it was bedlam compared to rural England. When darkness fell, every dog in the neighbourhood began to howl and bark, which in turn encouraged the cockerels to crow. On top of all that, people in Pugo loved to party with loud karaoke music until the early hours of the morning, and several singers couldn't sing! To make matters worse, the bridge in Bauang was being rebuilt. The rhythmic thud of pile-driving went on all through the night.

We had been waiting for our rice crop to ripen long after everyone else in the village had finished harvesting. The other farmers shook their heads and clicked their tongues at Peter. "It looks like you were sold a bad crop," they told him.

It was disappointing after all the hard work everyone had put in. But when Peter and Jose went to check progress later they were amazed to see so much rice on each stalk. No one else had such a good crop. My father had a great time with the men, harvesting and threshing. There was enough to feed everyone at LAMA House for a year, with extra to give away to Miracle Bible College and the regional jail at Christmas time. Another lesson in waiting: God's timing always brings the best result. Unlike us, He is never in a hurry!

Late one afternoon, I arrived back from the market with something to cook for the evening meal and found Oscar, Lito, Joey, Lazaro, and Almo on the roof. All of them young men now, they were having great fun blowing bubbles from a mixture of crushed hibiscus flowers. I shouted for them to come down and show me how to blow the massive bubbles. It made me laugh, until I realized they had completely missed out on their childhood. Suddenly it seemed quite sad. I decided at that moment we would always give plenty of time at LAMA House for childhood games – even with our teenage boys.

We designed a basketball court at the front of LAMA House and the youngsters from the barrio came to play at the end of their day. They thrived on the attention as we watched the game and cheered them on. It became a permanent LAMA tradition; more therapeutic than any other group therapy – for boys and staff alike!

At 5.30 p.m. as the sun went down, cooler air always beckoned everyone outside for a chat with their neighbours. The barrio children, arriving home from school, threw their schoolbags down and ran out to play with their friends, and the young men grabbed a basketball and headed for the nearest hoop. Housewives and husbands stopped what they were doing and sat on their porch for a while, gossiping. In the city or the barrio alike, everyone made the most of the cooler hours before darkness fell. Then they retreated back behind closed doors before the mosquitoes had a chance to get inside their homes. I tried to learn from their example – the Filipinos knew better than I how to live well in the tropics!

Chapter 16

Approval

**And don't think you know it all!... Do things
in such a way that everyone can see you are
honourable.**

Romans 12:16–17

The newly appointed assistant director at the DSWD Office didn't seem to like us. I had received a critical letter from him, in which he stated that Peter and I were not suitable to be directors of a child care institution because we had no qualifications in social work. I looked at the list of requirements, not understanding a word: accomplishment reports for the past two years; profiles of all clients served; profiles of employees; a service-users guide; staff policies and objectives; administrative policies and procedures; organizational structure; a strategic and operational planning system; work and financial plans for the next two years; medicals for all staff and boys; health and safety certificates; and so on and so on.

Many non-profit organizations had resorted to working without DSWD approval, unable to keep up with the many demands. Several Christian leaders advised us to dismiss them and get on with our work regardless. But when I prayed about it I knew that was not God's way. Romans 13:1, 3, 7 gave us clear instructions: "Obey the government, for God is the one who put it there. All governments have been placed in power by God. So those who refuse to obey the laws of the land are refusing to obey God... So do what they say, and you will get along well... give respect and honour to all to whom it is due."

I decided to do everything in my power to meet the DSWD requirements, thinking that maybe one day we would gain not only their approval, but also their commendation. But the guidelines they suggested seemed to exclude prayer, worship, spiritual gifts, and Bible-based counselling – and these things were the backbone of our ministry.

1 Corinthians 2:1 explains that we can't expect everyone to understand the work of the Holy Spirit; such spiritual things sound foolish to those who haven't experienced it for themselves. Often people simply cannot understand the religious language we use. Honour is one of God's requirements; without it we had no credibility as His workers. The assistant director was right – we were all under-qualified. And he was right to require us to hire a social worker, but it was difficult to find the right people.

Eventually we came across the kind of people we were looking for. Pastor Agusto, a friend from Miracle Bible College, loved being at LAMA House. As a teenager he had worked as a cigarette vendor and newspaper boy on the city streets and so he could easily identify with the boys. He readily accepted when Peter asked him to work with us as a house-father. He was a gentle man with a strong faith. His purpose in life was to serve others – that was just what we needed.

Cora, a senior social worker who had helped us obtain our foster parents' licence for Victory House, introduced us to Marion, a social worker with teaching experience. Her exuberance and genuine love for the boys was like a ray of sunshine. But before long she was leaving us to get married. Pastor Lito and Maureen also decided to move on to pastor a church.

My brother David had convinced me to buy a laptop computer and join the technological age. Full of good intentions, I took the Acer laptop out of its case and opened it, but afraid that I would press the wrong key and destroy the expensive gadget I closed it again and put it away. I repeated this procedure at regular intervals. So when I received a letter from Kelly Hodder in Wales, asking if she could do some volunteer work, I told her to come right away. Kelly had worked as a secretary for Project Taskforce, a non-profit organization in the UK. She taught me how to use the laptop and gave advice on how to write newsletters, create brochures, and print everything myself.

Up to that point I had relied on a Xerox copy machine in town to print out newsletters. She showed me how to organize the bookkeeping and office work on the computer, and keep the mailing list up-to-date and accurate. "You will wonder how you ever did it all without a computer," she told me. And she was absolutely right. A whole new world of possibilities opened up to me. It was a huge relief to have Kelly assisting me with administrative duties. But the time came around too quickly for her to return home.

Paperwork was now neatly printed out and spell-checked. Peter drove me to the regional office, where I proudly submitted the completed operation manual, yearly report, list of employees, and list of clientele, as well as the financial plan for 1996 and other "supporting documents".

Cora greeted us with a smile, placing the file on her desk. She was busy talking to a young girl with a baby, who was obviously in distress. She stopped mid-sentence and turned to face Peter.

"Pastor, isn't it you are licensed foster parents?" she asked in her Filipino English.

"Yes, but we are required to get a licence to operate a children's home," he reminded her, moving the file of papers closer to her.

"No, I need your help with something else today," she said.

She nodded in the direction of the pretty young girl sitting at her desk.

The girl smiled and shook Peter's hand.

"Hello, I am Janice... and you are Pastor Peter!" she said.

"Hi! How do we know each other?" Peter asked.

"When I was younger you and Maam Lesley used to come to our barrio, behind the disco bar and tell us Bible stories and sing!" she smiled.

She was one of our children from the red-light district! We laughed, pleased to be in the right place at the right time. She was very relieved to see us.

"Her teacher offered to take care of her baby and pay the hospital bill when she delivered. That is reasonable, but now the teacher wants to keep the baby. Janice wants her baby back, but the teacher insists she pay back all the money first – that is considered child-trafficking," Cora told us.

"Trafficking! It's that serious?" I asked, surprised.

"It is a big problem in our country. The law states that no money should pass hands when someone offers to take care of a child like this," she explained.

I remembered the difficulty we had persuading them to rescue Pekpek. They seemed to look the other way in that instance. It was confusing.

"Will you foster the baby until he can be returned to his biological mother? We don't have anywhere else to place him," she asked.

I looked at the baby and his frightened mother.

"You know Janice, none of this is your fault," I assured her. She began to sob. She was so quiet and vulnerable. I looked over at Peter and he nodded his approval.

Cora smiled.

The all-important paperwork suddenly seemed quite inconsequential as we walked out of the office carrying a three-month-old baby, a tin of formula, and a bag of baby clothes. It felt like God had timed the entire meeting in one of His perfectly executed plans.

"I wonder what Michael and the twins will think of this!" I said, laughing.

The lengthy application process for a telephone line to be installed at LAMA House was still ongoing and so I called home later from a public telephone in town.

"Mum, it's me! We have a new baby!" I blurted out, excited to share the news.

My mother was completely taken aback and assumed I was pregnant again. When I told her what had happened, she wanted to get on an airplane and help me.

"Oh, Lesley, what have you taken on now?" she worried.

Mama Adella was thrilled to have another little one to carry around on her back. Michael couldn't wait to get home from school to play with him. He was now six years old, and had won an award for "Best in conduct". I was so proud of him. By now Ana and Simon were three years old. They were not as talkative as most toddlers, perhaps because there were three languages spoken in our home. With someone so small to practise on, however, they sat for hours and chattered about this, that, and the other!

After two months Janice was given full custody of her son. We kept in contact with her, and the baby grew up into a very handsome little boy. They visited us often, whenever Cora needed advice. Cora had been obliged to visit us during the baby's stay and she became a solid friend and ally, learning to trust us and the way we worked. A devout Catholic, she began to understand our relationship with God. "Jesus was a social worker, you know!" she told me confidently, one day.

In turn, I gained a better understanding of the difficulties the DSWD faced. The lack of resources, often due to corruption in high places, meant they could never be effective. Our relationship with them developed into one of respect and was less stressful.

* * *

"I was wondering if you would like me to come to LAMA House with a team of interns, to provide a free clinic for the indigents," Dr Alviar suggested to me in February 1996. We had been talking with him about answers to prayer and he wasn't sure he believed in miracles but he said I had almost persuaded him. The word "indigents" always made me cringe.

"YES! I have been praying for that!" I replied, excitedly.

"So, I am the answer to your prayers," he laughed.

His occasional visits became quite an event in the barrio with hundreds of patients lining up outside the clinic door.

I also enlisted the services of Dr Christian Cordoviz from LORMA Medical Centre, who had become a close friend and "family doctor" for LAMA House. He always waived his professional fee, gave me free medicines, and told me to head straight to him at the emergency department instead of waiting in the outpatients' department for hours.

Watching him work, I thought he lived up to his name. Everyone was treated with dignity, regardless of their social status. I could imagine Jesus being just like him.

"There's a lot we can't do, but at least we're doing something," Dr Christian commented. "When I go biking around the remote areas, I check up on the children of poor communities. I'm a kind of missionary too."

"Yes! You absolutely are! This is what LAMA is about," I smiled.

It felt good to be practising my nursing again, in some measure. The three of us loved working together, despite the frustration of insufficient free medicine to hand out. Dr Alviar even said he would have liked to make LAMA House a hospital for the poor: "I could fix it all up with the World Health Organization – you could go back to nursing," he tried to persuade me. It was tempting. But it was not what we had designed LAMA House for.

For my thirty-sixth birthday Dr Alviar, Dr Christian, and his friend Dr Nelson Gundran came to help me celebrate. The following morning I turned on the television to see the news. To begin with I thought it must be some kind of hoax. They were saying that Princess Diana was dead following a terrible car accident in Paris. I kept the television on all day, and did my work around it listening to every news report. I felt utterly devastated, though I didn't quite understand why it had affected me so deeply.

Chapter 17

Dedication Day

... and in this place will I give peace, says the Lord of hosts.

Haggai 2:9 (KJV)

It doesn't always have to be breathtaking to be God's wonderful handiwork. We tend to overlook the slow processes of God. LAMA House had taken over six years to build, but it was all paid for, by ordinary people who gave the little they had. The villagers nicknamed it "The Mansion" because it looked so grand. During those six years of building work there were no accidents or disputes among the workers. There was something supernatural about that; it was a labour of love for everyone involved, brick by brick, year after year. God's work in the boys' lives was the same – it didn't happen overnight but He carefully fixed their broken childhoods.

Now, on 17 November 1997, we were ready for Dedication Day! We asked the governor of La Union to officiate the dedication service. Governor Justo Orros Jr had supported our work from its beginning in Victory House. He was a stately, dignified man who was loved and respected by rich and poor alike. It was a great honour to have him accept our invitation. He was another divine connection with whom God had blessed me.

The first visitor to arrive from England to the completed LAMA House was Kevin Hammond, from Hollybush Christian Fellowship in Yorkshire. My parents came next with Phillip White and David Dowling from Brunswick Baptist Church in Gloucester. Anxious to make a good impression, the barrio captain, the head of the village council, organized a team of men to clean up the roadway, ready for the governor's visit.

Dr Alviar came with news that boxes of free medicines had finally arrived for the clinic. My parents had brought a lot of medical supplies and equipment with them, donated by Dr Clarke, for use at the hospital. Dr Alviar was like a little boy opening Christmas presents!

It decided to rain for the first time in months, so planks of wood were put down in the driveway to prevent the official entourage from getting stuck in the mud. We wanted everything to be perfect, but as usual that was not going to happen.

Behind the scenes, a team of volunteers had started to prepare the feast. Dan-dan came with his father, and Ton with his new wife. Most of our extended family had come, including Alejandra, Pastor Fred, Uncle Rogelio, and Mariano. Pastor Abe arrived, then several from the Philippine Choir of Miracles and Miracle Sounds. What a grand reunion!

The service was scheduled to start at 9.30 a.m., but nothing ever starts on time in the Philippines. It is called "Filipino time". A crowd of villagers with their many children had gathered at the entrance, excited to catch a glimpse of the governor. By 10.30 a.m. he still hadn't arrived. "Maybe something else came up; maybe he can't come," I suggested.

Peter agreed. He asked Pastor España to start the service with a prayer. He prayed a very long-winded, rambling prayer – with one eye open, watching for the arrival of our honoured guest! Then he went on to acknowledge all those who had supported our work with their prayers and gifts. Letters were read out from the Chaudhary family (David, a close family friend, was a founding UK trustee) and others who could not attend. Still, no sign of Governor Orros, so honour was credited to the hard-working construction workers who had built LAMA House, followed by the staff and boys of the home, both past and present. Having totally exhausted the preliminaries, Peter asked everyone to stand as Gideon and Ditas, Condring, and Gina from Miracle Sounds led the congregation in worship.

Just at that moment, a commotion outside signalled the governor's arrival, along with the vice mayor of Bauang! He apologized as I led him to his seat; he had been delayed in Manila. The house was filled with the music of many people praising God. Governor Orros hesitated, clearly moved by the atmosphere of worship. There was a very real sense of the presence of God.

Then David Dowling read the Scriptures:

> *A promise for LAMA House, found in Isaiah 29:17– 19: "Soon – and it will not be very long… [LAMA House] will be a fertile field once again. And the fertile fields will become a lush and fertile forest. In that day deaf people will hear words read from a book, and blind people will see through the gloom and darkness. The humble will be filled with fresh joy from the Lord. Those who are poor will rejoice in the Holy One of Israel."*
>
> *And a promise for the boys at LAMA House taken from Isaiah 61:7: "Instead of shame and dishonour, you will inherit a double portion of prosperity and everlasting joy."*
>
> *A promise of provision and peace, from Haggai 2:7–9, "I will fill this place with glory, says the Lord Almighty. The silver is mine, and the gold is mine, says the Lord Almighty. The future glory of this Temple will be greater than its past glory, says the Lord Almighty. And in this place I will bring peace. I, the Lord Almighty, have spoken!"*
>
> *And so we ask the Lord, "Let your glory fill this place!"*

Quietly, David sat down and my father took his place behind the pulpit for the sermon.

*I want to talk to you today about the generosity of God,
from Psalm 145:16, which says, "When you open
your hand, you satisfy the hunger and thirst of every
living thing." Our God is a God who gives to all alike.
A glorious sunset is there for rich and poor alike. The
birdsong in early morning is for the weakest and the
lowliest, not only for the great. The eventide song of
the nightingale is heard by the poorest child, not just the
privileged. There is no colour bar nor class distinction
with regards to God's gifts. God's gifts are free, without
money or price! God's gifts are worth having. God's gifts
are varied – there are no two persons alike.*

*He has given each of us something with which to serve
Him, each slightly different from the other. God has an
imagination and gives a variety of gifts. Each has something
to exercise for the glory of God. He does things in a fantastic
way. He gives in abundance. This building is beautiful,
built entirely by faith, but there is more. Who knows what
God will do through even a few of the boys who come to
LAMA House and are transformed by God's love?*

Asking everyone to stand, my father prayed the prayer of
dedication:

*Having been prospered by the hand of the Lord and
enabled by His grace and power to complete this home
to be used for the glory of His name, we will now,
in His presence, dedicate this building to Him, to the
glory of God our Father, from whom comes every good
and perfect gift. We dedicate this home to the honour
of Jesus Christ, His Son, our Lord and Saviour, to the
praise of the Holy Spirit, the Comforter, Source of life
and light.*

*Almighty and Everlasting Father, accept the
offering of this home, which Your people have built to*

*the glory of Your name. Let Your ministers be clothed
with righteousness and all who work in this place. Let
Your people sing for joy. Put Your name in this place.
Let Your eyes be open towards it and hearken to the
prayers of Your people when they pray in this place.
And when You hear, forgive.*

*And now establish the work of our hands. And to
Your blessed name O God, whose we are and who we
serve, be honour and glory everlasting. Amen.*

Governor Orros cut the ribbon that had been fastened across
the front door, to symbolize the opening of the home. Everyone
applauded and cheered.

In the courtyard we had built a fountain. Susanna
dedicated it to the memory of Reverend Clyde Shields. She
spoke with her usual grand eloquence about the influence
Pastor Shields had had on so many lives, including my own.

"This fountain is dedicated to the memory of Revd Clyde
V. Shields, whose life and vision inspired many to give their lives
to the service of God," she said, reading, at the top of her voice,
the words inscribed on the plaque.

Governor Orros got to his feet. Everyone fixed their
attention on him. He always commanded such deep respect
from his people. He spoke from his heart, without notes.

*We are gathered here today to celebrate love and
celebrate life itself, and ask that it would be more
abundant, as God Himself has intended it to be.
We may not know exactly why we are all here, from
differing racial, geographical, religious, and social
dimensions and values. He has brought us together here
to dedicate our lives for the greater glory of God, through
whom all things are possible.*

*I was honoured to have been invited here, and to
also honour a good friend, Revd Clyde Shields. I was*

the Mayor of San Fernando when he passed away. He touched the lives of so many.

I am reminded of a story of a king who wanted to test his sons to see who would succeed him. He had three large rooms and asked them to fill a room each with something. The one who filled the room best would be his successor.

The first son filled his room with books, to enlighten the minds of the people. The king noticed though that the room was not totally full. The second son filled his room with flowers and trees, to make life more beautiful. The father noticed that there were still empty places. In the room of the third son there was a single lighted candle. The father asked, "Son, what have you done to this room, with such a small candle?" The son replied, "With this candle the whole room is full of light; there is no empty space at all!"

Our country was ruined when it was taken in the war. Many came to help, including Revd Shields who lit our province, our city, and our entire country. And again, your coming here with Revd Keenan brings more light.

But God has never forsaken us. We Filipinos have a strong faith. One theologian said, "The Philippines, through its poverty, is blessed with one shining jewel, a strong faith in the Almighty." And it is this faith that will see us through any crisis, through many difficulties. It is my desire to make this jewel shine even brighter and more steadfast in the years to come.

In Him, life is sacred and precious and can be more abundant. It is in this spirit that I am here on behalf of the officials of La Union to celebrate with you. We look upon this place as a ray of hope to young men, who might have blundered or strayed during their young life. But we know God never puts us in a challenging situation without the capacity to surmount *any difficulty, as long as we strengthen our faith in the Lord.*

We have problems in our country and in our municipality. Our prayers are being answered here in LAMA House. This is a gift from the Almighty, and Peter and Lesley and all who have supported it.

"A bell is not a bell until it is rung, a song is not a song until it is sung, love is not meant in the heart to stay, love is not love 'til you give it away!"

This is what you are doing today, in the dedication of this beautiful building of LAMA. Thank you for the light!

The crowd applauded loudly and stood to their feet. Governor Orros went around the room, shaking hands with everyone. He smiled and bowed his head as he greeted them.

Hundreds of people lined up outside for their plate of rice, noodles, fried chicken, roast pork, and vegetables. Excited laughter echoed around LAMA campus as the children played and adults chattered happily. Gradually the crowds dispersed and everyone returned home.

Eager to get started with his contribution, Dr Alviar came in the afternoon to conduct a free clinic. "C'mon Lesley, let's go. There is no time like the present!" he told me.

The service made a deep impression on the governor. He invited us to meet him at his office, with our guests from England. When we arrived there the following week he had postponed all his previous engagements for the morning. He wanted to know more about Jesus. Some distinguished-looking people were waiting outside his office to speak to him, but he didn't hurry or excuse himself as we shared our faith. Then he shared his plans for the province with us. We prayed for him, asking God's blessing on his work and life. It meant a lot to him that we did that.

Chapter 18

Order to Leave

When God said, "Have faith", he did not expect you to produce it – He simply wanted you to receive it from Him! Have faith!

Almo was truly one of a kind! The way he ate, dressed, and carried himself was outlandish to say the least. I tried to teach our staff to celebrate the unique personalities of each boy who came to live with us and Almo was one who tested that standard to its limit. Watching him eat spaghetti bolognese one evening, I had to laugh at the incredible mess he was getting into. "For goodness sake, Al! When you have a girlfriend don't order spaghetti on your first date. Promise me!" I joked. He laughed, opening his mouth wide enough to allow a mouthful of spaghetti to fall out slowly onto his plate. But not everyone found his quirky personality funny. One school day we were summoned to the principal's office to talk about his unusual behaviour.

"I don't know what to do with Almo," the tiny principal told us. "He lacks ambition, his work is untidy, and he doesn't speak when the teachers ask him something," she said.

I explained that he had some psychological problems due to bad experiences at a very young age. I considered it a major breakthrough when he was able to say "hello" or "goodbye", or even acknowledge the presence of an adult in the room. But she was unmoved.

"That should not be used as an excuse. You know, I was also a street-child. I don't know who my parents are, but look at me – I have made something of my life. He can do the same if he has the drive to do it. Life is what you make it!" she said.

She was right, in a way. But her approach didn't help Almo; it only pushed him further away. He finally gave up altogether and dropped out of school months before his graduation. He regressed, as if he were replaying the early days of his childhood. He didn't bathe, he didn't talk to us, and he didn't come home – choosing instead to sleep at the city Plaza with the homeless, eating what he could find on the street. We found him there one night and brought him home. He went straight to his room, where Peter and I sat on the bed, trying to reason with him.

Words are very powerful and I suspected his frustrated teachers had said some very negative things to him. I looked around his room at the sketches, on torn-off bits of paper, stuck on the walls. The artwork was impressive, but disturbing – pencil drawings of eyes, evil eyes like demons scowling back at me. "I'm taking these down, Almo! This can't be helping you," I told him.

"Pete, let's pray for him; this is a spiritual battle and we have to pray him through it," I said resolutely.

Almo began to sob as we prayed together, resting his head on my shoulder.

"We love you, Almo. Don't ever forget that. You are part of our family, for life. There is always a place for you here," I told him. Then, thinking about it, "Well, until you get married, anyway!"

He laughed. His trademark grin spread across his face. *That's better*, I thought!

I couldn't imagine him ever finding a girl who would accept his strange ways, but I didn't mind if he stayed with us for life. That basically summed up my treatment plan – I wrapped my arms around the boys and held on tight, until they learned to trust me and the God I represented.

At that moment, the darkness left him. He decided he would enrol in a vocational course to learn auto mechanics.

When he graduated from that, he went on to do night classes, finishing his final year of high school. His classmates at the National High School were older students like him, and former drop-outs. No longer the odd one out, he made friends quickly with three girls who were in varying stages of pregnancy, and two respectable-looking young men. He was very protective of the girls and felt terrible that their boyfriends were not providing for them. One evening, he brought them home to meet us.

"This is my Ma and Pa," he told them, nodding in our direction.

"Your mother is an Americana!" they commented, suitably impressed.

Almo had the features and pale skin of a *mestizo* (part-Caucasian), so it was not unlikely, but I thought he was a bit old to be my biological son. I shook hands with everyone with a satisfied smile on my face. That was the first time Almo had called me "Ma"! Perhaps, at last, he felt he belonged.

The process of getting birth certificates for Lito and Almo was extremely difficult as we had no information about their parents or their birth. That did nothing for their self-esteem. In the end, they were both issued with a "Certificate of Foundling", a constant reminder of their abandonment. Without their birth registration documents, children had difficulty registering in school. It left them in a very vulnerable position, as they did not officially exist.

Every two months or so, for the past five years, a motorcyclist had pulled up at LAMA House and handed Peter a brown envelope from the court. I came to dread those brown envelopes. In May 1998 we received another one that knocked us all for six. It informed us that we had lost the case. We were ordered to leave the property and demolish LAMA House.

"I've had enough. I quit!" Peter told me.

He had said that before, whenever a mountain towered over us. I knew that Jesus said if we have faith as small as a mustard seed we can say to this mountain be gone (see Matthew

17:20) but I couldn't find anything to say, unable to find the strength to lift him up this time. *But it would do no good to quit, no good at all.*

Why would God bring us this far, only for us to leave what we had begun? There was a long, empty silence between us. Did we misunderstand? What about all the promises God had given us? Peter went back downstairs, saying nothing. We were in a daze of disbelief and confusion. As was my custom, I locked myself in the bathroom and turned to God in prayer. I sank to the floor and sobbed until I could cry no more.

I remembered the story of Joseph in the Bible. His situation went from bad to worse before He received what God had promised him. Pulling myself together, I emerged from the bathroom feeling that somehow everything would be alright. LAMA House was God's work, not ours. If He wanted it to end, there was no point in our hanging on to it. Why should we doubt His goodness? Peter also found a measure of peace and clear thinking. The next day we went to show the letter to our lawyer.

"I can't believe this ruling," he told Peter indignantly. "Don't worry. There is no need to accept this. *Don't* move out and don't demolish anything! We will ask for reconsideration. We can win this! *God will indeed fight for us!*" he declared, like a preacher man.

I informed our trustees in England – my parents, David Chaudhary, and Phillip White. I half expected they would question our fitness to lead the charity. Instead they urged us to keep on doing what we were doing, regardless. My father suggested we visit Governor Orros and ask for his help. "Above all, keep an attitude of love and forgiveness to those who are falsely accusing you," my dad advised. He knew what he was talking about as he had dealt with more than his fair share of false accusations during his years in ministry.

Governor Orros was clearly disturbed when he read the letter from the court. He quizzed us about the sale of the land, then told us he would stand with us. But there wasn't much he could do to overturn the court decision. "Certainly, you can appeal. It might help to mention that the governor is backing you," he suggested, grimacing. So when our attorney met with the judge, Governor Orros's name came into the conversation more than once!

Not long afterwards, the woman who had filed the case against us died suddenly. The verse we read in Isaiah at the start of the court case came to mind, "Anyone who opposes you will die" (Isaiah 41:11).

Lord! I didn't want that to happen literally! I thought.

We assumed that the case would be dropped, but the woman's brother took it up instead. Remembering my father's advice about forgiveness, we decided to arrange a meeting with him. We met at the home of the barrio captain. The woman's brother was an elder in the Mormon Church, but he humbly asked Peter to open our meeting with a prayer. Peter prayed, asking God to fill our hearts with His love and to have His way in the decisions we made together. The Mormon Church had often opposed our work, instructing the village children to stay away from LAMA House, and openly mocking our beliefs. We had always tried to respond with grace. Now, unexpectedly, he asked for our forgiveness.

"We should be working together, not fighting each other," he said.

"I agree. That's the reason we came to meet with you, to show you that we forgive you," Peter told him.

As we left the house, the barrio captain's son stopped to talk to us. "I've never heard anyone pray like you did, Pastor Peter. You talk to God like a friend, even if you are not a priest. Please, can you give me a Bible?" he asked.

The secretary of the village council joined in the conversation. "Me too, I could feel something different in the house, as if God were there with us. I've never been present in a meeting like that before," she whispered.

Children at Miracle Children's Home, 1984 – Marcito, Reynaldo, and Ezekiel.

Pastor Bercero, Mrs Bercero, Sammy, and me at Sammy's high school graduation, 1984.

Mariano at Alejandra's graduation from Bible College, 1985.

Me and Peter with
our first foster son,
Ricky, 1985.

Mama Adella with
baby Simon, 1994

My parents at the Dedication Day, 1997.

The LAMA boys at Ifugao Rice Terraces, with Michael and the twins, 1998.

The LAMA Boys, 1999.

Our family, 2006.

Some of the staff and boys at LAMA House, 2012.

LAMA House courtyard.

The Keenan family, 2012. Left to right (back row) Esther, Linda, Philip, Simon, Ana, Andrew, Jessica, David, Carmel; (front row) My parents, me with Rain (Michael's son), Rachel, Ben, Rachel (Andrew's wife).

Dr Nelson Gundran, our friend and doctor.

Maam Stella, Ray, and Pastor Abe Duclayan.

Mama Jeanette with one of the boys.

Michael's 2nd birthday party celebrated with the children from the squatter village, March 1992.

Peter, Philip, Pastor Fred, and my father outside Pastor Fred's church.

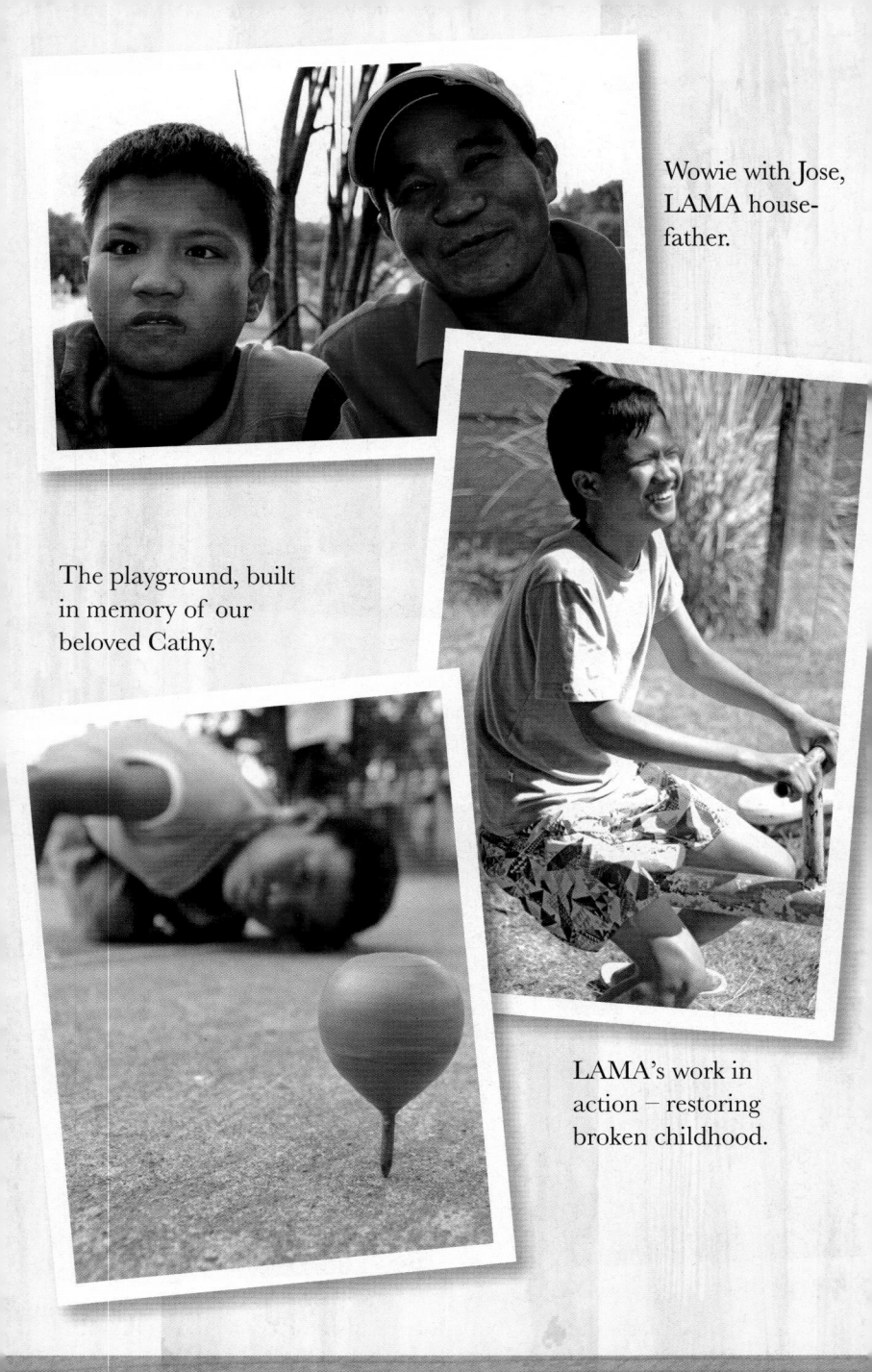

Wowie with Jose, LAMA house-father.

The playground, built in memory of our beloved Cathy.

LAMA's work in action – restoring broken childhood.

We felt sure that would be the end of it, but the man's lawyer persuaded him otherwise – he refused to settle the case.

Fidel Ramos was the president at that time and seemed to be doing a good job of running the country. But he inherited the corruption endemic in every government department in the Philippines. In June 1998 Ramos was replaced by Joseph Estrada, a handsome movie star. He played the hero in local action movies; the masses who voted for him probably assumed he would therefore save the nation. Politics in the Philippines seemed doomed to failure. I wondered if the odds were also stacked against us.

In March 1999, after a year of waiting for the judge's response, we received a letter with the verdict. "Motion for reconsideration: <u>Denied</u>."

I stared at the words in disbelief! *WHY was it so difficult?*

Feeling completely discouraged, I sat down with a cup of tea to read my mother's letter. One of my dad's devotions, torn from his desk calendar ten days earlier, fell out of the letter: "It's a fallacy to believe that if we obey God everything will go well. In fact, the gospel advances on disaster and suffering. Paul was in prison when he wrote the book of Philippians; he did not question his calling to preach the gospel after his arrest."

Of course, it was true. God's kingdom advances through suffering. Why was I complaining again? I was being "girded" with strength, like the steel bars that held our new building together during earthquakes.

We contacted our attorney, who again put our troubled minds at ease. He obviously knew how to speak to mountains! "Don't worry. We'll go to the Supreme Court and appeal. We can still win this," he told Peter. I admired his tenacity. We rested our case on the authority of God's word, rather than the authority of the court, and His peace settled over the whole situation.

Chapter 19

LAMA Boys

Can a mother forget her nursing child? Can she
feel no love for a child she has borne? But even
if that were possible, I would not forget you!
See, I have written your name on my hand.

Isaiah 49:15–16

After the dedication service, social workers began immediately referring needy boys to us. Two government-run children's homes in the region had closed down due to allegations of sexual abuse by an employee, so they needed our help. We visited one of the homes when we were trying to help Dan-dan, Noel, and Butz. The place was overcrowded, the boys institutionalized like dreary little prisoners. We left the place feeling appalled. Their forlorn faces haunted me for months. Only three boys from that home were referred to us. They were witnesses in the court case against the offender. *What had happened to all the other boys?* I wondered.

The three were accompanied to LAMA House by Analie, a kind social worker whom I instantly liked. Each boy carried a travel bag containing their scarce belongings. They looked frightened. Like street-boy prototypes their clothes were four sizes too big and the detached expressions on their faces said, "I don't need your help, anyway!"

We welcomed them, then Pastor Fred took them upstairs to show them their rooms. On the street the boys always slept in groups for protection, and in the other shelters they slept in a dormitory − so when they saw only two single beds in one room they were apprehensive. In the end, Pastor Fred wedged another bed inside the room and helped them unpack.

Downstairs, Analie explained their case histories. As I leafed through the notes I felt that these three were the reason for LAMA House, like Dan-dan, Butz, and Noel before them. They desperately needed what LAMA House offered.

The case notes stated that Franko had been abandoned at the hospital after his birth. The doctor who owned the hospital took him home, where he and his wife cared for him as part of their family. Franko lived with them until he was eight. Emotionally disturbed, he was not fully toilet-trained and often skipped school. Unable to cope with him, the doctor contacted the DSWD, who placed him in the children's home.

Ruben was found begging outside Jollibee (the Filipino equivalent of McDonald's). He claimed he was from Manila, but could not recall the exact address. I looked at the list of his family members:

Father:	*Whereabouts unknown*
Mother:	*Whereabouts unknown*
Siblings:	*Unknown*
Date of birth:	*Unknown*

He had run away from home because his parents were rarely there. When they did come home they were drunk and beat him. He had lived on the street for four years before being placed in the children's home, where he was repeatedly sexually assaulted by a male staff member. As a result he had become confused about his gender. He tended to throw his weight around and be a bully, but when he was challenged he cried like a baby. A psychological evaluation concluded he was mentally challenged, with a very low IQ.

Domingo had also grown up on the city streets. His parents were separated. His mother went to live with another man, taking her new baby with her, but then sold the baby to a childless couple. One younger brother and two sisters lived on the street with their father. Another sister with special needs was fostered by a Catholic nun who ran a mission in that city. *What a mess*, I thought. *What would happen to the rest of Domingo's family?*

As if she knew my thoughts, Analie answered my unspoken question.

"We would have placed Domingo's siblings in a shelter, if there were any places. With nowhere to live, they are all in danger. Their father tries to care for them but he is often drunk. Perhaps you can find out where they are now. I know Domingo wants to see his father soon," she told me.

"We'll definitely try," I replied.

"Franko is clever and does well in school but he is restless and a trouble maker, always trying to be the favourite. Domingo cannot concentrate in school. And Ruben has been expelled from several schools because he is disruptive and violent," she said, looking at me despondently.

"It's what we would expect. And, it is why we are here. We'll keep them out of school until they have adjusted and are feeling happier. Hopefully they will eventually finish high school. These things need a lot of time and patience," I told her.

"I know, I hope you all have enough of that," she smiled.

We shook hands and said goodbye as Pastor Fred came down the stairs with the three boys. "Goodbye boys, I'll see you again," she told them, looking relieved.

"I wish she worked for us," I whispered to Peter. She genuinely cared for the boys and wasn't afraid to show it.

Conscious that the boys were feeling anxious, I looked down at Franko and put a hand tentatively on his shoulder, feeling the muscles instinctively tighten. He had a metal chain dangling around his legs like a shackle, apparently the latest fashion accessory for teenage boys. A nasty boil had started to erupt in the middle of his forehead, no doubt due to the stress of this latest upheaval. His tough exterior did not fool me for a second.

It came as no surprise when straight away they began to test our resolve as substitute parents. They destroyed everything we gave them, and refused to obey us at every turn.

By this time we had a strong team – Mama Adella, Pastor Fred (who had returned to us), Pastor Agusto, Jose, Clarence, and Eunice, a licensed social worker.

Clarence worked as janitor. He was well known in the barrio as a self-taught chiropractor. When I sprained my ankle Peter asked Clarence to put it right for me. As he carefully massaged it it was very painful and I was sceptical of his abilities, but the next day it was back to normal. Through the years that he lived with us, he eased away migraines, bad backs, and various muscular ailments when conventional pain relief wouldn't work.

If the boys talked to anyone about their problems, it was Clarence. He was completely deaf but listened by lip-reading and replied in his own stilted Ilocano that most people had come to understand. I often found him sitting with one of the boys, counselling them through their life decisions. By this time I could understand Ilocano fluently and spoke it fairly well. I also understood most of the Tagalog (the national language of the Philippines). Even so, Clarence was the one person I could rely on to have a conversation with, and he was deaf as a post! He had nothing but a very poorly built shanty to call his own, so we helped him to build his house. Like many of the poorest people, he seemed more deeply convinced of God's love than those who had enjoyed a relatively easy life.

The three boys began to realize our concern was genuine and became less of a problem. God was healing them inside. For the first time in their lives they tentatively trusted the grown-ups. Still, in an effort to mark their new territory, they made sure everyone understood that they were, "The Original LAMA Boys!"

I overheard Michael talking to Franko, after Pastor Agusto had reminded him "for the last time" to have a shower. He nervously confided in Michael that he was afraid to go into the shower-room alone. "Don't be afraid; just trust in Jesus. He will always be there to help you," Michael told him confidently, in Tagalog.

Franko stood, quietly thinking about it. Michael was only eight years old. "Yes, yes. Jesus is a very kind man," he nodded, sure of it, too. The shower problem was solved.

Domingo was a gentle boy with fine features and a slight frame. He smiled a lot but I sensed that it was more a defence mechanism than a sign of inner happiness. He held no affection for his mother, whom he claimed he didn't remember at all. "All I remember is that she left us and took my sister and the baby away," he told me, bitterly.

But he couldn't wait to see his father, little brother, Piolo, and sisters, Michelle and Liza. He felt guilty that he had a nice place to live while they slept under the stars, on a vegetable cart. As soon as we could, we travelled to Urdaneta City, 88 km south of San Fernando, to visit them. We arrived at the market place, where Peter parked the van. Domingo knew exactly where to find his father, who worked as a "kariton" helper, collecting and delivering cartloads of vegetables to the vendors. We followed him to the back of the busy marketplace, where he stopped and stood awkwardly in front of a cart loaded with several plastic bags full of clothes. "This is it, Maam. This is our house. I'll go and find *Tatang* ['Father'']," he muttered, shrugging self-consciously.

Then he quickly disappeared among the stalls selling dried fish and salted eggs. We waited at the vegetable cart. A lump formed in my throat as I tried to comprehend what life must be like for them... *How did they live like that?*

Before long, his father appeared, with the other children trailing along behind him. Like Domingo, he was small in stature. He had a friendly face, weather-worn, and framed with shoulder-length grey hair.

"This is Michelle, Liza, and Piolo," Domingo said proudly,

pointing to his sisters and little brother. They smiled, and lifted my hand to their forehead politely. They were all painfully thin.

"Let's go and eat somewhere," I suggested.

Domingo linked arms with his sisters as they led the way to a stall inside the market that served home-cooked meals.

"We usually just ask for some soup," Michelle instructed me.

"Not today – you can have whatever you want," I said.

They chatted happily as they tucked in to chicken with green papaya and soup. I could see that they loved their father very much. That was the first of many visits, in which we came to know the family very well. But our many efforts at helping them were doomed to failure. They had become accustomed to, almost reliant on, living in crisis.

Because the sea of needs was so vast, the DSWD tended to concentrate on one "Clientele Group" each month: "Anti-Child Abuse Month"; "'Anti-Child Trafficking Month"; and so on. I noticed that every four or five weeks we would have a different set of referrals, all with the same sort of problems. The beds began to fill up and soon there were fourteen boys living at LAMA House. During "Child Slave Labour Awareness Month", the DSWD raided dubious businesses that had been under surveillance. Rescued boys were brought to us for safety until they could be transported back home to their families on other islands. On one such occasion an extra sixteen boys unexpectedly turned up who had been working as slaves at a nearby rice mill.

During "Anti-Sexual Exploitation Month", undercover operations were conducted at disco-bars and "Members Only" nightclubs. Underage boys and girls were rescued from prostitution. The girls were placed in the DSWD Home for Girls, while the boys were referred to us. These referrals were the biggest challenge for me. Many had been taught from a very young age that there were no rules in sexual conduct. For them, what was unacceptable became acceptable and was rewarded.

Sadly, we had to refuse some of them in order to protect the other boys in our care, as well as our own children. That proved to be the wound most difficult to heal, and the behaviour too stubborn to modify. It seemed we would never really find a satisfactory solution. They needed to be cared for exclusively with professional counsellors, but we could find nowhere in the entire country that was equipped to solve this, the Philippines' biggest problem.

Laws had been passed making child trafficking, child prostitution, and sex tourism illegal but they were rarely enforced, as with most laws in the Philippines. There were no laws against the sale of child pornography, which was sold openly in marketplaces across the country (a law against this was eventually passed in 2009). There were often cases where children were abducted from schools. More than once my children came home from school with a written warning from the principal, telling parents to personally pick up their children at the gate because of recent abductions in the area by a suspected paedophile syndicate. Because of the extreme poverty, children were used as currency by their mothers, or paedophiles befriended women with children and then abused their children.

"You are pretty enough to marry a foreigner," I overheard one mother telling her fifteen-year-old. It appeared to be something to attain to, regardless of the foreigner's age, looks, or even character! Apparently the love of money outweighed every possible negative.

Peter and I were invited to attend seminars organized by the DSWD, and became members of the Council for Protection of Children in La Union. The full extent of what we were dealing with was uncovered, like a can of worms. We learned that each tourist destination throughout the Philippines specialized in various aspects of the child-sex trade: Cebu was cited as the place where children were brought to be "processed". The former US army bases of Angeles, Subic, and Olongapo were notorious for offering children for sex. Pagsanjan was advertised as a "gay paradise". Busloads of tourists arrived at resorts across the country, on scheduled sex tours, to exploit the pretty young girls, or boys.

Social workers warned me that the international syndicates would go to any lengths to continue their lucrative trade. Anyone serious about taking them on had to know exactly what they were doing. "Foreign paedophiles are very well connected, with positions in industry and politics, so any efforts to apprehend them usually come to nothing," Cora told me.

As the only foreigner present at the seminars I felt uncomfortable. Perpetrators were mostly foreigners – I had little to say. I felt ashamed to be "white". The frequent accounts of perverted sex and unspeakable violence were deeply disturbing. Only Paul's advice in Philippians 4:8 helped me cope: "Fix your thoughts on what is true and honourable and right. Think about things that are pure and lovely and admirable. Think about things that are excellent and worthy of praise."

Once, after dealing with some grim obscenity in one boy's life, I purposely went to a garden centre and bought a beautiful, fuchsia-coloured bougainvillea plant to position at our doorway. When I arrived home, it silently reminded me that God's world was still filled with lovely things.

Every boy that passed through the doors of LAMA House quickly learned how to pray. We often took Communion together. There is power in remembering Jesus' death. As the boys experienced God's presence and His purity in worship the ugliness eventually washed away. Often without a lot of fuss or excitement, they were set free from the things that bound them.

It took sustained effort on the part of our staff before the boys could begin to trust again. But eventually they relaxed into God's love and knew for certain that we cared for them – and that God was the best kind of dad. The day would come when I would look at them in church and see God's gentlemen.

Chapter 20

Mysterious Ways

**Everything big starts with something small;
all God needs is something to start with. What
did the disciples say to Jesus just before He
fed 5,000? "There's a young boy here with five
barley loaves and two fish. But what good is that
with this huge crowd?" (John 6:9)**

My children were usually fully occupied with school and homework. With no girlfriends in the house, Ana spent a lot of time at her friend Cathy's home, which was just around the corner from LAMA House. They were both lively, fun-loving girls who loved barrio life, and everyone in our area knew them. It seemed that we could travel almost anywhere and someone would greet us with, "Hi Ana!"

On restless nights, while everyone else in the house was sleeping, my thoughts often drifted back to memories of my own childhood at the Old Vicarage. It was another life completely; how I wished I could duplicate it for my children and for the boys at LAMA House.

As the vicar's children, our friends in Yorkshire supposed we were as Victorian as the big old house we lived in, which was built in the 1850s by renowned architect William Butterfield. We lived completely separated from the rest of the village by a canal. In fact, we were not at all grand; more often than not we could be found laughing until it hurt, over some ridiculous joke my father had told us. My brother Andrew's best friend

Richard was not intimidated. He came often to help mow the acres of grass in our vast garden and the adjacent churchyard. Andrew, Philip, Esther, and I helped to rake it all up, which usually ended in "mown grass fights". One of our favourite games was racing around the house on our bikes, then all falling off in a heap when we reached the yew tree. We called the game "falling off each other's bikes". When we were not in school, all our time was spent playing outside in the garden, our imaginary kingdom until Mum shouted for us to "come inside for tea".

In summertime we had an abundance of pears, apples, and plums from the fruit trees, as well as gooseberries, strawberries, and red and blackcurrants. The scent of wallflowers, roses, lilac, and orange blossom filled the air. My mother and I would gather armloads of flowers to arrange in church or in the house. Birds of every British kind would visit the bird table.

At the back of the house was a walled-in cobbled yard. Fan-tailed pigeons lived in a little house on top of the old stable block, which was converted to a garage for my father's old Humber car. This was the "tradesman's entrance", which led into the scullery, where one Christmas morning I discovered my present hiding in a cardboard box – a Jack Russell puppy! I loved my dog more than anything. On our long walks together I learned to commune with God and find the quiet place in my soul.

On Bible study night the church people packed into our sitting room. There were so many that they overflowed into the oak-panelled hallway and up the grand stairway. Three of the choir ladies, Beryl, Joyce, and Eileen, stood by the piano to sing gospel songs, and everyone joined in at the top of their voices. Our social lives revolved around church activities, which to me was a lot of fun.

The Old Vicarage had five bedrooms. Esther and I shared one of the larger ones, which had an unused fireplace and looked out over the churchyard and on to the primary school.

This was our world in a nutshell.

The childhood memories of our boys at LAMA House stood out in stark contrast to mine. I felt I had been granted an unfair advantage. LAMA House was designed to set them free. One day, we would have fruit trees and blossoms, pigeons and puppies, bikes and swings. We would sing at the top of our voices, dance, and laugh until it hurt!

As wonderfully sheltered as our secret garden back home was, I had not been completely isolated from the realities of life. Part of my father's duty as vicar of the Parish of Pollington-cum-Balne was being the chaplain of the borstal. He sometimes invited a few of the young inmates to our house for afternoon tea. At first I was scared of them, but I soon realized they were no different from anyone else.

A number of times people who were down-and-outs came to live with us, until they could get back on their feet. I never forgot "Irish Peter", a homeless man my father brought home for tea and cake. We all sat around the wide kitchen table, staring at the bedraggled mess in front of us as Irish Peter tried to lift the cup of tea to his mouth. His hands shook so violently from alcoholism that most of it was lost in his lap. I cautiously moved forward and held the cup to his cracked lips to help him. At twelve years old I didn't understand why I felt such a gut-wrenching compassion for the man. After he had gone, I went to my bedroom and wept.

Another day, my father found a woman wandering around York, drunk and confused. He brought Gay home and she lived with us for several weeks. Her sallow, sunken face and bony body were the stuff of nightmares. Another lady from church helped her for a while. We bumped into them at Hollybush Christian Camp in Northallerton in the summer. I was pleased to see Gay again, but she looked worse than ever, and when I hugged her she was nothing but skin and bone. Not long after that my parents received a call. The police had found Gay in a public toilet with her wrists slashed. She was dead.

Reminiscing about it all, I realized that Irish Peter and Gay had only enriched my childhood. In school, I tried to practise loving everyone – even Christine, the school bully who it was rumoured had been expelled from nine schools. I had absolutely no desire to enjoy an easy life surrounded by comfortable things. The silent adventurer in me loved that Jesus was always eating in the wrong houses, hanging out with the wrong people, and healing the sick on the wrong day! My favourite name for Him was "Friend of sinners".

Instead of asking God to protect them, I began praying that my children would give their lives to ministering to people in need. Surely it was the most fulfilling life they could have.

As is often the case, when I had come to that place of acceptance, God revealed an even better plan for us. I woke early in September 1998 aware that God was waiting to speak to me. The Schofield family were on my mind. Our missionary friends still lived in the second-floor apartment in front of our previous home. Thinking about their planned return to Ireland, the thought occurred to me that we should move into their place in San Fernando. My immediate response to God's prompting was that I would rather not. Peter had put a lot of time into making our apartment at LAMA House just right for us, with no rent to pay. But where had that thought come from, if not from God? I knew it was pointless to argue with Him!

I opened my *Daily Light* devotion book on the bedside table to read the Scriptures for the day. "Then people go off to their work; they labour until the evening shadows fall again" (Psalm 104:23). That was a new concept! Since we married we had lived at work, and were "on call" twenty-four hours a day, seven days a week. Going off to work was not what we did; it was permanently around us. I read the next Scripture in Hebrews 4:9–10: "So there is a special rest still waiting for the people of God. For all who enter into God's rest will find rest from their labours, just as God rested after creating the world."

It sounded like God's guidance to me. When I told Peter about it, he agreed. But we told no one that we planned to move because we didn't want our staff to panic. Even so, when the time came, enough money had been donated in our account to buy everything we needed to set up home again. We left most of our furniture at the apartment in LAMA House so that visiting guests could stay there comfortably.

The apartment in San Fernando was next to the main road. It was constantly noisy with the sound of traffic and dirty with pollution from exhaust fumes. To make matters worse passing trucks routinely honked their horns through the night right outside our bedroom window, as if there was a sign there instructing them to do so. The only place to hang the washing was on the flat roof of the building, which I had to navigate carefully to avoid tripping over pipes or protruding steel bars, thereby plummeting to my death.

But Michael, Ana, and Simon were happy – they loved their new school – and were even happier when they discovered a family living below us with children their age to play with. Peter and I realized that we had expected too much of ourselves and our children by living on the job.

However, as I opened our front door one evening to tell the children to come inside, I heard an ominous scurrying noise. Looking down at the yard where the children were playing, I could see hoards of rats scampering around with them. When I hurried them inside to safety, they thought it funny that I was trembling. They wouldn't hear of "never playing down there again"! When I went to put our rubbish bin out the next day I found the massive pile of rotting garbage that had accumulated at the back of the building. No wonder there were so many rats and cockroaches. Foolishly, I tried to burn some of it and very nearly had to call out the fire department.

Then I discovered some other unwanted guests – head lice passed on by the children's new-found friends. Peter shrugged it all off and told me not to worry, but it was as far from my ideal as we could possibly be. I had to laugh at God's sense of humour.

Despite everything, we had a certain peace about the move and felt it was in God's plan. Still, sometimes I would lie awake at night listening to the traffic, hoping it was very temporary. One advantage of our new location was that it was closer to the children's new school: "Brain and Heart of a Christian Institution". I always thought its name was rather grandiose, but it was an excellent school. With classes starting at 7 a.m. it made life easier being close at hand.

Whenever we were in the city, I kept my eyes open for "House for Rent" signs. When we passed through a quiet sub-division one day, we noticed a large bungalow. There was a wide garden at the front and back. Designed like an American ranch house, it was different from anything else in San Fernando.

"Look at that place, Pete! *That* is where I would love to live!" I said.

He agreed, without a moment's hesitation. Both of us dreamers, it mattered little that the house was quite derelict. It had obviously been empty for years. But it was not for rent.

It was April 2000 before we found another place, not far from Pastor Fred's church. The newly built apartment block was complete with a fitted kitchen, new toilet and shower, fresh paint, and new floor-tiles. Not a cockroach in sight. I wasn't sure how long we could afford the higher rent, but on my last trip to England our trustees had made me promise to take better care of myself – so we decided to trust God for the money, month by month.

I was delighted to find that one of our neighbours was British, originally from Robinswood in Gloucester, where I had lived for three years. Another neighbour was from South Africa and we instantly got along well together. Their children quickly made friends with Michael, Ana, and Simon. It felt great to have English-speaking company next door, who appreciated the value of a good cup of tea and a chat. Communication became even less complex with the purchase of a mobile phone. Calls and texts were cheap, so I could call my parents often.

At the same time, I learned to appreciate the value of email. Anson Sia had converted what was formerly Victory House into an internet café, which he called "The Master's Work". Now a keen evangelist, he played Christian music there and gave out gospel tracts to his customers. With no internet at home I visited The Master's Work often, praising God as I turned into the alleyway and stepped inside the doorway of our old home.

Time sped on, and soon the boys would be out of school for the Christmas break. At home a pile of correspondence had accumulated on my desk. Mulling over each letter, I prayed for God's blessing on friends who helped us. I re-read a letter from Jackie Pullinger. We had been praying for healing for John, whose liver was giving up. She had written to tell me he had passed away. Wiping away tears, I thanked God again for the privilege of knowing them both, and the opportunity to recently spend time with John at a conference about ministry to the poor. I prayed that Jesus would be right there with Jackie – then realized He always was. Once again I had to admit that I didn't really know how to pray.

By this time, several former boys from LAMA were married with children. Oscar and his new wife were expecting their first baby. Joey was also married. Incredibly, Ricky and Marcy had four children. And Ton was married, and had a beautiful little daughter. They all often called on us to help them cope with the challenges of marriage and family, and they came "home" for Christmas and New Year. We invited Domingo's family to stay at LAMA House for the holidays, too. His little brother Piolo looked even thinner than before, so I took him to the hospital for a thorough check-up.

"It's bad news, I'm afraid," Dr Christian told me, showing me the X-rays.

"He has advanced tuberculosis and will have to take medicine for at least two years to get rid of it. On top of that he is anaemic, malnourished, and has pneumonia," he frowned.

Tuberculosis again! I bought a supply of medicines so he could start treatment right away. When the rest of the family went home after Christmas, Piolo stayed on to get well. But after three months his mother returned, insisting she take Piolo back to Urdaneta with her. I handed her the medicine with strict instructions to make sure he took it continuously, but doubted she would comply.

March 2001 crept up on us – the long summer holiday was fast approaching. The boys were usually excited to start the school year with their new uniforms and shoes, school bags, and books, but towards the end it became more of a struggle. Our thirteen-year-olds were in classes with seven-year-olds, so the teachers had a difficult task. Despite being teenagers they often acted like naughty toddlers, being manipulative and hyperactive. The pocket money for their mid-morning snack was, however, enough of an incentive for them to attend classes to the bitter end. Without an education they wouldn't stand a chance in the workplace. Even to stack shelves at the grocery store employers wanted a graduate of a four-year college course.

After much preparation, we travelled home to England for the summer break, leaving Pastor Fred, Eunice, and Pastor Agusto in charge. My parents were semi-retiring and needed help packing up the contents of the vicarage in Cornwall. Their new home in Worthing in Sussex was much smaller than their current home so much of what they had accumulated over the past twenty years had to go.

As I rummaged through the stuff I had got stored away I found my secondary school tie, art work since I started school, and old report cards. There was a suitcase full of school projects and neatly filed notes from my nursing assessments. Sifting through the pile of projects, I remembered the feeling of panic in my final year at Snaith Secondary School, because I didn't know what subjects to choose.

What did I choose, in the end? I wondered. I couldn't remember. Lifting the folders one by one, I could hardly believe my eyes: social services, world affairs, immigration and child care, child development, and children with special needs! For my biology paper I researched amoeba, not knowing that in the future I would experience it first-hand in the form of amoebiasis!

Intrigued, I found my GCSE certificates from the sixth form at Goole Grammar School. I had good qualifications in child care, social studies, sociology, and typing. With absolutely no intention of ever becoming a secretary, why had I taken up typing? At the time, of course, I was blissfully unaware of all the paperwork that was required by the Department of Social Welfare and Development in the Philippines!

"What?!" I laughed, as I found my thesis from my final year of nurse training: "Twin Pregnancy and the Care of Twins"!

Throughout my school life I always felt I was below average, but as I looked at my old report cards I was surprised to find that my grades were reasonably high in secondary school. In the excitement of leaving school, I had not paid much attention to any of the teacher's parting words. I started to chuckle as I read their comments, as if for the first time. "She must not shy away from problems but admit them and set about surmounting them," wrote Mr Hetherington, my English teacher.

If only he could see the problems I had set about surmounting, I thought with a grin. Where others chose a relatively simple path, I had chosen an obstacle course. Art was one of my better subjects, but even Mr Kibler had to boost my confidence: "Always playing safe, must take some risks in life," he wrote.

Finally, Mr Lawrence, the principal, had concluded, "Lacks confidence but always does her best."

In a small box I found another treasure – my old autograph book. It opened at 28 November 1976 where Bishop Coady from America (introduced to my family by Revd Clyde Shields) had written from Proverbs 3:5–6, "In all your ways acknowledge Him, and He shall direct your paths."

On another page a journalist, who wrote a newspaper article about my father, wrote, "A happy life – many travels!" I was fifteen at the time.

I often doubted I was the right person for the job, but when God calls you it is pointless to question His wisdom. As I sorted out the paperwork of my life I could see He had indeed directed my paths.

Chapter 21

Loved by God!

We often joined forces with Silungan, a halfway house in Baguio City, to find families and help homeless boys in the area. On one such visit, as we talked with Flor, one of the social workers, I noticed an older boy washing dishes in the kitchen area. He didn't look anything like a street-boy. Something about his demeanour saddened me – he appeared to be completely lacking in self-esteem.

Flor explained that he was from a nice home, having been unofficially adopted as a baby. But his adoptive parents kicked him out of the house when he reached eighteen. They didn't want him anymore. Felipe looked at me bashfully as she introduced us, then he politely lifted my hand to his forehead in the traditional greeting.

"He is eighteen," Flor cautioned, knowing the age bracket for LAMA was ages nine to nineteen.

"That's OK. We could help him find work," I said.

We often extended our age limit, in both directions. The shelter in Baguio could not be so flexible – they could only offer their services for a maximum of six months.

Felipe's sweet nature and gracious manner were a welcome change for us at LAMA House. The younger boys were drawn to him and he became their gentle leader. Unfortunately that was not always a good thing, as he had a penchant for body-piercing and tattoos. Before long all the boys at LAMA House were sporting their own earrings, nose rings, and homemade tattoos. For him, it was a form of self-harm; he was expressing how dissatisfied with himself he felt. I met him one morning as he was coming downstairs. I couldn't help but notice the number 666 recently tattooed on his arm. He knew I disapproved and looked at me apologetically.

"Do you know what it means?" I asked him, frowning.

"Not really," he shrugged.

"The Bible talks about it. It is called the number of the Antichrist. The Antichrist hates Jesus," I explained.

He looked back at me woefully, as if to say, "Why am I so stupid?"

I wished I hadn't said anything; it only made him feel worse – after all, what could he do about it now? I prayed he would come to know Jesus as his friend as it would undoubtedly reverse the way he felt about himself. The next morning he came downstairs with a third-degree burn on his arm in the shape of an iron. He had burned the tattoo off. It was not an act of defiance, but of submission. "Oh, Felipe – what have you done?" I cried, trembling. I put my arms around his neck and hugged him. "Lord, do for Felipe what I can't," I prayed silently.

Felipe and Almo were the same age and quickly became good friends. After working in an auto repair shop for a while Almo became the school bus driver at Brain and Heart of a Christian Institute – BHC for short. Unlike most Filipino drivers he was very careful behind the wheel. For the first time in his life a principal had something good to say about him.

After six months at LAMA House Felipe was anxious to mend the relationship with his adoptive parents so he decided to return home. But they refused to allow him back and instead he managed to find work in a local grocery store in Bangued Abra (140 km north of San Fernando), renting a room in the town. (It was much easier to find work like this in the towns rather than the cities.) It often took years to convince our boys of God's love for them; I wasn't sure six months with Felipe was long enough. *Had he accepted God's grace?* I wondered. *Did he understand that he was of great value to God, or did he still consider himself utterly worthless?* The lines of communication were kept open by mobile phone – through Felipe's initiative. Curiously, he always sent messages of encouragement to Peter, rather than the other way around.

One afternoon we were travelling back from Manila and stopped off at McDonald's in Urdaneta, ninety minutes from San Fernando, for something to eat. As we headed back to the jeep a street-boy tapped my arm, begging for food. From his shaven head down to his dirty bare feet I could tell that he genuinely needed help so I reached in my purse for some money to hand him, then hurried to catch up to Peter.

"Pete, did you see that little boy? Can you come and talk to him, see if he has parents anywhere? He is so thin, maybe we should try to get him in LAMA," I pleaded.

Peter looked back at the boy, who was staring after us.

"It's Piolo! Didn't you recognize him? He had his head shaved," Peter laughed.

"Piolo," I muttered, rushing back. I held his face in my hands and he smiled shyly, not knowing where to look!

"Piolo, I am *so* sorry – I didn't recognize you without hair!" I said.

I laughed quietly, but felt like crying. He was not at all well. We found his father in the market place. He told us that Piolo's mother had left again after a short time back with the family. Piolo often resorted to begging outside the restaurants. Reluctantly he agreed to let him stay at LAMA House with Domingo, where he could get better and go to school. "We'll bring them back here to visit you often," I promised.

Piolo was only eight years old. He was much smaller than Ana and Simon who were five years old. As I suspected he had not continued his medicine. With the possibility that his body had become resistant to the drugs I took him back to LORMA Medical Centre to consult Dr Christian Cordoviz and have another X-ray. I didn't expect a good result and neither did Dr Christian. He looked at the X-ray report several times, comparing it with the first one, then asked the radiologist to take another look.

"I don't understand this – it's a normal result! There's no explanation, other than that you people really know how to pray," he said, puzzled. We looked at each other and giggled.

"Good news! He's been healed then," I concluded.

"Yes… good news!" he smiled. "Well done, Piolo!"

"Yeah! And well done God!" I smiled.

We enrolled Piolo in elementary school. As it turned out, he was very clever. Several of our boys at LAMA House tried very hard at school and were rewarded by being promoted to higher grades at the end of the school year, an advantage given to only a few in the province.

* * *

Philippine law requires that cases involving children should be tried within one year, but it never seemed to work out that way. Domingo, Ruben, and Franko suffered the trauma of hearings being postponed almost every month for three years. Sweat poured off Ruben before every hearing. The stress didn't help matters in school. But because he appeared tough on the outside his teachers were not sympathetic and he eventually dropped out of school.

Fortunately, we found a special education (SPED) teacher who could help him. Dr Obana had worked in America for much of her career. Recently retired to the Philippines, she rented a house in the city where she helped children with special educational needs. After testing Ruben, she found he had profound learning difficulties. She offered to provide him with a special tutor, a lovely, motherly lady who was genuinely delighted to see him every day. She was an answer to prayer for Ruben, whose poor self-image was relegating him to a place of anger and rebellion. In a short time, he grew into a respectful, responsible helper at the school. We were amazed at the patience and gentleness he showed with children who had severe physical and mental disabilities.

Then the day he had been dreading finally came and it was his turn to testify in court. He sat in the dock, only just tall enough to see the man who had destroyed his soul, who was staring at him menacingly from the front row. Ruben panicked and changed his testimony at the last minute. The perpetrator was sentenced to thirteen years in prison. At that time in the Philippines the sentence for rape was the death penalty. Ruben was frustrated and mad at himself. Analie, the social worker, had helped him prepare his testimony and practised it with him, but when it came down to it he could not do it. As we made our way back to LAMA House she spoke softly to him, reassuring him that at least it was finished and now the three friends could get on with their lives.

As we prayed together I put my arm around his shoulders, and noticed with some satisfaction that he didn't flinch away from me. Perhaps he could begin to trust people. The other two boys had not suffered as severely as Ruben. Domingo's response was to opt out generally from life with a "whatever will be, will be" attitude. Franko was still stuck, in many ways, at the age when his adoptive parents rejected him. He hoarded his possessions, and "collected" other people's things, locking them all away in his cabinet with several padlocks.

* * *

In June 2000 a letter from the DSWD Central Office arrived at our door – the licence for LAMA House had finally been approved! Now I had to apply for accreditation.

I was always looking for workers who would stay. More than anything the boys needed continuity. One young man came to LAMA House looking for work, having recently graduated from Bible School.

"Hi, I'm Jun," he said, shaking my hand.

"I'm Lesley," I replied.

"Yes… my stepfather has told me all about you," he replied, excitedly.

"Who is your stepfather?" I asked.

"Art!" he said, smiling.

I couldn't believe it! After all these years – Art's stepson… a pastor! The stepson of the man who had lived most of his life in prison and who had been one of our first residents at Victory House!

Jun joined our team of house-parents for a two-month trial period. He was an enthusiastic evangelist and arranged for the boys to attend a youth camp in Baguio. It was a lot for him to organize, but turned out to be a turning point spiritually for many of our boys, as if God sent Jun for a specific assignment. He left shortly after that, deciding instead, like many of the Bible College graduates, to pastor a church in the mountains.

Mama Myrna joined Mama Adella as house-mother. They had worked together before at Miracle Children's Home, where I first met them. Rico, whom we later hired as a house-father, worked at BHC, as a security guard. I could tell right away that he was a Christian, and told him that I admired the way he dealt with the students. When Peter asked him to work for us he was eager to be involved in Christian ministry. Pastor Jim also joined our team. He and Pastor Agusto were cousins, and were gifted with the same quiet, patient nature.

Pastor Fred suggested we join his church, Christ's Church in the Philippines (CCP), where Pastor Julius Mamaril was associate pastor. We laughed, surprised that none of us had thought of it before. Peter and I had supported CCP church in Paringao in Bauang since our days at Miracle Bible College. To begin with the boys felt awkward integrating with the other youngsters, but when they began to make friends the church family experienced a wonderful healing effect.

Standing next to Larry in church one Sunday I marvelled at the change in his life over the past year. At sixteen he was maturing physically, but mentally was still a child. I remembered his first week at LAMA House. At night he would wake everyone up with his screams. He could hardly speak, so we never found out why he was so disturbed.

At the time, missionaries from Ezer Fellowship in Korea were visiting LAMA House, so I asked them to pray for Larry's emotional healing. They gathered around him, gently laid their hands on his shoulders, and prayed quietly for the Holy Spirit to minister to his unknown needs. The change was instant. The night-screaming ceased and his sweet nature emerged. He surprised himself when he managed to graduate from the first year of elementary school. Now our eyes met as he sang at the top of his voice, the words incoherent. He smiled back at me shyly and I could see peace in his face.

Another pastor began to attend CCP church with us. Pastora Vicky had emigrated to Hawaii from the Philippines and was approaching retirement. As many Filipinos do, she planned to retire to her homeland, so was building an impressive house, not far from the church. She was an old-school, fiery Pentecostal preacher who loved to sing. Her enthusiasm was contagious, and Pastor Fred usually asked her to preach whenever she was in the country.

One Sunday morning she preached on the familiar Scripture John 3:16: "For God so loved the world that he gave his only Son, so that everyone who believes in him will not perish but have eternal life."

Speaking simply about God's love, she told stories from her own experience of his faithful, undivided attention. I watched the boys lean forward in their chairs, listening carefully to every word. It was a message they really needed to hear and understand. Pastor Fred had noticed too. He didn't want to embarrass them by singling them out but was aware that our LAMA boys particularly needed prayer as the sermon came to a close.

"I would like all our young people to come forward please, and we will pray for you," Pastor Fred announced.

Several walked forward and stood in front of the pulpit. Heads bowed as Pastora Vicky put her hands on their heads and prayed powerfully for them. I noticed little Piolo leave his seat and move forward. He didn't consider himself old enough to be a "young person", but wanted to come anyway. Big tears rolled down his cheeks. Squeezing past the others he positioned himself right at the front, sitting on the floor with his legs crossed. He pulled his T-shirt up over his face and sobbed.

He sat there, as if at Jesus' feet, as people started to leave to go home. He clearly understood, for the first time in his interrupted young life, that somebody really did love him and wanted the best for him, and that somebody was... GOD!

Chapter 22

God's Work

There is faith for life, and then there is a darker faith for death. There is faith for miracles, but also for pain. There is faith for God's will when it's our will too, but there is also the grace to trust God when His will is not what we would choose.

Pete Greig in *God on Mute*

Revd Andres Gomez had spent fifty-one years in ministry with a passion for winning souls until his last breath. When "Papang" hugged me before leaving the Philippines for his flight back to Hawaii, I sensed that it was his last goodbye. He was eighty-five and had been ill for some time. I had so much respect for him and felt honoured to be a part of his family. He died 10 December 2000. We went to Hawaii for the funeral. Despite the huge feeling of loss it was good to be with the rest of Peter's family again, some of whom we hadn't seen for seven years.

The monsoon season in 2001 was particularly wet in the Philippines and the river that ran close to LAMA House burst its banks. The year was spent rebuilding homes on the beach – all of which had been washed away – and repairing damage in and around LAMA House. We were thankful for no loss of life. But in 2005 and 2009 the disaster was repeated, each time worse than the last. News reports blamed mismanagement of one of the dams. Floodgates were opened late, releasing an incredible volume of water into our low-lying rivers. Many lives were lost in nearby Pangasinan. Many were saved because LAMA House had a second storey. It became the official evacuation centre for the barrio.

On 11 September 2001 the world was shaken by the news of the terrorist attack on the World Trade Center in America. It didn't seem real. Another war was imminent.

Franko became increasingly restless. As a natural leader, that caused uneasiness in many of the boys. Looking over his case notes, I came across the name of the barrio where his mother used to live. We had been told that she didn't want any contact with him, but I decided to launch our own investigation. It would probably come to nothing but at least we could say we tried.

We made the ten-hour journey south to Pangasinan. With no specific address, Peter stopped the vehicle outside a house we came across and asked for directions to the home of the barrio captain. The barrio captain knew Franko's family. "I'll accompany you to the home of the boy's auntie," he told us. To our surprise, he led us back to the house where we had asked directions. The auntie welcomed us cheerfully, curious to meet Franko.

"His mom was a lot of trouble since she was a teenager. They say she sold her children to pay gambling debts, and changed her husbands after bankrupting them!" she whispered. "When he was born the doctor told her to leave the baby at the hospital until she could pay the bill. When she returned with the money no one knew anything about it. She came home without him."

It may have been for the best, I thought. I saw Franko's shoulders relax, as if pleased to know his mother had tried – that maybe she had intended to keep him. Back at LAMA, he was more at peace.

* * *

When a social worker arrived at LAMA House with a "new boy", all the boys quietened – as if afraid they might add to the brokenness of their new housemate. He cowered on the floor like a frightened animal as the social worker went over his case history with Eunice. Peter tried to talk to him, but the only information we could get was his name – which sounded like Herman. We guessed he was fifteen. The social worker didn't know if the multiple cuts and bruises were due to a severe beating or a road traffic accident. He couldn't bathe himself, feed himself, or use the toilet. It would be difficult for our staff to cope with another child with special needs.

A month or so earlier we had accepted an older boy who was severely autistic. When we first met him in the shelter in Baguio he was called "Mr X" as no one knew his name. We went there to talk to the social worker about another case, but Mr X didn't take his eyes off us all the time we were there. And as we left, he followed us to the door.

"That's strange! He has never done anything like that before. He usually sits alone, staring into space," the social worker told me. That was enough reason for me to take him home.

We named him Andrew. The boys welcomed him and treated him with kindness. He needed help with feeding and going to the toilet. He sat in a foetal position all day, rocking to and fro. But after a few weeks, he began to make progress. Then one day, to everyone's amazement, he stood up and began to play basketball with the other boys – he played like a pro.

Herman and Andrew were with us when a team from Hawaii came to visit us to see the work that LAMA was doing. They brought scooters with them for each of the boys. Max, who had earned a reputation for being accident prone, decided he would scoot down the stair rail. Thankfully he didn't break anything, but he came away very shaken with a spectacular black eye. The week previous to that he had decided his eyebrows were too hairy, so he shaved them both off. Consequently, he was nicknamed "alien" by the other boys.

The Hawaiian team had hired a driver for their trip to San Fernando. Strangely, the driver recognized Herman the minute he saw him. "I've seen that boy before, hanging around outside the Victory Bus Terminal in Olongapo," he told Peter. It couldn't possibly be a case of mistaken identity. Peter decided to follow the lead, and took Herman to Olongapo after the Hawaiian team had gone home.

But he didn't recognize anything as Peter drove around. Getting nowhere, Peter decided to try the DSWD office, but none of the staff there could help either. He sat on a bench outside the social worker's office, with Herman lying on his lap. "Now what shall we do?" he asked Eunice. A social worker arrived and asked if she could help. She recognized Herman immediately. Forgetting her other business she took them to his mother, who was working in the market place. She had been searching for weeks for her lost boy.

"But his name is not Herman; it is Immanuel! I have been praying that some good people would find him and bring him home," she said, overjoyed.

The social worker arranged for him to attend a day-care facility while his mother was at work, so he wouldn't wander off again.

"Immanuel – it means 'God with us', you know. God must be watching over you," I told Immanuel's mother, explaining the course of events that had led us back to Olongapo City. There was no doubt – He had answered her prayer.

Eunice searched for a more specialized institution for Andrew and eventually found a place in Bicol, operated by a group of Catholic monks, called Missionaries to the Poor. Almost 700 km away, at the most southern point of Luzon, they had a large facility for adults and children with mental and physical disabilities. Pastor Jim and Eunice accompanied Andrew on the twelve-hour journey. Pastor Jim and Andrew had become good friends so it was difficult to say goodbye. But we stayed in touch with the director by telephone, who assured us Andrew had settled in very well.

The intense heat of summer was taking its toll on my health again. I phoned my mother. *Poor Mum, I always call her when I need someone to complain to, or when something terrible is happening,* I thought, waiting for her to answer the phone.

"Top of the morning! Vicar speaking!" my father sang down the line.

"Dad, it's me," I said, trying to sound cheerful.

"Ah! Lesley. How is everything? I'll call Mum," he said. I smiled. He always said the same thing, and so did I. My mother asked if I was OK. I explained that my period was worse than ever, literally draining me.

"Mum, why doesn't God heal me?" I asked, not expecting an answer.

"I don't know, Lesley. You are like the woman in the Bible who had 'an issue of blood' for twelve years; the woman who touched the hem of Jesus' robe and was healed," she answered.

We talked for a while longer about anything and everything. More often than not I felt better having called home, but this time I put the phone down and retreated to the bathroom, where I always went to pray. I cried out to God, fed up of having no energy.

"Lord, if You were here and I could physically touch the hem of Your robe, you know I would. But I don't know how to do it. Show me what to do and I *know* that I will be healed," I prayed.

That Friday afternoon I decided to join the team going into the regional jail. I hadn't been able to go with them for some time and I wanted to meet Will Vincent, a young man who was over from London to help out. The prison ministry was like a tree that bore fruit in season with very little help from us. I never ceased to be amazed at the spiritual growth of the inmates who gathered for the hour-long service run by LAMA.

"He is facing the death penalty for rape but insists he is innocent," Mrs España whispered in my ear, as the inmate assigned to give the sermon began to speak.

He spoke about faith, about holding on to God for answers to prayer even if it takes a long time. And he mentioned the woman in the Bible who touched the hem of Jesus robe' and was healed after twelve years of illness. I knew God was speaking to me, but my mind was dull and I didn't recall my bathroom prayer.

Leaning over to Peter I told him that I wanted to ask this man to pray for me after the service. As soon as I spoke the words to Peter it felt like someone had thumped me in my chest. "This is how you will touch the hem of my garment," God said, almost audibly. Then I remembered that I had asked God to show me what to do, and *knew* I was about to be healed.

Immediately, doubts crept into my mind – *you cannot ask him to pray for you!* But there was no doubting that God had spoken to me, so when the service closed I approached the inmate-preacher. He looked surprised when I asked him to pray for me to be healed. He nervously beckoned several inmates to join him. They were not sure what to do exactly, but when they prayed their words were full of faith and authority. I found it difficult to walk out of the prison gate to the car because I was trembling from head to foot.

That evening I called my parents. Struggling to get the words out sensibly, I cried as I described what had taken place in the jail. Mum listened quietly.

"Last Sunday a missionary from Lithuania was at our church," she told me. "You might remember her… you met her last year when you were home? She asked how you were doing in the Philippines, so I told her you were still having health problems," Mum said, her voice trembling, too.

"Yes, I remember her," I said.

"Well, I got a bit aggravated with her – she must know we have been praying for you, but she asked if you had touched the hem of Jesus' garment!" Mum told me, crying and laughing at the same time!

A week went by and I didn't actually feel any better physically. But I remembered hearing a preacher say that faith comes by hearing and by hearing God speak to you personally. And I knew that God had spoken to me personally.

That Sunday there was a guest speaker at church, the wife of a pastor I had sponsored in Bible College eighteen years earlier. Her sermon was about the woman who touched the hem of Jesus' garment and was healed!

By this time, even the hardest sceptic would have to believe. But outwardly, there was no evidence of my healing; I still felt tired and weak. I woke in the night and decided to go downstairs and get a drink of warm milk, hoping it would help me sleep. Picking up a devotional book by Selwyn Hughes from the bookshelf, I opened it to the message for that day: "In Genesis 41:32 before he interpreted Pharaoh's dream, Joseph told Pharaoh, 'The reason the dream was given to you in two forms was that the matter has been firmly decided by God and God will do it soon'," it read.

And so it was that gradually my health improved.

Chapter 23

A Life Poured Out

**Jesus teaches us to measure our life by
sacrifice, rather than self-preservation, by
what is spent on others rather than lavished on
ourselves.**

David Roper in *Our Daily Bread*

At the end of March 2002 Michael celebrated his twelfth birthday. His graduation from elementary school raised questions in my mind. The system of education in the Philippines was very different from that in England. In some ways it was better, with less bullying and good moral teaching, but in other ways I was dissatisfied. Should we go home to England for Michael's secondary education? How would we do that? If we stayed, what would his future be in the Philippines?

At that time, Franko and Domingo also graduated from elementary school, at the age of sixteen. Three of the boys at LAMA received honours at the end of the school year; even Ruben got an award for being, "Most Industrious". They were so pleased with themselves! I hoped their success would influence all the boys to do well, but there were still those who just could not make progress.

Christopher and Curt, both aged eleven, had been passed around since birth from one mother figure to the next. Christopher was from the red-light district in San Fernando; Curt came from Manila. They were good-looking boys, which gave them the advantage of being able to get what they wanted just by being cute. There were a couple of times when Curt didn't come home from school. Days later he called us from Manila, having saved up his pocket money until he had enough for the bus fare. He visited a man he called "Uncle", but the man left him to run wild in the big city.

Christopher eventually decided to stay with his Mama Rose in the red-light district. During one of his short stays at LAMA House he fell off the roof of the jeep – having been told not to climb up there.

I waited in the hospital while Dr Christian put a plaster cast on his broken arm. "Have you met my sister, Judith?" he asked, introducing me to the young woman waiting next to me. I recognized her and her husband as their children went to BHC school with Michael, Ana, and Simon. She stood out from other women.

"I think we have met at BHC," I said, smiling. She was obviously ill, leaning on her husband's shoulder, huddled in a blanket.

"We are very close – like twins," Christian said, smiling at her.

"It's good to have a brother who is a doctor," Judith said, trying to smile.

"It's good to have a doctor like your brother!" I told her.

Dr Christian had completed his studies in the Philippines and, to my mind, was one of the best doctors I had ever worked with. Yet he had no desire to leave his country for better pay. *Maybe my children will do fine with their education here*, I thought. If Michael, Ana, and Simon turned out to be anything like Dr Christian then that would be terrific. *It is in losing your life that you find it,* I reminded myself, thinking of Matthew 10:39.

The plaster cast put Christopher out of action for weeks on end. It made me smile, seeing him lying contentedly on Peter's lap. He felt sorry for himself, but at least he was getting some tender loving care out of it. For once he let his guard down. But after two months he couldn't take the boredom anymore and took the cast off himself.

I took him back to the hospital, apologetically. Thankfully, Dr Christian's careful work was not completely wasted, and another X-ray showed the bone was healing nicely. He used the bottom half of the old cast and wrapped it with a crepe bandage to keep it secure for a while longer.

Dr Christian was quieter than usual. "Would you pray for my wife?" he asked. "She is pregnant… due any day now. I just hope everything will be OK."

I had never seen him anxious about anything before.

"Of course we will pray," I assured him.

I told the boys that evening, as most of them had the pleasure of meeting Dr Christian at some point! Many first prayers were offered up during our evening devotions, before the boys settled down for the night. We prayed for Dr Christian's wife, and for boys who were no longer with us, asking angels to watch over them. I loved to listen to the boys talking to God, without all the fancy rhetoric that religious people get caught up in.

As I settled my three children in their beds it occurred to me that most of the boys at LAMA had never had a goodnight kiss from their mother. They had no memories of being kissed better when they had grazed a knee or lost a tooth; indeed they had never had any physical affection shown towards them. The attention of a girlfriend poses a problem for most teenage boys, but for these boys it was an absolute minefield, often resulting in unplanned pregnancies.

It irked me that the men on staff, including Peter, were unwilling to tackle the subject. At a loss, I asked God what I should do, and felt Him prompt me to talk to Dr Christian about it. So I visited the hospital to ask him if he would come to LAMA and talk to the boys about sex. He was amused by my request, but agreed to come one evening and help me out.

"By the way, thank you for praying! My wife gave birth to a baby girl and everything is fine. My other daughter is thirteen, you know. She has cerebral palsy," he told me.

I didn't know. He was always so full of the joy of living that I had no idea of the difficulties he faced every day. He was thrilled to bits with his new baby girl.

"They say she looks like me," he said, grinning, the way only a new daddy can.

As promised he took time out from his hectic schedule to talk to the boys. As a keen cyclist and weight-trainer he promoted sports as a way to channel their untamed energies. I hovered in the background while he instructed them about the finer details of their sexuality, glad that it had not fallen to me to do it.

Pastor Fred was also a cyclist, so he and Dr Christian persuaded Peter to join the cycling club. Eventually we were able to buy bikes for the boys who were interested. It turned out to be a brilliant idea as cycling became part of the programme at LAMA House.

We were in town one Saturday with Michael, Ana, and Simon, after buying art materials for a school project. Peter stopped to look, for quite some time, at the latest fully equipped cycle on display in the cycling shop. As I waited with the children, Dr Christian came around the corner of the store, dressed to the nines in his cycling gear.

"Hello Princess, how are you?" he said, smiling at Ana.

She smiled back and hid behind me, suddenly shy!

"How is Christopher? Is he staying out of trouble?" he asked.

We chatted until Peter had his fill of window shopping. Ana and I couldn't help giggling as we watched Christian hobbling to the door of the shop in his cycling shoes, which had grips for the pedals and were not designed for walking.

"Are you laughing at me?!" he asked, winking.

"I'm walking like I've just been circumcised," he teased Michael, who thought that was hilariously funny.

"He keeps calling me Princess!" Ana whispered, blushing.

* * *

As locating Immanuel's mother had been miraculously easy, I began to look through the case notes of the other boys, in the hope of finding a nugget of information that would lead us to their parents. We decided to take Larry back to the place where he was found wandering in the rain. Four years had passed, but perhaps we could find someone who knew him. Peter drove around the town for hours, accompanied by Pastor Fred. They stopped at places Larry recognized, and interviewed a few people that he appeared to know.

"That's my uncle," Larry said, pointing to a man.

The man looked at Larry and smiled, obviously drunk!

"Oh, Larry!" he nodded.

Interesting, he knew Larry's name! But there was no further information forthcoming, and it appeared Larry was answering "yes" to everything, whether he knew the answer or not. Not knowing the correct answer he just said "yes", or made up an answer.

Pastor Fred also noticed that Larry had his name tattooed on his arm in large letters for all to see, courtesy of Felipe. They laughed and laughed, remembering all the people they had talked to and homes they had visited with hopes high. Exhausted from the madness of it all, they returned home, having achieved nothing at all. The other boys ran out to meet the jeep as it pulled up in the driveway at LAMA House.

"Did you find his mom?" they asked expectantly.

"Nope! We didn't find his mom – but we thought we found his uncle!" Pastor Fred said, laughing again.

* * *

A couple of months later my sister Esther was due to arrive in the Philippines for a visit. We were on our way to Manila to pick her up when Peter received a call from Pastor Fred. "Dr Christian is in intensive care at LORMA! He's critical. He was in a car accident," he said.

We couldn't believe it! I wanted to rush back home, but we had to wait for Esther's flight, then stay overnight in a hotel. I prayed quietly, frantically, for the rest of the journey. *He is a strong man; surely he will pull through,* I told myself.

When we arrived back home the next day we went straight to the hospital, where a nurse told us what had happened. He had been hit by a speeding car when he was cycling to Baguio. The driver was drunk. Because the nurse knew me, she went against protocol and allowed us into the intensive care unit. I peered through the glass partition, unable to accept that the motionless body, surrounded with machines and IV lines, belonged to Christian.

"If anyone deserves a miracle, Lord, it's Christian," I murmured, turning away to face the window so no one could see my tears. *Surely he will get through this. He will fight it,* I thought, trying not to despair.

I was hanging out the washing, at the back of our house, when Peter came to tell me he had just had a telephone call. I saw the pain in his face.

"No!" I wailed.

"He told the nurses and doctors to stop... he just decided to go, said to just let him go," Peter sobbed.

Dr Christian was thirty-seven, just four years younger than me. He had four children, two boys and two girls – his new baby girl was just eighteen months old.

He was gone. The grief swamped me and took away all my strength. Hardly able to stand, I leaned on the desk for support. I glanced at my desk calendar, the Bible verse for the day 21 July 2002:

As for me, my life has already been poured out as an
offering to God. The time of my death is near. I have
fought a good fight, I have finished the race, and I have
remained faithful. And now the prize awaits me – the
crown of righteousness that the Lord, the righteous Judge,
will give me on that great day of his return.

(2 Timothy 4:6–8)

I caught my breath and read the verse again.

"Pete, look at this! *How* does God do that?" I asked in astonishment.

Of all the verses in the Bible, none could have been more comforting on that exact day. We knew he was with the Lord and enjoying his reward.

Dr Christian was one of those rare people who lived every day as if it were his last, not for himself but for others. He had lived a life poured out. He lived more in his thirty-seven years than most people do in eighty-seven! I wanted to live like that.

When the children came home from school I carefully told them what had happened. Later we went to the hospital, where the coffin lay in the hospital chapel. Judith was sitting in the front pew when we arrived. I sat next to her and held her hand, but I couldn't find any words to say.

More than anything, I wanted to attend the funeral in Baguio, but my body collapsed with what seemed like recurrent typhoid fever, confining me to a hospital bed. In the hospital car park, Peter watched with a crowd of hospital personnel as the coffin left.

For years I couldn't visit the hospital without crying, especially when I saw his desk in the emergency department. Whenever I saw Judith at the school we hugged each other tightly and talked about how much we missed her brother. Not long afterwards, her life was also cut short by cancer. She never really came to terms with the grief.

Homesickness followed me around, like a shadow. In the past I had been able to overcome it easily: just waking up in the morning and feeling the sunshine on my face would dispel any longing for cold, grey England. But Dr Christian had been like a brother to me. I longed for home and family. I needed someone to hold me up, someone who expected nothing from me.

Sitting outside, as the sun began to go down at 5 p.m., I remembered the words on my desk calendar on 21 July and they managed to pointed me away from the awful feeling of grief that I had been experiencing. How wonderful that God would have prepared that thought for the day for me.

I felt the breeze, cool against the back of my neck, and closed my eyes. It took my breath away – as if a dear friend had just crept by and greeted me gently with a kiss. I thought I heard Him whisper, *"Eternity!"*

Chapter 24

Dirty Feet

**But we make His love too narrow by false limits
of our own. And we magnify its strictness with a
zeal He will not own.**

Frederick Faber

It made everything worthwhile whenever one of the boys
decided to follow Jesus and be baptized! If all we provided
were food, shelter, and education it wouldn't be enough in
the long run. The only real hope we could offer was a personal
relationship with the God who answers prayer and gives peace
and hope amid the harsh realities of life.

Pastor Fred had postponed the baptism service several
times, waiting for Pastor Julius to be in better health. It was
now September 2002 and the day we had all been looking
forward to had arrived. In all, there were thirty candidates to
be baptized in the river at Suyo, Ilocos Sur, 65 km from San
Fernando, including twelve boys from LAMA House, our
house-father Rico and his wife, and Clarence. The sun shone,
despite forecasts for rain. When the last person came up out of
the water, Piolo asked me if he could be baptized, too.

"I think you should wait for a while, when you understand
it," I told him. *Did he really understand that it symbolized the end of
self-will and surrender to God's ways?* I wondered. He sulked all the
way home.

His bad mood vanished when Sarah arrived at LAMA
House to volunteer for six months. She was a teacher, and one

of the young people at the church where my parents were now based, in Worthing. Her experience teaching children with behavioural problems and learning difficulties was exactly what Piolo and the boys needed. And the first time she joined the boys for devotions, she cried the whole time.

A month later, the inspector from the DSWD's head office in Manila came to scrutinize LAMA House for accreditation. She told me she had already failed four other institutions in her own department. Having said that, however, she approved our accreditation. I was quite proud of myself!

The way I saw it, our mission was simply to follow the example of Jesus, when He washed the feet of his friends at the Last Supper. There were often times when the mundane transformed into something marvellous as I remembered to "carry a towel and washbasin" with me wherever I went (John 13:5). That was really *all* I wanted to do.

But among the daily grind some of our team started to grow tired of washing dirty feet. Often the boys came to us very dirty; their little feet were just a picture of what had happened to them on the inside. I could see a couple of our staff slipping into personal resentment when dealing with bad behaviour. It robbed them of any power to help the more difficult boys. And their attitude was contagious. I needed people who could habitually think kindly – some would say too kindly – of the boys. I reminded those team members of the need to spend quiet time with God, so He could refill them with His Holy Spirit. But quiet time did not come naturally in Filipino culture.

"They are not Bible School students – they are recovering street-boys!" I told Peter, feeling hopelessly frustrated.

Perhaps I expect too much of my staff, I thought. To add to the pressure, Peter was ill in hospital with typhoid fever. I decided to call a staff meeting anyway, anxious to find a solution and discuss the problems they were having. I looked around at a bunch of stony faces; they didn't want to hear my non-Filipino opinion.

All I knew was that I loved the boys. I fully expected them to have behavioural problems while they worked through the mess of their lives. And the boys in question had reached adolescence; seventeen was always a difficult age, but it wouldn't last forever! My words fell on deaf ears. *Perhaps I am being too soft on the boys?* I thought. So I gave in and gave Eunice permission to discharge the boys in question. But where would they go? Everything in me wanted them to stay, but I appeared to have no one backing me. I was at my lowest point.

When Peter came out of the hospital I felt completely drained, but there was no food in the house. I decided to walk to the city centre instead of taking a tricycle. It was a long way to walk in the hot sun but I needed to think. I had been in a kind of fog for the past few days. I tried to focus on what is lovely, what is pure, and what is true but I just couldn't bring anything to mind. *Surely I have not lost hope? If only I could find professional staff who actually liked teenage boys with problems. How hard could that be?* I smiled cynically. When I arrived home later I had a clearer perspective. The walk had done me good. Jesus had been walking with me, as He had done since my childhood.

Of those who were discharged, Roco went back to Manila to an auntie, where he worked without pay, but at least he had a roof over his head and food in his stomach. Domingo went to live with his mother and sisters in a shack that a landowner allowed them to use. Lucas returned to the red-light district with his brother Juno. For a while they worked as dancers in the gay bars, which I hated. But they attended church most Sundays, usually to ask for a little money. I didn't mind; I was just glad to keep tabs on them. Lucas died seven years later, aged twenty-one, from miliary tuberculosis. I was with him until the end. His brother Juno was arrested on a drugs charge shortly after his brother's death; his case was acquitted two years later because of lack of evidence. At age twenty-five, he too had miliary tuberculosis. When we met him in the city after his acquittal he told us that his dad was dying and he wanted to see him one last time. When we offered to pay his bus fare he broke down and cried.

Larry went to stay with a friend in the city, where he collected junk for recycling. He enjoyed his work and the boss provided a place for him to stay. Whenever I saw him I brought him food or clothes. He was usually in church on Sundays – not smelling very good, but no one minded! As far as I was concerned, I would never give up on them.

I had no idea where to place Franko. His auntie suggested he stay with his sister, whom he had never met. When we dropped him at her home she suggested he talk to his mother on the phone. Franko tensed up, obviously petrified at the thought of talking to his mother for the first time in his life. As his sister handed him the phone the colour drained from his face. "Hello?" he said, nervously. It was more of a question than a greeting. He listened as his mother cried and apologized. After sixteen years of feeling nothing but anger towards her, he showed little emotion. I hugged him for a long time, then Peter and I left for home.

A few weeks later he decided to look for work close to LAMA House, and he found somewhere to live with an old school friend. I told him I was glad to have him close by, but I could tell he was unconvinced. He had regressed and he no longer trusted me.

My heart ached for each of them. Talking about it with Sarah, she reminded me about children leaving the nest. It wasn't easy but the boys were going to learn to fly. Her advice came from a heart that loved the boys as much as I did. She was, of course, that member of professional staff who actually liked teenaged boys with problems. I entrusted my brood to God's care.

Months later, Franko visited church. I went to sit next to him, and held his hand through the service. That wasn't a very good move culturally, but after that he sent me texts from his cell phone every day. His texts would often read, "I luv u Ma", and I would reply, "I luv u 2!"

The fact was our older boys still needed a lot of help after their eighteenth birthday. Most of them had nowhere to go. After Sarah returned to England, she got busy organizing a fundraising event to buy goats. The idea took off. We had enough money to buy a piece of farmland where we could build a small home for the older boys. I was apprehensive about buying more land, as the court case over LAMA land had dragged on for over ten years. But it was useless to live in fear of making a wrong decision. The owner this time was a good friend, an attorney whom we had known for years, so we went ahead with it.

Ton returned to work for us as caretaker of the "goat land". Although quite a distance from Pastor Fred's church, he was always there on Sundays. He had a beautiful family. God had to develop in us the ability to wait well. Ton's life was evidence to me that waiting and trusting worked.

In August 2003 our lawyer turned up at LAMA House, waving a brown envelope in the air. He had received the verdict from the Supreme Court.

"The Court case is finished and LAMA House can never be taken away from you! To tell you the truth, my colleagues can hardly believe it! They couldn't see me winning. But I knew God would fight for us! *We won!*" he laughed triumphantly.

Sometimes I wished that God would shout. His ways were so gentle that I often missed what He was saying in my spirit. I wrote Isaiah 50:4 in the flyleaf of my Bible as a reminder that the Lord was eager to teach me if I would stop to listen: "He wakens Me morning by morning, He wakens My ear to hear as a disciple [as one who is being taught]" (Isaiah 50:4, AMP).

I made an arrangement with God: if He woke me very early in the morning I would listen "as one who is being taught". Getting out of bed at 6 a.m. was usually the earliest I could manage, so if I did wake up before that time with a sense of purpose I knew it was God. Instead of trying to get back to sleep I tried to listen for His still small voice, expecting that He had something important to tell me.

This led to a fascinating tradition. When I was a little girl my dad woke me early for school with a cup of tea. This was something like that.

One morning, I woke early with the thought, *I should go with Peter to McDonald's for breakfast!* Peter usually stopped at McDonalds for breakfast after he dropped the children off at school, but I preferred to stay at home with a cup of tea and marmalade on toast. Funny as it seemed, I recognized God's voice and decided to act on it.

As I sat at one of the tables with a Sausage McMuffin and coffee, I noticed our old social worker friend, Cora, coming through the door. She didn't usually frequent McDonald's either. We hadn't seen her for a long time. We told her we had received accreditation for LAMA House, and updated her about Almo.

I noticed she was wearing a little black badge on her dress, a sign of mourning.

"My husband died suddenly; pray for me," she asked, as she kissed my cheek to say goodbye.

"So sorry… yes, we will. If you have any babies that need a home, we'd be happy to foster again," I blurted out, remembering she had registered us as foster parents.

Peter looked at me questioningly, as if to say, *What did you say that for?*

"You're as bad as me, taking on other people's problems," she laughed.

"There's no rush though," I added, realizing I had just volunteered for something that Peter wasn't quite ready for.

That same evening we had a telephone call from Cora. "Lesley, you won't believe this – I have a baby boy for you – can you come and pick him up?"

She was right: I didn't believe it.

"See how God works! After meeting you in McDonald's, I went to Urdaneta on business. While there, someone informed me about a baby that had been abandoned. I knew instantly what to do," she said.

Peter had to agree: it was God's handiwork. So we went right away to the DSWD office where we were handed a baby boy of just three months old. I always thought it strange how relatively easy it was for us to foster a baby than operate a home for teenage boys. It all happened so fast we could hardly catch our breath and had no time to make any preparations. Fortunately Cora had bought a few things to get us started.

A young man the same age as Almo had been caring for the baby. He would have kept him, but he had to work all day. Almo was thrilled when the little fellow formed an immediate bond with him. He hurried home to hold him every day, and loved it when the baby cried because he was leaving.

"Maybe you should adopt him, Almo," I joked.

But the baby didn't stay with us long. After a few weeks a couple applied to adopt him. When they came to collect him, the mother couldn't hold back the tears.

"We have wanted another baby for some time. The other night my daughter prayed before she went to sleep that God would give her a baby brother, and the next day we got a call from the social worker telling us they had a baby for us!" she told me.

We handed him over without hesitation, but for weeks Almo mooched around like a dog that had lost its puppies.

Another frightened little boy arrived, accompanied by a friendly policeman. "We found him sleeping in a waiting shed [something like a bus stop] in San Juan," the policeman informed us. "He said his older brother brought him from Manila and left him there. He was frightened; as it's near the cemetery, I don't think he got much sleep!" he winked.

He was nine years old, and looked vulnerable in clean clothes and with a neat haircut. He was not a street-boy. Surprisingly eloquent, he gave us plenty of information and seemed to be under the impression that his mother was working as a nurse in Canada. He claimed he didn't know his father. "My father left us after I was conceived," he explained.

I smiled at his candour – he knew a whole lot for his age.

He told us his name was Klyde Lusano and wrote down an address in Manila where his mother Cherry used to live, including the number of the house. We placed the missing ads on television, radio, and in newspapers, but as usual no one came forward with any information. Peter took him to Manila but they found no one of that name at the address. The Barangay officials had no record of a Cherry Lusano living in the area; no one knew her.

Peter and I both hated going all the way to Manila, only to achieve nothing. Klyde didn't seem to know if his mother was in Canada or Manila. We had to give up looking for her. "Let's try to visit Roco instead," I suggested, and Peter agreed to try. There are not many street names to follow in the back streets of Manila so the map I was navigating from was practically useless! Nevertheless, we found the house eventually, after making several wrong turns. Seeing Roco again made the hassle worthwhile. He recognized our jeep as we pulled up outside the house, and cried when he saw us.

"I am doing OK here. I changed my name: it's Ewok now! My father still avoids me, but I have friends here," he told me.

I noticed the sadness of rejection in his eyes as we talked. That sad countenance on the boys' faces usually lifted after a couple of months in the LAMA family. I always looked for it, and felt sorry that it was still there in Roco's eyes. I hugged him as we said goodbye before returning home. He must have sensed my own uncertainty. "I have Jesus in my heart," he said as if to reassure me.

Back at LAMA House, one of the boys said he'd overheard Klyde talking about a classmate who lived in Baguio. So Peter took him to Baguio and they searched up and down several streets where Klyde thought his home was, but they came back to LAMA House even more confused.

I studied his file, trying to find clues but they always escaped me. He was such a delightful, well-educated, and polite little boy that I was sure someone must be looking for him. In another newsletter, I asked people to pray about it. Meanwhile, Klyde made himself at home in LAMA House, spending most of his time with Ana. He was like Ana's other twin!

When we returned to England for the school holidays in April 2004 Peter came with us. LAMA boys attended the youth camp again in Baguio during our absence. As they relaxed together at the campsite Klyde suddenly remembered which *jeepney* he should take to go home. Without warning, he wandered off. When it was time to eat Pastor Agusto noticed Klyde was missing. A frantic search party was organized to find him. Jose, our house-father, returned to one of the streets where Peter had tried unsuccessfully to find Klyde's home before. There he was, standing at the side of the road, hugging his mother!

She told them that his real name was Geirone! No wonder no one responded to the newspaper and radio ads. The name he used as an alias actually belonged to another little boy in his class at school. And his mother's name was not Cherry.

"He must have run away from home when he heard me talking about going to work abroad. When I went to Manila to follow up my application he must have thought I'd left already! He was gone when I got home," she explained tearfully.

In England, we received a phone call from Pastor Agusto to tell us the exciting news. For six months he had maintained that his name was Klyde Lusano. His real name was much fancier – Herbert Geirone V de la Luna! He had really led us on a wild goose chase, but we couldn't be angry with him as he was such a sweet little boy.

The first thing that Ana wanted to do when we got home was visit Klyde in Baguio. Klyde and Ana kept in touch with each other for years. We continued to call him Klyde – even though that was not his name!

Chapter 25

Kit

**[We] need a God whose promises are certain; a
God… [who] can walk with me and counsel me
and pray for me and prepare a place for me and
who can even make all things work together for
good… [He] loves us completely, is all-powerful
and will ultimately make all things new.**

Pete Greig in *God on Mute*

Pastor Julius never fully recovered. His sons accompanied
him to church as he was too frail to make the journey
alone. I could hardly believe it as I shook hands with
them – they were as tall as me. "I can still remember when you
were only the size of my hand," I told Joshua.

In one way I admired Pastor Julius's disregard for all things
temporal; he was always longing for his home in heaven. He
died on his fiftieth birthday, at the end of 2004. I felt privileged
to have worked with such a dedicated man.

For a while proceedings at the church faltered. Pastor Fred
hesitated, not sure if he could replace what had been lost. He
asked Peter to take over the Bible studies on Sundays. Peter was
also nervous about filling Pastor Julius's shoes, but God took
their weakness and humility and used it to bless the church.

"What about Kit? He didn't come to church again today.
What are we going to do?" Pastor Fred asked me after the
service.

The next day, I studied Kit's case notes, trying to make sense of the jumbled case history. Sixteen-year-old Kit had been in a dark depression for the past month or so, only coming out of his room to eat his meals. He covered his bedroom window with a blanket to block out any trace of light, and he wouldn't talk to anyone.

It all started before the Christmas holiday, when his teacher asked the class to write an essay about their family. For a long time Kit sat at his desk staring dejectedly at the blank sheet of paper in front of him, feeling that it summed up his worth. He could find nothing to write about, so stood up and walked out. He came home in tears, went straight upstairs, and shut himself in his room.

I was angry with his teacher because we had carefully explained who we were and the difficulties LAMA boys were facing. I looked for anything that would help us find a family member, but the information in his file was confusing; even his surname was incorrect. There was no way we could possibly find his mother.

According to the report, he was abandoned outside a grocery store when he was three years old. A couple, whose surname he was now using, found him and took him home. It appeared that they sold him to a woman. Sometime after that he ran away from her house because she treated him badly. Another man found him on the street and took him home to Ifugao, where he left Kit with his brother and sister-in-law. He stayed with them for four years.

When he was late for school one day, he explained to his teacher that he had to do a lot of work before coming to school. He complained that he didn't feel like he was part of the family. Concerned, the teacher asked a social worker to investigate. She found out that the couple had no legal claim to Kit, and she immediately removed him from their care, placing him in a children's home. At the children's home Kit became very difficult, refusing to go to school or do any of his chores. After less than a year the director of the home transferred him to a DSWD temporary shelter, unable to cope with him.

He was transferred to LAMA House when he was ten years old. Angry and confused, he set about wrecking the place, destroying all the doorknobs and windows. He continued his mission of mass destruction while I constantly reminded our house-parents to be patient with him.

Eventually his wounded expression was replaced with a lovely smile. He devoted his spare time to reading his Bible and prayer; not out of duty but because he enjoyed it. And I noticed he was genuinely concerned for other boys left to fend for themselves on the street. On the odd occasion when one of the boys didn't come home, Kit volunteered to search and bring him back. He had been doing well, until this latest setback.

When he did let me talk to him, he told me that he spent every night crying, pleading with God to help him find his parents. "I have prayed and prayed. It doesn't work," he told me. I didn't know what else to do. *Lord, send someone who can help Kit, someone he can relate to*, I prayed silently, as we sat together on his bed in the darkened room.

"We'll try our best to find them soon," I promised.

He was still locked inside his room when, days later, Ariel arrived. He was ten years old and had been found wandering the streets. Pastor Fred and I laughed when we saw him, because he looked exactly like a younger version of Kit.

"That's odd! It's Kit – again!" he joked.

It was like going back in time, reliving Kit's arrival at LAMA House six years before. We were still giggling about the uncanny resemblance when the lunchtime bell clanged and everyone headed for the kitchen. Kit came down the stairs to join us at the big kitchen table. The mood grew sombre.

"We would like to welcome Ariel, who will be joining us here," Peter announced.

Everyone applauded and cheered to welcome the new arrival. Kit lifted his head and saw Ariel, sitting directly opposite him. He blinked, as if unable to believe his eyes, and then laughed out loud. That started Pastor Fred laughing again, and soon everyone was caught up in the happiness of the moment. I could almost see the gloomy spirit fleeing the building.

"God sent Ariel to remind you that He has chosen you. He brought you to LAMA House for a reason," I told Kit. He smiled back at me.

He went back to school and received honours that year. In June he started high school. But the longing to belong took over his thoughts again, and he found it difficult to concentrate on his studies. I hadn't forgotten my promise to find his parents, and neither had he.

Thankfully, Pastor Jim built up a rapport with him and discovered that Kit wanted to find the family in Ifugao who had taken care of him for more than four years. He considered them his parents. That changed everything. It made the search possible, as there were names and an address for that family in his file. But the social worker's report claimed that they had abused and neglected Kit.

I had to ask Kit about it.

"No Maam, that's not true! They treated me kindly," he told me.

Had we known that before, things would have been a lot easier. As usual, it was more important for the paperwork to look right. In the Philippines, it seems appearance is more important than accuracy. That's why at restaurants the menu looks varied, but a lot of items are always unavailable. It made me very angry with the system.

Peter made immediate plans to travel to Ifugao, but the remote village was at least an eleven-hour drive away, and our vehicle was under repair. Pastor Fred volunteered to make the journey in the Pinoy jeep, which had seen better days. He was confident it would get them there – eventually! Kit insisted that Ariel come along, just in case they found out that he was a distant relative. Like us, he was learning to expect the unexpected.

The tiring journey, mostly on dirt roads, ended with a crossing of the dam on a bamboo raft. It was as if they were in another world: bamboo homes were balanced on stilts over the water. When they finally reached the village, the group went from house to house asking if anyone knew the family, but thirteen years had passed since Kit was placed in the children's home and nobody recognized the name.

They were about to give up when one man came forward with some information.

"I know the man who brought this boy to Ifugao," he told Pastor Fred.

He ran off to find him.

The man was shocked when the news reached him, and he set off running. When he caught sight of Kit he didn't slow down, but met him with such force that they both fell to the ground, hugging each other and weeping uncontrollably! With a band of villagers following behind, he took the travel-worn team from LAMA House back to his home and gave them a meal. He showed them photos of Kit as a little boy. Then he took them around the homes of his neighbours, where more photos were on display.

"I tried to find you after that social worker took you away from my brother, but I didn't know the address of her office. Please, stay here with us now," he begged, holding on to Kit.

But Kit had enrolled in a driving course during the summer vacation, and had plans to go to Bible College. He was satisfied just to know – without staying – though he still wanted to find his foster parents. So his "uncle" wrote down an address in another province, where we might find them. Then, with emotional goodbyes and promises to visit again, Pastor Fred and the team began the long journey home to La Union.

Kit arrived back at LAMA House excited to share his story. But there were mixed emotions among the boys. I studied Max's face as Kit recounted his adventures. Max was referred to LAMA House around the same time as Kit. According to his case history, he had run away after witnessing the murder of his father, when he was ten years old. He claimed he came from Manila, but that was all he remembered. I put my arm around his shoulders as he sadly stared at the floor and blinked his eyes, trying not to show any emotion.

That night, without telling anyone, Max left LAMA House. A tricycle driver told one of the boys that he saw him boarding a bus bound for Manila. He had gone to find his mother. For three days we worried about him, and prayed that he would somehow find his way back to us. Unfortunately, he was terribly absent-minded and was always getting lost. We always asked, "Have we got Max?" whenever we were ready to return home from an outing with the boys. So when he returned home safely from his excursion to the big city, everyone cheered. But he was not happy.

A memory had been sparked in his mind and he thought he knew where to go, but when he got to Manila he couldn't find the right place. Peter promised him that they would go back to Manila together soon to find the landmarks that he remembered.

Almost six months passed before Peter had time to follow up the next lead in the jigsaw that was Kit's life. After another long, dusty drive they found Kit's foster father, who was delighted to see Kit and asked him to stay. But Kit had finished the driving course and was now determined to study in Bible College. His prayers had indeed been answered. A new joy and confidence grew inside him, along with a very real sense of purpose.

We had a farewell party at LAMA House before Peter took Kit to college in the Mountain Province. He had a big smile on his face as we gathered outside to wave goodbye.

When he came home that Christmas he had a good report from the teachers. However, it was an entirely different culture in the mountain region, and some of the students picked on him because he was a "lowlander". The familiar feeling of not fitting in began to haunt him again, but he persevered through the first year. Back at LAMA House for the summer break, the boys were impressed when he led their devotions every night, and taught Bible studies.

When he returned to the college his books and belongings had been stolen. Feeling completely disillusioned with his classmates, who he suspected were responsible, he decided to come home and go back to high school instead. We supported his decision. Despite his treatment by the other students, the experience had been good for him.

However, he was embarrassed when the principal at the school asked for his birth certificate. He still didn't have one. Peter decided to travel back to the town where Kit's foster father lived, thinking that a Certificate of Foundling would be the best we could do, but he was no longer there. Even so, the mayor of the town was very helpful. Many of his constituents were not properly registered, so he had some experience in securing birth certificates for people. With the information that was now available to us he registered Kit's birth and issued a certificate to him. At last Kit had proof of his existence, even if it was faulty.

Oddly, as soon as Kit got his birth certificate and found peace with himself, Ariel decided to go home to his mother in Zambales, 200 km south of San Fernando. He had been there for a couple of visits, but it didn't go well and he was always happy to return to us. Now he had decided to stay with his mother, as if he considered his mission accomplished. But his mother was not so keen to have him back. After a few months he went to live with his grandma. Later, we heard that he had linked up with his old friends, street hawkers who sold popcorn in town fiesta celebrations. Every now and then he paid us a visit.

Kit tried to finish high school but struggled with the lessons. When he failed to do his school work his teacher asked Peter and me to visit the school to discuss his progress. His self-esteem had plummeted again.

"I feel stupid," he told us.

The other children stared and whispered to each other as Peter and passed by their classrooms.

"Americana!" they giggled, pointing at me.

We talked to the teacher for a while, who was willing to help Kit get through the school year. We told her we would try to motivate him to do better. Then we waited outside Kit's classroom, to take him home with us.

"Is that your mother?" one girl asked him, as they left the classroom.

He smiled at me, paused, and then said, "Yes!"

I don't know who felt more proud – him or me. He straightened up, and we smiled at each other. He held his head high as we linked arms and made our way out of the schoolyard.

But Kit never did finish high school. He got distracted by a beautiful girl who lived near the older boys' home in Naguilian. Maricar's parents had eight daughters, all of them very pretty. Their father told us that he had barred all young men from coming to the house to visit his daughters, but when he met Kit he relaxed the rules.

"He told our daughters when they are ready to marry they should choose one of the fine boys from LAMA House!" Maricar's mother told me.

We accompanied them to the mayor's office to get a marriage licence. "It's a good thing you got your birth certificate – you can't get married without one," I told him. I brought along his case file for reference and leafed through it as we waited. I came across an old progress report. According to the unusually detailed report, when Kit walked out of his class the principal had summoned him to her office. She told him off and poked at his shirt.

"What is this? Clean yourself up!" she shouted.

"Don't hurt me! Don't touch me!" he told her, instinctively pushing her away.

"You are disrespectful! That must be why your parents abandoned you!" she retorted.

I couldn't believe what I was reading. Why hadn't our social worker told me this? Kit was left holding on to those cruel words, while the solution slipped slowly through my fingers.

"When will they realize that to delay telling us about a problem only makes the problem a hundred times worse?" I asked Peter. Then I realized it was likely that he was informed, but didn't tell me. It was so frustrating.

It was time for us to talk to the mayor. I watched as he interviewed Kit and Maricar, filling in the necessary forms. "Who are your biological parents?" he asked Kit. He looked down at his feet in embarrassment. "He doesn't know, but we are his guardians," I quickly answered. He lifted his head again and smiled. His bride gave his hand a squeeze.

Chapter 26

The Calendar

Peter's brother Jerry had worked as a taxi driver in Manila and knew all the unmarked nooks and crannies of the capital that were not included on a map. He offered to take Max and Hilary, our new social worker, on the next search. They motored around for some time hoping to come across something that Max remembered, but it seemed futile.

Then Jerry had an idea. "I don't know if this will work, but let's try to search the list of voters at the COMELEC building. Your family name is not such a common name; we might be lucky," he suggested. They studied the list of names and Jerry asked questions, naming landmarks he was familiar with in each location. Max remembered living near a school, so Jerry made a note of all the addresses that had schools nearby. Then they set off again for the first address on the list.

When they reached the place, in a slum district, Max stayed behind in the jeep while Jerry found the house. He introduced himself and asked if the family had ever lost a ten-year-old boy.

"Yes, we lost a boy, but that was many years ago. He's probably dead by now," the woman replied.

"Can you tell me the child's name?" Jerry asked.

"Yes, his name was Max," she said.

"Really, it's Max?… Wait here," he said, his eyes welling up with tears as he ran back to the jeep.

Max had quite distinctive features and the woman recognized him right away, despite the fact that he was now a teenager. The family started to shout for joy and soon the whole neighbourhood came out into the street to see what all the commotion was about. Max stood there, stiff and uncomfortable, as everyone clamoured to hug him. He was a very quiet boy and didn't know how to react to so much excitement, but a wide smile crept across his face. Jerry laughed, tears in his eyes. "It's Max!" he kept saying over and over.

The woman was Max's auntie, his father's sister. She asked them to come inside their small house and be seated.

"Your father died, you know," she told Max.

"Yes, that's all I remember," he replied.

"Your mother left home; we lost contact with her. Your sister was adopted by a wealthy couple in the city. She is studying at one of the private schools, but we never see her and don't know how to find her," she continued.

Max nodded. He remembered having an older sister. He wanted to find her.

The search party returned home happy, feeling as if they had been part of another miracle.

When Max was ready to return to his auntie's, I went with them to meet the family. We arrived in the early evening, turning off the main street into the slum district. Peter was nervous about leaving the vehicle parked on the side of the road. We made our way along a very narrow alleyway between the cramped homes. Remembering the way, Max walked ahead of us, and as he came to the house the door opened – they were waiting for him. I could hear frantic whispering as we neared the shanty.

"Americana! Go and get some Coke!" the auntie ordered.

As we entered the small home a young girl dressed in a miniskirt and halter neck top squeezed past me to go to the sari-sari store. When she came back, I realized she was actually a young boy, dressed up in transvestite gear. I glanced at Max, but he smiled at me reassuringly. *Were we doing the right thing?* I wondered.

Back home at LAMA House, we missed him. The boys had nicknamed Max, "Steel", because whenever he hurt himself he didn't cry. He was always falling off or being hit by things! The boys told stories about his escapades as we gathered together to pray for him one evening.

Max stayed in Manila for six months and then decided to come back to LAMA House. Life had been difficult there, and he got into bad company, probably the only company available to him in that place. On a positive note, his time in Manila had given him more self-confidence and he took on the role of older brother at LAMA House. Before he left he was very nervous about talking to anyone, but he returned having found his voice, as well as his own opinions. We had to smile as he debated world issues with the boys as if he had been in university in Manila rather than in one of the worst slum districts. In 2012 he returned to his auntie and this time he was stronger. He found work in Manila. When he came home to visit I noticed he was no longer one of my boys – he was a man. He stood for a while before leaving, waiting for me to give him a hug. "I love you! Take care of yourself," I told him. "No drinking!" He nodded and smiled bashfully. "Yes, mom," he agreed.

Meanwhile, Curt and Christopher both spent time in jail for theft; Curt in Manila and Christopher in San Fernando. Their choices were often weak. I still believed that if they would give their lives to God His grace would be sufficient for even their unwise choices and He would use it all for his glory.

Curt paid us a brief visit after his release from jail. He was fourteen years old. He proudly displayed a tattoo he'd got when "inside" – in large Gothic letters across both shoulders it read, "Christian". I didn't know what to think.

Sometime later, I was tidying the boys' rooms when Pastor Agusto approached me. He was obviously distraught. "Maam, there's a new boy in the office with Maam Hilary – just been referred," he said, his voice trembling. He wiped tears from his eyes with the back of his hand. "I have never seen anything as bad as this, Maam."

At the office, Carlos sat huddled between Hilary and another social worker. The referring social worker stood to greet me. Hilary passed the folder of papers over to me. I glanced at Carlos, so frail and covered in bruises. He was twelve years old but small for his age. He didn't lift his face to meet my concerned gaze.

"Oh, Lord," I muttered, a lump forming in my throat.

I quickly read the case report then looked away – it was too upsetting. The little fellow seemed completely broken. Putting the folder down on the desk, I lifted Carlos up and sat him on my knee. It was like lifting a rag doll.

"It's alright, you will be safe here," I told him with tears in my eyes.

Everyone in the room was crying as Pastor Agusto gently lifted Carlos's T-shirt to show me the bruises and scars. All except Carlos – he had no more tears left.

"I had to take care of their chickens. When one of them died, my uncle lifted me by my jaw, pinned me to the wall, and punched me in the stomach. He threw me down on the floor and kicked me. That's when our neighbour rescued me and brought me to the DSWD," he told Hilary.

Pastor Agusto introduced Carlos to Piolo and Bong who had come into the office to investigate the new arrival.

"Let's go and watch cartoons," Bong suggested.

Piolo put his arm around his shoulders and they went to join the other boys in the television room. I reopened his folder and took a deep breath, bracing myself to read the full story.

Carlos was very small when his father died and so he didn't know him. His mother was confined in a mental hospital in Manila, due to drug addiction. They had not been married. For a while, his grandmother took care of him. They lived in a district of Manila notorious for drugs and crime and his other grandmother was also a drug addict. When she could no longer cope, the grandmother gave him to her son and his wife, who lived in an upper-class neighbourhood and had a nice house. Carlos went to school there and was taught to help out with household chores. He was an obedient and helpful little boy.

Things changed when another uncle joined the household. He blamed Carlos if anything in the house was lost, and whipped him for the slightest mistake. One evening, when he came home from work, he grabbed Carlos and tried to tie him to a chair. Carlos managed to wrestle free from him, so instead his uncle pinned him to the floor and whipped him with his belt. There was no reason for the uncle's outbursts, except that he too was a drug addict.

The abuse was repeated whenever his uncle came home from work; whenever they were alone together in the house. The neighbours knew about it as sometimes his body was almost completely purple with bruises. But everyone was too afraid to report it to the police. If one neighbour hadn't been brave enough to finally intervene, Carlos would have no doubt lost his life. He was taken to the hospital with multiple injuries. The DSWD filed charges against his uncle.

Carlos quickly made friends with everyone at LAMA House. They all had questions and he related his story as if they had been friends for a long time. He obviously felt safe, at last. He was relaxed and enjoyed playing with the other boys, politely addressing those older than him as "*kuya*" or "*ate*" (older brother or older sister).

"Can you show me where to have a shower?" he asked Bong, when he finished eating. I smiled as several boys stood to help him, pleased to see them caring for one another. To everyone's surprise he volunteered to clean the kitchen, mop the floor, and wash the dishes. When one of the boys was unkind he went immediately to Pastors Jim, Agusto, or Fred for protection. That was something he had never been able to do before.

I was very protective towards him in his first few weeks with us, as I was with all our new boys. I could see that rare coping mechanisms had already developed in his personality that helped him not only bear what he had suffered but begin to use it to help others. But sometimes he argued with someone, and words would come out of his mouth that reminded him of his abuser, or he would hurt one of the smaller boys. He hated it, but it was like a reflex action.

I've seen it happen often; the beaten-up soul can harden and tend to beat up others. But God was working His magic at LAMA House, slowly but surely. As we prayed for the boys and as they surrendered to his loving ways He was melting the hard places and making them tender again.

***

At the end of November 2004, I learned how to design a calendar on the computer. Each month had a colour photo of one aspect of our work. It was costly to print and mail, but I knew it would remind friends to pray for those whose photos appeared each month, and for that alone it seemed worth it. I sent out over 300 copies with the Christmas newsletter. It could not have been a coincidence that I chose Domingo and Piolo's family picture to grace the page for March 2005.

Domingo was eighteen and Piolo thirteen by this time. Both boys visited their parents and sisters often. I was determined to help the family get back on their feet, but in reality they never had been on their feet to start with. Everything we did to help them came to nothing, but we kept helping. We paid tuition fees in high school for Domingo, so he could finish his education. He didn't do well, but attended classes most days, arriving late wearing multiple earrings and his uniform dishevelled. When we visited the school the principal couldn't understand why we involved ourselves in the muddle. She threatened to suspend him, so we took him for a haircut and told him we would only pay his fees if he tried harder. He promised he would.

"It's hard, Maam. Sometimes Tatay [Dad] doesn't have money for food. I can't think when I'm hungry," he told me.

It appeared the only constant was that Domingo's father would work every day, carting vegetables for the vendors, having had a few drinks to help him on the way. Domingo and Piolo felt they could depend on him, whereas their mother could hardly be depended on for anything at all. They loved him deeply, and he loved them.

I listened closely during evening devotions as Piolo prayed for his family. His mother had visited that day. She told him that the landlord had threatened to evict them again. We had given her the rent money, but she used it for something else. Piolo asked God to help his father make more money.

The next morning, the phone rang in LAMA House. Hilary answered. It was Piolo's older sister, Michelle. She was crying. Hilary handed the phone to him. "Tatay has gone, Piolo. A truck hit him last night as he was pushing the cart along the highway. He died before anyone took him to the hospital," she said.

When I arrived at LAMA House I found Piolo in the television room, staring at the screen as if in a trance. He didn't notice when I put my hand on his shoulder. He had gone into his own world, pretending that it wasn't true. We immediately travelled to Urdaneta. I put some music in the cassette player to break the silence as Peter drove. Sitting behind me, Piolo began to sing along, his voice shaking and tears streaming down his cheeks.

"I will give you all my worship. I will give you all my praise. You alone I long to worship, you alone are worthy of my praise." He had memorized all the words of the songs, even though they were in English, and kept singing until the cassette tape stopped. I felt like my heart would break with his.

After a couple of hours we arrived at a clearing, outside a small cluster of houses.

"This is where Liza lives now with her husband," Piolo explained.

"Her husband… how old is Liza?" I asked.

"She's sixteen, Maam. They're not really married; she lives with him," he told me.

We were met with the usual disorder. Piolo's mother didn't know what to do about a wake, because they had no home in which to place the coffin. Stepping out of the jeep Piolo stood motionless while people shouted insults at each other, trying to find someone to blame. There were no comforting hugs or words of sympathy, just noisy confusion.

"Piolo, go and gather up your father's things," his mother ordered.

His father's belongings amounted to two plastic bags full of old clothes, and three more bags full of pieces of cardboard, which had been folded neatly and tied in bundles ready to sell to the junk yard for recycling. Piolo went over to one of the houses and moved the bags from there to where his family were standing. It was a pointless gesture.

"Where is Domingo?" I asked.

"He's in school. He doesn't know that Tatay is dead," Michelle told me.

"What? Someone should tell him," I said, finding it hard to understand what was going on. Michelle was a pretty girl, despite being far too thin, and she seemed more sensible than anyone else in the group. She left immediately to go to Domingo's school.

Domingo came to the classroom door to meet her.

"Tatay is dead," she told him bluntly.

"What?! But I saw him yesterday; he gave me some money," Domingo replied. He excused himself from the class, arriving at Liza's place in a daze.

"Where have you been? Your father is dead!" his mother yelled.

"I didn't know," Domingo cried, clearly confused.

"Why didn't you know, you should know!" she shouted in his face.

No one had told him, so how could he have known?

When everyone had calmed down, Peter persuaded Liza's partner to hold a wake for a few days at his home. We offered to pay for the necessary snacks. The truck driver had already accepted responsibility for the accident and agreed to pay all the funeral expenses. As soon as Peter mentioned the financial situation everyone began fighting again about the money and how it should be spent. I imagined their father looking down on the uproar with a smile, never dreaming he would have left a penny behind for anyone to argue over.

Reluctantly, we left Piolo there to attend his father's wake. When we came back to pick him up I could see he was exhausted and disturbed by the week-long ordeal. Meeting him at the door, I handed him one of the calendars, showing him the photo for March. It was a lovely family portrait of his family with his father smiling back at him. His face lit up with amazement. He thought only politicians and pop-stars were featured on calendars.

Chapter 27

Weddings and Funerals

"I should warn you – I've run out of teabags," I joked with Peter.

The telephone rang.

"Hello?" I said.

"Hello," a woman with a British accent replied.

It was Joy Pegg from Tewkesbury in Gloucestershire. I was delighted to find out that she and her husband Steve were teaching in a Bible school not far from us. We arranged to go and visit them that afternoon. Whenever I found British company it was like a conversational dam bursting; we talked non-stop until evening. "A little something for you from England," Joy said as we left to go home, pressing something into my hand: a packet of Twinings tea! When we arrived back at our apartment there was a parcel outside the door from Bert, our South African neighbour, who had recently moved out of the apartment next to ours. He had also sent me some tea! That same evening, Caroline Bickersteth phoned from England to tell me that some of her friends from London were planning a visit to Pastor Abe's children's home in San Fernando. "Is there anything you would like them to bring?" she asked. "I would love some Typhoo tea," I laughed. It was the only thing I found it difficult to do without. Thankfully, God understood that.

On Saturday night, our neighbours were having their usual "happy hour" drinks party until the early hours of the morning. Absolutely no air circulated in our apartment, sandwiched as it was between two others. I gave up on sleep and tried to concentrate instead on who needed my prayers.

Lito came to mind. A couple of days earlier he had phoned us. He was visiting us so regularly to ask for money that Peter had talked to him about it. "You can't keep running to us when you need money," he told him, encouraging him to take responsibility as provider for his family. Lito hung his head and looked down at his feet; he didn't say anything. It upset me to see any of the boys looking so useless. I would have willingly given him more money, but I knew in my heart that it was not the answer.

He hadn't said much on the phone either, which left me perplexed. Why had he really called? I could remember the conversation, word for word.

"Maam, I'm sorry," he said, in a voice so quiet I could hardly hear.

"No, you don't have to apologize. It's alright," I told him.

He was silent.

"Are you OK, Lito? What is it?" I asked.

"Maam, I'm sorry," he said again, and put the phone down.

"Lord, save him from any trouble he may be in. Help him to budget his salary better. Let him know how much you love him, and we love him," I began to pray. Unsure of what to say, I asked the Holy Spirit to help me and started to pray in tongues, knowing that God hears our hearts more than our words anyway. This was the language of my heart, of acknowledging God and not leaning on my own understanding. Suddenly conscious of God's presence, I felt compelled to stop talking and listen. *What is it, Lord?*

In an instant my thoughts shifted to 1975. I could see myself sitting in my father's church in Pollington, listening to the Philippine Choir of Miracles. The same overwhelming feeling I felt as a girl swept over me again; it was God's unmistakable calling on my life. I began to cry, trying to be quiet so I wouldn't wake Peter. The Holy Spirit reminded me of the times when I thought I was mistaken. Under pressure, I sometimes argued that He should have called someone more capable. I trembled with the knowledge that there was no going back on God's call, and tearfully asked Almighty God to forgive me. Humbly I renewed my commitment to abandon myself to His wisdom and obey Him at any cost.

As we rushed to get ready for church in the morning, I told Peter about my sleepless, prayerful night. I began to tremble and cry again. I could see Peter thought I was just being hormonal.

When we came home from church, three hours later, there was a message on the answer machine of our phone.

"Pete, this is Pastor Lito. There were two policemen at LAMA House a while ago. They came to inform you that Lito Lausa is dead," his message told us.

"What on earth is that? What is he talking about?" Peter asked me.

"I don't know. There must be a mistake; maybe it's another Lito Lausa, not ours," I replied.

"There are no other Lito Lausas!" he retorted, as he rushed out of the door.

"Lito Lausa's body was found this morning at a girlfriend's house. It appears he had hung himself," the police officer told Peter at the police station.

"His girlfriend... are you sure? He is married. We were in church with his wife and children this morning," Peter objected.

But as the police officer began to uncover the body, Peter recognized the boots. He stepped back in shock – there was no arguing with the fact that it was Lito's body lying there.

"His friends and neighbours told us he had been taking drugs and drinking. Apparently, the girlfriend was pregnant," he explained.

The shock was too much for us to take in. We shut down, unable to think, but our team of pastors banded together to hurriedly arrange the funeral. Lito's wife and children came to stay at LAMA House, until Peter could take them home to her parents in far-away Bicol.

Numb with grief, I watched Lito's body being placed in the grave, without tears or emotion, as if we weren't really there, not really burying one of our boys.

If God had not met with me the night before, and spoken so clearly to me, I would not have been able to carry on. There was no going back.

In April 2005 I travelled to England with Michael, Ana, and Simon. My mind was blank. I struggled to promote our mission, feeling a complete failure as far as Lito was concerned, but tried to keep my discouraged thoughts to myself and see through the itinerary.

"There is someone here to see you," Mum announced, as I tried to relax with the children, watching television. "It's Elizabeth. I met her when I spoke about LAMA House in the Methodist church a while back. She really wants to meet you. She's a lovely Catholic lady. Can you show her your pictures of the Philippines?" she asked.

"I don't feel like it, Mum. I'm sorry. I have lost all enthusiasm," I moaned.

But the sitting room door opened and in walked Elizabeth, all smiles and hugs. I smiled back politely as she sat down next to me. Reluctantly, I picked up the photo albums from the coffee table. As we leafed through the albums I felt a little better, showing her pictures of LAMA House and the boys. Then we came to a group photo of the boys laughing with Pastor Fred. My hand touched Lito's face in the picture.

"You look tired," Elizabeth said, taking hold of my hand. My eyes met hers and I could see she had walked through deep sorrow herself.

"I'm OK," I assured her, trying to smile.

"I lost my way as a youngster," she told me quietly. "In a drug-induced trance I thought I was going to die and go to hell. Then suddenly I felt rescued by God's mercy and love. He met me where I was, and brought me out. God can reach people even when it seems impossible, *even when they are close to death*," she said.

I looked at her without saying a word. How could she know what was going on in my mind?

"I have a mental illness you know, but I love Jesus, and His mercy is beyond our understanding. Can I share with you one of my poems?" she asked, still smiling.

I nodded, sensing that God was speaking through her. She began very quietly to recite one of her poems: "Don't you know that you are loved with a love beyond your wildest dreams? Don't you know there is a peace, a peace this world cannot conceive?" it began. The words escaped me until she recited, "… it is the love and peace of Him who hears a sparrow fall."

She squeezed my hand and stood to leave. *The love and peace of Him who hears a sparrow fall*, I thought. Elizabeth smiled and recited the whole poem all over again, as if to make sure I got it. Unable to say the words out loud, I didn't tell her that Lito had committed suicide. She kissed my cheek, and left as unexpectedly as she had arrived. My mother stood behind me at the front door, waving goodbye to her as she wandered down the street. I closed the door slowly.

"Did you tell her about Lito?" I asked my mother.

"No, I brought her straight in to see you," she said.

"She really ministered to me, as if she knew all about me," I wept. And Mum wept with me. I felt I had been visited by an angel.

I knew it was true: His love and mercy know no limit. God is not limited by time or location or any other box we try to put Him in. He could speak to someone in a prison cell or at a party, on a lake or in a bar, not only in a church pew. It didn't matter if Lito was tangled in a mess of his own making; God could still reach him in the darkest place.

It seemed like we were constantly battling against spiritual forces of darkness in the Philippines. *I do this work for God, not for success, or for happiness in my spirit, or anything else*, I told myself.

Our trustees were right when they had suggested I visit England every year, so that my mind and soul could recuperate. But it rarely was any kind of restful. My times in England were always crammed with visits, phone calls, trustee meetings, appointments, and speaking engagements. When I arrived back in the Philippines in June 2005, I felt nothing but utter weariness.

Lito's death had left us all feeling bewildered. As we went over events preceding his death, and conversations we'd had with him, there were a lot of unanswered questions. But there was no inquest, and nothing we could do to find out more information.

To add to the sense of loss, Pastor Agusto handed us his resignation. It was a huge disappointment to me, as he understood our work better than most, and loved the boys with all his heart. But like every other graduate from Bible school his dream was to have his own congregation.

I received a text message from Severina to remind me that I was scheduled to preach at the morning chapel service at Miracle Bible College. It wasn't the first time I had forgotten all about my schedule and I was glad she thought to remind me. After the short service Pastor Valdez shook my hand warmly. "Thank you! God will overflow blessings on your family," he said, slowly, meaningfully. His words took me by surprise and I wasn't sure how to reply, so I just smiled and thanked him. We stood for a while, smiling at each other silently.

As I walked down the mountain road to go home I wondered what he meant. The way he said it, it sounded like a sort of prophecy.

Peter was in Mindoro, another of the Philippine Islands, when Almo approached me in the kitchen at LAMA. I could see he wanted to talk, so waited patiently for the words to come out.

"Ma, my girlfriend is pregnant," he said.

I wasn't aware he had a girlfriend. He was twenty-five, but had no savings and no house. "O, Lord!" I muttered. I didn't feel at all ready to tackle another problem.

"Are you going to get married?" I asked. She nodded, but Almo shook his head.

"Do your parents know?" I asked Arlene.

"My mother knows, but no one dares tell my father," Arlene explained.

I looked at her pregnant tummy. *He must know*, I thought. Peter wouldn't be home for a week or more. What was I going to do?

"We have to go and talk to Arlene's parents about it, don't we?" I asked Almo. He nodded.

"We'll get married. It's the right the thing to do. I'm not going to run away from my responsibility. But I'm not ready," he explained, making the clicking noise with his mouth that he did when he felt inferior.

The atmosphere was very uncomfortable at Arlene's home when we arrived. The whole family were there – her parents and sisters and grandparents. I was struggling to find the Ilocano words to explain my foster son's regret and discuss what action we would be willing to take, when, with surprising courage, Almo took control of the conversation. I had never heard him speak so many words at once – particularly under such pressure. I expected the grandparents to tell us off and lecture us about how relationships were conducted "in their day", but they were most amiable and helped ease the tension. Long silences, where no one knew what to say or do, made me feel very awkward but they all seemed quite content to sit and look at the floor.

"They have decided to get married," I said, anxious to move the discourse along. Arlene's mother broke the silence, asking Almo how he would pay for everything, where the service would be held, and who would prepare the food. As Almo did most of the talking, I prayed silently that God would help us with it all. I felt as much out of my depth as Almo did. When everything was arranged and the family seemed satisfied, we shook hands and took our leave.

In the jeep, I looked over at him, "Well, that went well. We are all still alive," I said, breathing a deep sigh of relief. He started the engine, laughing nervously. As we made our way back to LAMA House, he and Arlene relaxed and chatted happily with each other. It seemed he had found someone he could easily talk to. *Lord, thank you!* I breathed.

The wedding was held in Pastor Fred's church. Three of the boys from Lama House were groomsmen. Our son Michael was the best man. The reception was at LAMA House. I watched happily as friends congratulated Almo. Evidently Peter and I were not the only ones who loved Almo. There were over 600 people there.

Shortly after the wedding, Pastor Jim drove Mama Adella and Hilary to San Fernando to stock up on groceries for the month. At sixty years old Mama Adella was feeling the weight of stress. We had all been on an emotional roller-coaster ride. Lito's sudden death had reminded her of when she lost her husband, leaving her to care for the children alone. It had all been weighing heavily on her mind lately. She leant against the wall while Pastor Jim loaded up the jeep with the boxes of groceries. Her head was pounding.

"Mama, are you alright?" Pastor Jim shouted.

She collapsed onto the ground. When he went over to her, she couldn't speak or move. She was barely conscious when he and Hilary lifted her into the jeep and rushed to the hospital.

The CAT scan revealed that Mama had had a stroke, leaving her without speech and paralysed on the left side of her body. Peter was miles away in Bicol, having taken Lito's wife and children to her parents' home. He would be gone for several days. I called him to tell him the news.

Like many Filipinos Mama was not accustomed to vacations, and hardly ever took time off in the fifteen years she had lived and worked at LAMA House. She preferred to stay at home, but that meant she never fully rested, like most mothers.

She spent several days in the hospital. When she arrived back at LAMA House the mood was sombre as Pastor Jim lifted her limp body out of the jeep and carried her to her room, placing her on the bed. I couldn't bear to see her like that. I tried to find a wheelchair for sale or rent so that she could get around, but there were none available. Her son Ezekiel came to live with her at LAMA.

Expecting a long, difficult recovery ahead I emailed all our friends abroad, asking them to pray. The boys prayed every night that she would be able to walk and talk. We arranged for a physiotherapist to visit. After the first few days of exercises, she insisted that Ezekiel get her up out of bed. Leaning heavily on him, she dragged herself around the courtyard of LAMA House. The next day she did the same thing, but this time with a stick. I couldn't believe my eyes: in less than a week she was walking around unaided and speaking clearly. Having nursed a lot of stroke patients I knew that recovery was possible with regular exercise, but I had never seen a recovery like that.

Our Mama Adella was going to be OK!

Chapter 28

A Sign

With Him, the calf is always the fatted calf, the robe is always the best robe, the joy is unspeakable, and the peace passes understanding.

Haddon Robinson

A new set of neighbours had moved in to the apartment next to ours. The middle-aged Australian men were obviously sex tourists as they had two underage Filipina girls living with them. Loud, drunken parties had become the norm. In another apartment block adjacent to ours a string of prostitutes visited one man regularly. Our home was no longer a haven for our children.

Directly opposite, the owners had decided to invest in gaming cockerels for a new cock-fighting arena that had been built in Bauang. There were far too many cockerels welcoming the dawn every morning, and at regular intervals throughout the day and night. Peter could sleep through anything, but I was not getting enough sleep. The time had come for us to find somewhere else to live.

At one time we imagined we could one day build our own house, close to the beach near LAMA House, in a beautiful spot near the river. But after the freak tsunami in Indonesia on Boxing Day 2004 that idea was quickly abandoned. We didn't have the money for it, anyway.

There was a lot to be thankful for, but how I wished we had a garden where we could sit in the shade of a tree, and where our children could run around safely. I hated having to caution them not to talk to the neighbours or *ever* go inside their house. *Perhaps I should ask God for a sign*, I thought. But I was hopeless at recognizing signs – I usually forgot what I asked God to do.

A family of kingfishers had taken up residence on the riverbank near our apartment. The river was often dirty, with garbage floating in it, but I walked there every day with our newly acquired dog Shilo, hoping to catch a glimpse of the gorgeous, turquoise birds. They were unbelievably beautiful.

"Lord, if you want us to stay here we will. Make our family shine brightly in this place, like this family of kingfishers. If you want to move us on again, show me a sign," I prayed. It was worth a try!

A few days later we visited one of the suburbs of the city, to find out information about Bobby's background. Bobby was eleven when he came to live at LAMA House. I looked at the ID picture attached to his file. I had never seen such a forlorn little face. *He looks completely rejected, bless him*, I thought.

Peter stopped the jeep outside a nice house, where the man who used to take care of Bobby lived. He confirmed that the information in our file was correct.

"Bobby really wants to find his mother," Peter told him.

"But she doesn't want to meet him," the man told us. "She was working in my club when she got pregnant. She left him when he was a year old, promising to come back when she had a better job. She never came back. When my wife died, Bobby was eight. I couldn't cope with him on my own so I asked my nephew to get him."

We talked for some time and he told us that Bobby started to skip school and ran away from the nephew's home to stay with someone else. Before long he ran away again and stayed at another friend's home. When one person asked him to leave he returned to the next, until finally he was placed at LAMA House.

As Peter drove home I read Hilary's comments in the case notes: "Bobby wants to look for his mother and be with her for his lifetime. He also said he would like some toys on his birthday."

"Bless him," I whispered.

Peter took the road through Namnama Village, onto the airport road going to San Fernando's city centre. We passed by the derelict ranch house that we loved.

"Pete, look! It has a For Sale sign outside," I gasped.

"Wow! Let's have a look," he said, pulling over.

The place was more derelict than we had imagined. But we still loved it.

"Did you see the garden at the back? There's a big mango tree and a tamarind tree – it's even got a broken-down swimming pool," I chattered excitedly.

"It needs a lot of repair though. But it seems to have been OK in the rainy season," he replied.

"I wonder if they would rent it instead," I suggested.

"Let's get the number and give them a ring," he said, adding the contact number onto his cell phone.

We giggled like excited children as he drove the short distance back home. As I washed the dishes that evening I imagined what it would be like to rent the property.

"Did you see the sign?" a quiet voice said.

I turned around, but no one was there. Had I imagined it? *The sign?* I thought. *Oh! The For Sale sign!*

Peter came through the door, arriving home from LAMA House.

"Lesley, I think we should go back and look at that property again tomorrow. Maybe God wants us to buy it," he said.

I started to cry.

"Pete, it's the sign, the For Sale sign. I asked God to show me a sign and he showed me the For Sale sign. Don't you see? It's so obvious!" I explained.

"What on earth are you talking about?" he said, laughing.

When we went back to the house in the morning, the real estate agent was outside. We introduced ourselves and asked how much the house was selling for.

"You are a pastor? Where is your church?" the man asked.

We told him about Pastor Fred's church and LAMA House. He was excited about our faith.

"I am also a Christian. I attend the Christian Community Church in the city. We are fixing the place up, and have done quite a bit of work already inside. Come, I'll show you around. The asking price is 6 million pesos [£61,000]," he told us.

I gulped. *Six million! What were we thinking?*

Inside the house the floors were ridiculously uneven. The walls had a new coat of white paint but we could still see cracks. "Is this earthquake damage? What is the foundation like?" Peter asked. The estate agent assured us the foundation was sound.

"I don't know. The kitchen would have to be rebuilt, and the roof – is that asbestos? Those floors – can they be fixed?" I questioned Peter.

He looked at the agent. "I'll be honest with you – we don't have the money. But we love this place. We'll pray about it and see what God will do," Peter told him. I explained that we lived "by faith".

"OK. OK, I understand. My wife and I love this place too. We would buy it ourselves if we didn't already have a house of our own. It's unique. I know it needs a lot of work but the land alone is worth the price. This is considered a prime location," he told us.

"We'll come back next week and see you again," Peter suggested.

"I am also a man of faith. I'll be praying for it too. If you don't mind me asking, how much money do you have available?" he asked.

We looked at each other, not knowing what to say.

"Well… we have less than 1 million, but we might be able

to get a mortgage from our bank," Peter winced, expecting him to laugh at our audacity.

"That's OK. You visit the bank and let me know what you come up with," he said, unperturbed.

We shook hands and left to go home. My heart was pounding.

"Less than 1 million... we have a *lot* less than 1 million! What just happened there?" I asked Peter.

"I don't know! It looks like we are buying a house!" Peter laughed.

"He probably thinks I'm a rich white woman! Where on earth will we find 6 million?" I asked, thinking how absurd the whole thing was, but at the same time how wonderfully "possible with God" (Luke 18:27).

In the following weeks we spent quite a bit of time talking to the bank manager, working out how we could possibly take on a mortgage. We didn't expect the bank to loan us such a big amount, but he saw that our account had always had a steady amount coming in and based his assessment on that alone, rather than the fact that we did not receive a regular income. Standing order donations coming into our personal account only amounted to £250 each month, and we didn't take a salary from LAMA Ministries. It was obviously not enough. When we went back to talk to the estate agent, we had put together a mortgage that was payable over fifteen years. The monthly amount we would have to believe for was scary.

I thought I should write to the people in England who supported us to inform them of our plan to take a mortgage out, as they might not approve of us taking such a drastic step. The response was not what I had supposed. Many friends said it was "about time" and said they wanted to help us.

"We might be able to do it; I don't know. The Lord is providing us with much more than we anticipated," I told the agent.

"Well, we prayed for it! In fact, for you I'll drop the price to 5 million. God is doing His part; I will do mine!" he offered.

"Five million? That would still be out of reach for us. What about four-and-a-half?" Peter bargained.

I nudged Peter. "He's already knocked off 1 million," I whispered, embarrassed.

"Shhh! Let me handle this," he muttered back, looking at me knowingly.

"Right! Let's say four-and-a-half [£46,000]. But that is the absolute minimum, right there!" the agent smiled.

As the days went by, more donations from friends were sent to my parents. But I was still concerned about taking out a mortgage, so I made lists, regularly readjusting the amount that we would need to loan from the bank. A month later I had a telephone call from my mother. She told me about a lady who had sponsored me since I left England in 1983.

"Somehow she hasn't been receiving your newsletters lately, so didn't get the news about you taking out a mortgage. But she came across a copy at her friend's house. She wants to give you £17,000! She wants you to get the house," Mum almost shouted down the phone.

We were amazed. This was not a ministry project, and we hadn't asked people to help us. I looked at my latest list – the full amount had just been covered. The following week, we met the estate agent in his office and paid in cash.

"God is so good! Enjoy your new home!" he laughed.

I wrote letters of thanks to friends who had been so generous, but I couldn't find an address for the lady who gave the final, big amount. Her name was familiar to me, and I wondered for how long she hadn't been receiving my newsletter. How strange it all was. Fortunately, my mother had her name and address in her address book.

Months later, my brother Philip came to visit us with my mother. As they walked around the house I could see they were not convinced. It needed loads of work to make it liveable. Philip worked as a builder in England and had a lot of experience in renovating old barns. "Well, it's a lot like one of my old barn renovations. Let's get started!" he said, rubbing his hands together.

My mother stayed for three weeks and Philip stayed for three months. He got straight to work with Mario, Arnold, Clarence, and Glen – part of our faithful construction team who built LAMA House. While work was going on at our new home, I tried to keep our homelife as relaxed and normal as possible. Whatever else was happening, I had to be around for my own children when they came out of school, usually with loads of homework to accomplish before bedtime.

We decided to move out of our apartment and back into the flat at LAMA House for a few weeks. We were not "at home" in the apartment any more and didn't want to be paying rent. The children were keen to go back to LAMA House for a while. The decision could have been a serious mistake had we not been covered by God's grace.

There were several new arrivals at the home. Aldoni, a young man with autism, was found in the market place begging. He needed a lot of care, but like Mr X he responded well to life at LAMA. It amazed me how gentle our rough-and-tumble boys were with him. They had learned not to laugh at those different from themselves.

Another little boy with special needs couldn't speak clearly. We didn't even know his name or how old he was. The boys named him Wowie. He was probably only seven years old. He had a large scar on the back of his head and was cross-eyed. At first I thought he had Down's syndrome, but the neurologist told us it was likely the head injury had caused brain damage.

Patrick also had special needs. Probably nine years old, he was found wandering the streets. Evidently he had been sexually abused. We had no information with which to find relatives for Patrick or Wowie... ever.

Eleven-year-old Jun had come from prison. When his mother was arrested and charged with possession of illegal drugs, no one was left to take care of him, so he was jailed with her.

Brent was a year younger, but he was very small for his age. He came from the tribal region of Kalinga, where he had witnessed the brutal murder of his cousin in a tribal war. His mother was mentally ill, and no one claimed to be his father. Because he had experienced such terror, he himself was a terror. They were both very difficult cases, Brent having been exposed to extreme violence and Jun to sexual perversion in prison.

Shortly after we moved back into the upstairs flat at LAMA another boy arrived. He was sixteen and had been moved around from one shelter to the next. He had serious psychological problems as a result of sexual exploitation. He had been labelled as being out of control, so none of the shelters were prepared to keep him.

Clearly, I had moved my children out of the frying pan and right into the fire.

But an unmistakable assurance came over me when I picked up my *Daily Light* devotional on the morning of 10 August 2005: "I'm not asking you to take them out of the world, but to keep them safe..." (John 17:15). This was a verse that God kept bringing me back to. He was asking me to trust Him on a deeper level.

One evening, Michael came home from school with a terrible skin allergy. He became hysterical as red, itchy hives appeared all over his body. It was so severe that we rushed him to the hospital, where doctors struggled for three hours to get it under control. After several injections, he finally calmed down.

We returned home exhausted. Then in the morning, it returned with a vengeance. As Peter drove us to the hospital again, I sent text messages on my cell phone to ask for prayer. Psalm 91 came into my mind. The Holy Spirit reminded me of that psalm so many times that I had memorized it.

> *He that dwelleth in the secret place of the most High shall abide under the shadow of the Almighty. I will say of the Lord, He is my refuge and my fortress: my God; in him will I trust. Surely he shall deliver thee from the snare of the fowler, and from the noisome pestilence. He shall cover thee with his feathers, and under his wings shalt thou trust: his truth shall be thy shield and buckler.*
>
> Psalm 91:1–4, KJV

I was afraid Michael was going into shock as he began to struggle to breathe.

"You can *not* touch my family because we dwell in the secret place of the *most High!*" I shouted.

Immediately, Michael became calm and began to breathe normally. I looked at his skin. The redness and angry hives had all disappeared in a moment.

"The itchiness has stopped," Michael said, surprised, straightening up in his seat.

We arrived at the emergency department, where our friend Dr Nelson Gundran met us. But I had nothing to tell him, as all the symptoms had gone. I explained what it had been like on the way there, and told him we had prayed. He had heard before about our prayers for healing, and smiled knowingly.

"Just get these antihistamine tablets, in case," he said, writing a prescription.

We laughed as we made our way back home at a more leisurely pace.

"You certainly told the devil where to go," Peter joked.

Michael didn't need to take the tablets. I kept them in case, as Dr Gundran had advised, and threw them away when they expired. Neither Michael nor I ever forgot the dramatic healing that he experienced that day, or the power of God's Word when spoken with conviction.

As we set about the renovation work, I could see we would need more than our initial daring – a good measure of rational thinking might help, particularly as the first job was to replace the asbestos roof.

"You will dispose of it properly, won't you?" I asked Peter.

"Yes, don't worry," he said.

Since there were no designated facilities for this, I knew he wouldn't.

I enjoyed having a house full of busy people and took on the marketing and cooking as my low-profile contribution. The builders were suitably impressed that I could cook Filipino food for them.

By October, after two months' work, we were able to move into our new home. It was absolutely wonderful. I quickly had everything unpacked and put away. Picking up my journal, I went to sit in the garden with a cup of tea. The garden was actually a pile of rubble, as the builders were still rebuilding the existing kitchen, but it felt good to sit outside under the mango tree. I flicked through the journal, looking for a blank page to write on. I came across pictures I had cut out of a magazine a year earlier, showing the styles I liked if ever we had a home of our own. I peered closely at a picture of a bathroom and bedroom with wood panelling around the walls. Another picture showed a curved driveway at the front of the house, and another French windows looking out onto a garden.

It took my breath away. Everything I had cut out and stuck into my journal in 2004 was right there, in the home we had just moved into. We even had the red-brick tiled floors that I loved in the Old Vicarage, my childhood home!

"Are you alright?" Philip asked, joining me, with his cup of tea.

I was crying again!

Chapter 29

Covered in Grace

If you pull back each time you reach what seems like your limit, you will never know how much you can trust God.

In August 2006 Mama Adella retired from her work at LAMA House. Several families from the village joined us at the front of LAMA House to wave a tearful farewell to her. It was the end of an era. Her health was good and there were no obvious signs of the recent stroke, but it was time for her take it easy. She went home to the Mountain Province to take care of her own grandchildren, and her garden. My parents were fully retired by now and moved from Worthing to Seaford, right on the white cliffs of the East Sussex coastline.

We hired a lady called Elsie as the bookkeeper for LAMA House. At last I could hand over that part of the charity's work to someone who knew about accountancy. That freed me to fill Mama Adella's place to some extent.

* * *

When Amado heard the news that his stepfather had died suddenly, he wasn't sad. He and his sister had both been placed in Pastor Abe's children's home because of their stepfather's cruelty. He was transferred to LAMA House after a few years, while his sister returned home. At home, the stepfather raped her. He was imprisoned, but after a few months her mother withdrew the charges so he was released. Amado's sister was pregnant with her stepfather's baby at the age of thirteen. It had all been a very heavy burden for Amado to bear.

When he came home from the funeral, he told me the full story. "He slashed his wrists, Maam. Some of the neighbours said he had been bitten by a dog with rabies that made him suicidal. Others said it was the weight of guilt that made him do it. I don't care. It's better he's gone."

I looked into his face. Something was different. He looked more like a boy instead of the sixteen-year-old who had grown old before his time.

* * *

I had been searching for a man to fill the position of social worker, supposing that the boys would feel more at ease sharing their struggles with a man. But like teaching, social work was considered a woman's job in the Philippines and any men we came across were decidedly effeminate. But when Frederick arrived to submit his job application, everyone thought he was a police officer. There was something very sturdy about his manner. I wasted no time accepting it – after all he was male, he spoke English, he had a keen sense of humour, and he was an Anglican. He became a strong member of our team. I always smiled when I read his reports.

Of Raffy he wrote:

He portrayed/made a very impressive progress as noted/ commented by the house-parents, and he continues/ sustains his desirable attitude. Accordingly, he does his household task/daily routine and displays a skill/talent for dancing and related activities. Accordingly, his teacher has endorsed/recommended him to take the Accelerated Test which is slated/scheduled on 17 February 2008.

Reading his report was like reading a thesaurus! So after a few months of this wordiness, I asked him to stop using two words when one would do. He very graciously complied, but he retained his favourite word, "accordingly"! Still, his case study reports were like a breath of fresh air to me, because he always looked for something positive to say, unlike many others I had read in the past.

One example is of Raffy's arrival at LAMA House. The social worker who referred him to us had this to say (written in Filipino English): "During his time at the DSWD Centre he was hard-headed (would not accept correction), naughty, insisted on what he wanted, stealing others' money and belongings, fabricates, harms his playmates when teased, eats a lot and always put plenty on his plate at mealtimes."

From the moment Raffy settled in at LAMA House I couldn't recognize any of the disagreeable traits she described, except for occasional theft, which was one of the few things his father taught him how to do. I found him to be quite the opposite of the report's findings. Frederick noted as much in his reports… accordingly!

Like most of our boys at LAMA House, Raffy's deepest longing was to find his mother but she didn't want to be found. She had remarried and had another family. When Raffy was three years old an attorney and his wife fostered him and his older sister. At some point his sister was returned to the DSWD after continually running away and stealing. At age nine, Raffy was also taken back to the DSWD centre. He was heartbroken.

"He has distorted values carried down from parents. He needs a family who would provide him with time, effort, love, understanding, patience, commitment and caring," the social worker's report concluded.

Another long list, but I felt sure we could do something with this one.

There was something different about Raffy – despite his travels he had escaped exposure to the horrors of street life and had retained an air of respectability. I wanted to write to the attorney and his wife and tell them that he was growing up into a fine young man. But they had emigrated. Perhaps that was the reason they could not keep him. At the time, the social worker told little Raffy that he was "not welcome in their house anymore".

"God has kept you in His hands, Raffy. You were kept safe even when you were running away and staying with people you didn't know," I told him. That evening, I used his story to explain to the boys about angels. "It's only natural to rely on what we can see, hear, or touch," I told them. "But there is another world that is just as real; it exists all around us. There are thousands and thousands of angels helping us every day, and nothing in this world can stop them."

That Sunday when Raffy stood to his feet in church to give a testimony, thanking God for watching over him, I knew he had taken my words to heart.

One of the older ladies also stood up to give a testimony. She spoke about her husband who was a fisherman. "We have been hard up lately as my husband slipped and fell last week. The doctor told us he knocked the kneecap right out and tore all the ligaments. He needs surgery. We don't have any money. We could lose our income altogether. Please pray for us," she asked.

"Times are hard for the fishermen. They can't take the boats out to sea during typhoons," Pastor Fred explained, "and those bigger fishing trawlers are constantly entering our territory and using explosives. They grab big hauls of fish and we are left with nothing. It's illegal and destroys the reefs as well as our livelihood. I don't understand why the authorities do nothing to help us."

He asked the congregation to stand, and we prayed for the injured fisherman. He rebuked the authorities and demanded they do something about it... even though there were no coastguards or policemen in our congregation. I had never heard him pray with such authority.

The following week, the fisherman's wife stood up again in church to tell us what had happened. "When they told us that the operation would cost 28,000 pesos I prayed to God. I told Him I wasn't going to borrow from anyone to pay the bill but would trust Him to do it. Thank God, the operation was successful. I went to the cashier to pay our bill, expecting to give a down payment and pay the rest in instalments," she told us. Trembling with emotion, she paused and took a deep breath. "You won't believe me... it came to exactly ninety pesos! They didn't even round it off to one hundred!" she said, laughing.

That was almost £1! Everyone applauded and cheered. Our incredible God. There were often stories like that, as God used all kinds of people in all sorts of ways.

A couple of weeks later we watched, puzzled, as three policemen arrived at LAMA House on a tricycle marked, "Special Police". When I saw them I thought one of the boys was in trouble with the law. But then they lifted several large buckets of fish from the sidecar of the tricycle and presented them ceremoniously at Peter's feet!

"We are seizing the hauls from the illegal trawlers in the bay, and though it best to donate it all to you," they told us.

I remembered the prayer Pastor Fred had shouted in church. Like Jesus' miracle on the Sea of Galilee, we had so much fish donated every week that we were not able to contain it. When we passed some on to Miracle Bible College the students told us they had been praying as food was short.

Like a lot of Filipino men, Peter was a storyteller, and he enjoyed telling the "beach children" the stories of Jesus' life on earth. I loved watching them as they squatted on the floor at his feet to listen. Our modern-day fish miracle prompted him to relay the story of the miraculous catch of fish. "The disciples struggled all night and caught nothing. Jesus told them to try putting down the nets on the other side of the boat. It seemed a silly thing to do but they obeyed. And they caught a load!" Peter told them. They applauded with amazement. Jesus was such a super-hero!

One such Sunday evening, as people climbed into the back of our truck to get a ride back to the beach, one couple stayed behind. "Pastor, will you pray for our daughter, Jennifer? She is very sick and the doctors can't tell us what is wrong with her. She is only sixteen," Manong David told us, tearfully.

We knew Jennifer as she had attended the children's vacation Bible school that Pastor Agusto organized during the summer months. Her father, Manong David, did all the glasswork for the windows in LAMA House.

"Yes, of course. I'll come down there tomorrow morning early," Peter replied.

"I'll come too," I promised.

Like all the homes on the beach it was a very poor place. Several relatives and friends had gathered around Jennifer's bed. Her condition had worsened in the night, so they were already mourning, waiting for her to die. She lay motionless, hardly breathing, on a bamboo bed that took up most of the room.

"She hasn't eaten for over a week," her mother told me.

The scene reminded me of another Bible story about Jairus's daughter, the little girl who died (Mark 5:35–43). "Jesus, what would You do?" I prayed silently. The thought occurred to me that in that case He told the mourners to leave. I looked around at the bleak faces, but didn't have the nerve to suggest they leave the room. We prayed for God to heal Jennifer. But there was no immediate improvement.

"I think you should take her to the hospital. We will help you," I suggested, feeling inadequate.

Peter lifted her tiny body inside our jeep and drove to LORMA Medical Centre, where she was admitted to the intensive care unit. But the doctors were baffled. They could only give her IV fluids and nourishment through a nasal tube to relieve some of the symptoms. After a few days, her family decided to bring her home again.

"We have tried everything, including the witch-doctor," her mother confessed to Peter. She looked embarrassed. The family had become Christians when we first began church services on the beach, and they knew we disapproved.

"Why did you do that? It's better if you look only to the Lord," Peter told her.

I knew Peter was right, but at the same time realized that my faith had been miserably small, too. Miracles require the kind of faith that doesn't need other people's approval. The kind of faith Noah had, when God asked him to build an ark, and there was no sign of rain. We prayed for Jennifer again, and with Manong David and his family, affirmed our trust in God alone.

"Lord, forgive us for doubting. This illness seemed so big and we feel so small. But we put our small faith into Your hands, like the little boy who gave You his bread and fish. This is our step of faith and we trust You to heal Jennifer completely," I prayed.

The next day, Jennifer's father came to LAMA House. He was smiling, like a father who has just witnessed his first baby being born. He couldn't wait to tell me: "Praise God, Maam! Jennifer got up out of bed early this morning! She ate a big breakfast and has been washing clothes with her mother at the water pump!"

Chapter 30

Hearts Tuned for Praising

**... to stand speechless in the presence of Jesus,
hearts beating wildly, staggered and stunned by
what God is doing...**

Mike Yaconelli in *Dangerous Wonder*

Almo had been married for more than six months before his friend Felipe was able to visit. He told us he was also planning his wedding. He had been living with his girlfriend for some time and they had a baby girl. "There won't be many there – just simple," he said, bowing his head.

In evening devotions he asked Peter if he could say a few words to the boys. Still quietly spoken and self-conscious, he told them about his short time at LAMA House. "I didn't pay much attention to the staff when I was here," he confessed, shyly. The boys leant forward, listening to every word. "It was only when I left here that I realized the impact it all had on my life. One night I surrendered my life to Jesus, and now I am trying to live for Him. My advice is to listen to the people who care for you here, and give your life to Jesus. Ask Him to fill you with His Holy Spirit. It's the best thing you can ever do," he told them.

Peter and I looked at each other with tears in our eyes. Evidently God had been working behind the scenes to finish what He had started in Felipe's life. He is the author and finisher of our faith.

Everyone at LAMA House travelled north for the wedding day. Felipe and Jane exchanged vows in a stately

Catholic church that dated back somewhere to Spanish colonial times. Jane was a lovely, gentle girl. I thought they fit perfectly – she even had a discreet tattoo! After the simple wedding ceremony, the priest also dedicated their baby girl to the Lord. On one side of the massive church Jane's parents, relatives, and friends were seated. Representing Felipe, on the other side, was LAMA House family. If we had not been there Felipe's side of the church would have been without a single soul. I thanked God for bringing us together. We felt God's blessing and peace in the old church, knowing Felipe wanted to honour God in his marriage.

The boys all shouted congratulations as we waved goodbye. Felipe cried tears of gratitude and joy. I felt my heart would burst. To Peter, Felipe became like Barnabas who is mentioned in the New Testament as one whose name means "son of encouragement".

The boys persevered in school and I was very proud of them. Delbert was the first of the LAMA boys to be enrolled at college level. Piolo beamed throughout his graduation ceremony from elementary school; he was so pleased with himself. He received an award for "most obedient student"! Much older and taller than their classmates, Amado and Cesar stood self-consciously at the back of the class for the class photo. We celebrated their achievements at LAMA House with everyone's favourite party food – goat.

After he graduated from elementary school, Amado decided to go back home to live with his mother and take care of his sister and the baby. His mother was an alcoholic so I was concerned about him returning to the rough neighbourhood. It was a lot of responsibility to take on. But he found a job as an ice-cream vendor, and made enough money to feed everyone. Whenever he could he visited LAMA House and attended church with us. I was impressed by his maturity. He too let go of the bitterness in his heart and focused on what he could do to build a brighter future for his family.

At the same time, our son Michael graduated from high school. At sixteen he had no idea which career he wanted to pursue. Most of his classmates, both male and female, opted to train as nurses, not because they were interested in nursing – they were not – but because it provided an opportunity to work abroad. I had searched the internet for online courses and had written to several colleges in England for information. But none of that looked like it would work out. Almost every night throughout the school holidays we prayed and discussed together what he should do.

College courses seemed limited to nursing, computer studies, and business management. The university offered a wider range, but it was poorly equipped and classes were regularly cancelled because teachers failed to turn up. The Maritime College and College for Criminology didn't appeal to Michael. After trekking around each centre of learning in San Fernando in the search for information, it was clear I was never going to find anything that was on a par with British standards. It all seemed so haphazard and disorganized. However, as June approached a decision had to be made so Michael opted for a BS in Business Management at LORMA College.

With that hurdle navigated, there was still time in the summer holidays for some fun and relaxation – for our youngsters at least. They joined a youth camp in the mountains with 200 young people from various churches. LAMA boys joined the basketball competition and the choir. They won awards in each singing category – choir, solo, duet, and trio. Interestingly, the basketball trophy was given to a rougher team.

For years Pastor Fred pleaded in the Sunday announcements for more people to join the prayer meeting on Wednesday evenings. But the same faithful handful of middle-aged ladies turned up, along with Ike. In his forties, Ike had attended the prayer meetings every week with his mother since childhood. So one Wednesday, Pastor Fred asked Ike to pray that the young people would meet God in a special way at their youth camp. He was a quiet man, and he prayed quietly, sincerely. Then suddenly he began to pray fervently in tongues; the Holy Spirit praying through him!

The youngsters enjoyed the four days of fellowship, but in the end there wasn't much in the way of rest and relaxation. They had to get out of bed at 5.30 a.m. for devotions. If they didn't make them they missed breakfast. And showers at 6 a.m., in icy cold water, were a shock to the system! They were thankful to come back to our warmer climate and the city lifestyle to which they were accustomed.

In church the following Sunday everyone could see that they had again grown closer to God and each other. They each gave a testimony, telling us about the different food, the cold showers, the games, and the awards they had won. Michael told the congregation about the times of worship. He loved being part of such a crowd of young people dancing and singing. "I wish we could always worship God like that," he told the congregation. I recognized it as a calling on his life.

Later in the service, as several of the young people led worship, Jerome suddenly leapt down the aisle from his seat at the back of the church. He was followed closely by Piolo, dancing with their hands in the air. Jerome was usually so restrained. Their enthusiasm was contagious and the congregation erupted in joyous praise.

As we sang one of my favourite songs I glanced over at Raffy, who was standing with both arms stretched to heaven, completely lost in worship, tears rolling down his face. We were singing a song called "I Am Yours". It spoke about belonging to Jesus, who always hears us calling and always catches us when we wander away or fall. I thought of Raffy's wanderings, and how God had always been there with him. "Thank you, Lord. They might not be anyone else's, but they are Yours!" I prayed, weeping unashamedly

The Holy Spirit was doing something new and exciting in our youth group – there was a revival. It continued through the summer holidays, into the next school year, and long afterwards. The Friday night youth group grew quickly, from around twenty youngsters to over fifty. Among them were several teenagers from Pugo, including Ana's friend Cathy. I noticed that everyone smiled when she entered the church one Friday evening. Perhaps it was those deep dimples, or the twinkle in her very dark brown eyes, or just the fact that she was always so happy.

"Isn't Cathy a lovely girl? Something about her lights up a room," I whispered to Peter, smiling broadly too.

"I know! She has always been like that! I think LAMA boys have noticed as well!" he replied.

On Easter Sunday 2006, Pastor Fred arranged for a baptism service at the nearby river. There were twenty-nine candidates for baptism, including Piolo, Raffy, Carlos, Erwin, Ariel, Bobby, and Bong. Joining the LAMA boys were Michael, Ana, and Simon, and Pastor Fred's children, Hoven and Alaika. They were determined to commit their whole lives to following and obeying Jesus. Piolo could hardly contain his excitement. He had been waiting since 2002 for his turn.

Michael's previous words had been like prophecy. Every Sunday during worship the atmosphere in church was electrifying. Everyone lifted their hands, with tears falling down their faces in adoration. Every week, people were added to the church, many of them young people and children. The youth group began to spend all their free time worshipping together. They watched videos of Hillsong United concerts from Australia or practised their music, often missing meals so they could get straight to church. They were being consumed by worship.

The Wednesday prayer meetings usually started around 8 p.m., but at 7 p.m. Michael was eager to leave for church. His school friends were becoming jealous of church, because he hardly ever went out with them anymore after school.

"C'mon Mum, leave the dishes – we've got to get to the prayer meeting. All the young people are there already," he told me, pushing me out of the door. When we arrived there were forty young people waiting quietly for the adults to get there. Towards the end of the prayer time Ike began to pray again for the young people – that they would know His guidance for their college plans, for jobs, and wisdom in their relationships. His voice was shaking; he trembled as he spoke.

The atmosphere became charged with an almost tangible sense of God's glory. Ike felt he could not speak to an almighty God. He bowed his head and began to quietly speak in tongues. As he prayed, I became conscious of the fact that I had often taken for granted the privilege of prayer. I loved being able to talk to God as my dearest companion but suddenly I was aware of *whom* exactly I was talking to when I prayed! "The Lord Most High," I whispered, as everyone in the room bowed, their faces to the floor.

A couple of weeks later, as the congregation worshipped, I prayed silently that God would pour out His Spirit on us. *Immediately* everyone in the church began shaking and crying and speaking in tongues. I was completely taken by surprise, and for a while dared not open my eyes to look around.

The little children were playing outside, as they usually did after their children's church. They quietly filed in and sat on the floor at the front. No one had told them to. The young girls who had been dancing with tambourines were bowed down, their faces to the floor in worship. My heart was beating fast… something extraordinary was happening. We were in the presence of God, and I felt nervous and amazed. All I wanted was to remain that intoxicatingly close to Him, every day!

Chapter 31

Seizure Disorder

Remember to relax into God. He is the one who never fails.

As told to me by my "uncle", Wallace Brown

In August 2006 the older boys moved into their new home. They enjoyed their new-found independence and kept the house surprisingly neat and tidy, like house-proud women. But as Bobby approached his eighteenth birthday he was undecided about moving on to the "Older Boys Home" that we had established for boys over the age of nineteen. He didn't cope well with change; it made him ill.

"I'll be going now," he told me one evening, having decided to give it a try.

I saw a shadow of sadness creep across his face. For a moment he resembled that ten-year-old little boy who arrived at LAMA House, lost and alone. I hated seeing that old mask reappear. I had nicknamed him "Mr Smiley" because he had such an amazing smile. I had hoped it would be a permanent fixture on his face. "It's only in the next town, Bobby! You are not going abroad!" I told him, and his fabulous smile returned, lighting up his face and mine.

Both he and Carlos had been diagnosed with stomach ulcers. Peter took Carlos to the emergency department one Friday night, after he collapsed in excruciating pain during the young people's service. When Dr Gundran examined him he couldn't understand why someone so young would have such symptoms.

"We usually see this in CEOs: middle-aged men with high-powered jobs," he told me.

"He came to us from a very bad situation. He was very badly abused," I explained, quietly.

"Poor boy, he must have lived constantly worried. It's an indicator of how much he has internalized," the doctor told me.

Sometimes I questioned how the boys could forgive the wrongs done to them, but for their own peace of mind they needed to. Those who held on to the hurt struggled to find joy. The ability to love and trust again evaded them at every turn. Only a supernatural work of the Holy Spirit could cover it. In quiet times, I often revisited my own experience of the baptism of the Holy Spirit, and remembered God's immense love pouring over and into my life. That was what I wanted for them. It had the power to make all things new!

On Friday morning, I stopped to look at the Bible reading for the day – 1 Corinthians 6:9–11:

> *Don't you know that those who do wrong will have no share in the Kingdom of God? Don't fool yourselves. Those who indulge in sexual sin, who are idol worshippers, adulterers, male prostitutes, homosexuals, thieves, greedy people, drunkards, abusers and swindlers – none of these will have a share in the Kingdom of God. There was a time when some of you were just like that, but now your sins have been washed away, and you have been set apart for God. You have been made right with God because of what the Lord Jesus Christ and the Spirit of our God have done for you.*

Powerful words! They echoed in my mind as I left the house to meet up with Pastor and Mrs España for the prison service that afternoon. I thought about the inmates who had found soul-peace inside the jail. A visit to the prison always did me good; it was more like attending a well-established church than visiting inmates.

A new prison had been completed at the outskirts of the city. It was one of the best prison buildings in the country, a huge improvement on the old dungeon-like facility. It could house more inmates, in roomier cells, with a recreation area and chapel. Prisoners were allowed to have fresh food brought in, which they could cook themselves in a kitchen area. Security was tighter and there was a separate wing for female inmates. The only problem was the shortage of water, as it was situated so far from the city. To begin with this caused several riots, but eventually a better system was put in place.

"Maam, you will be our speaker today," Pastor España told me when I arrived. I usually protested when asked to speak with no prior warning, but this time I knew what God wanted me to say.

"OK! I'm ready," I smiled.

The armed guard unlocked the gate and accompanied us through to the chapel area, where fifty or so inmates had gathered. I greeted them happily as Nestor, one of the inmates, stood up to lead the singing. He still bore the image of his old transvestite lifestyle, with tattooed eyeliner like Cleopatra. Looking around nervously I began to have doubts. How could I read those verses? What if there was a riot before I reached the happy conclusion? I would be addressing a crown of adulterers, thieves, and swindlers – in fact all of the above! "Lord, are you sure about this?" I prayed silently, feeling increasingly uneasy as the time for the sermon approached.

"Now Maam Lesley will come and share God's Word with us," Pastor España announced.

I asked him to interpret, so that there would be no misunderstanding.

"Let's read from 1 Corinthians 6:9–11," I said, and began to read slowly, careful not to make eye contact with anyone.

It was noticeably silent, until we came to the verse about those who practise homosexuality, where several giggled uncomfortably. Then Pastor España read the verses again in the Tagalog version, slowly, as I had done.

"… But now your sins have been washed away". I heard everyone exhale. "… You have been set apart for God. You have been made right with God." As they fully realized that Jesus had taken their guilt, their sigh of relief was followed with a loud, united, "AMEN!"

I giggled with delight, and went on to describe the scene in a courtroom, where one stood accused, waiting for the verdict, knowing he was guilty. The inmates nodded; they knew exactly how that felt.

"But before the judge could pass sentence, Jesus stood up. He took the blame, allowing the guilty man to walk free," I said.

All eyes were on me. I looked into their faces and watched as disbelief turned into immense gratitude. *Could this really be true*? they asked wordlessly.

"Who among you would like to be washed clean today?" I asked.

Everyone immediately lifted their hands up in the air.

"*Yes!*" they almost shouted at me.

God's Word was so exact, so sharp! I prayed that I would never again hesitate to preach it. And I knew that it would perform what it set out to do.

As we approached the school holidays in April 2007, Hilary resigned from LAMA House. She was getting ready to emigrate. Frederick had to take six months off so he could renew his expired licence, which left us again without a social worker. Fortunately, Hilary knew someone who could help us. Veronica had worked in a children's home in Manila; she offered to fill in for six months before joining her fiancé in England. Veronica was an absolute godsend and I tried my best to persuade her to call off her engagement and stay at LAMA House instead. But it was not to be!

Mama Myrna needed to move on too. "You have to take care of yourself," I told her, remembering Mama Adella. Pastor Fred's mother-in-law, Mama Norma, took her place in the kitchen.

Michael, now seventeen, had become hopelessly frustrated with college. His class schedule had long hours with nothing to do and he was studying maths and science at a level at which he knew more than his teachers. Impatient, he dropped out after the first year. Instead, he enrolled in a six-month culinary course. He loved it and hoped to go on to diploma level and become a chef.

When I went to England with the twins for their summer holiday, Michael stayed in the Philippines with Peter to finish his course. At my parents' bungalow in quiet Seaford, I was assigned the small bedroom and the twins shared a room. With a few weeks to relax before I started travelling, we explored the beautiful East Sussex countryside together, enjoying the unusually warm spring (springtime in England is summertime in the Philippines). It was perfect.

Towards the end of our visit, in the middle of the night, Simon woke up when he heard a thump and strange rasping noises. He got out of bed and went to switch on the light, stumbling over something on the floor. When he put the light on, he saw that it was Ana. She had fallen out of bed and was shaking violently on the floor, foaming at the mouth. Frightened, he ran into my room and woke me up.

"There's something wrong with Ana!" he cried.

My mother and Esther woke too. Ana was still fitting on the floor. It had never happened before. We were all very worried. The next morning, Ana couldn't remember falling out of bed. She was embarrassed when Simon told her what had happened.

"It's too much television, and sitting in front of that laptop," my mother insisted.

"It could be the orange juice. I read somewhere that it has something in it," Esther offered.

We hoped and prayed that the seizure was an isolated incident as I was leaving the next day to stay with my brother David in Aylesbury in Buckinghamshire for a few days, having been scheduled for follow-up tests at the hospital there. David was at work in London when the phone rang. It was Mum.

"Ana had another seizure in the night. We got an ambulance and took her to the hospital. She is OK now, but you'll have to have her checked when you get back to the Philippines," she told me, nervously.

"I'll be home soon," I said, not knowing what else to say. *Lord! Please not this*, I cried silently. Inside I was panicking.

Throughout my nurse's training the one illness that frightened me was epilepsy. I remembered sitting in the classroom as our teacher explained that its cause and cure were something of a mystery. In the Philippines, like in medieval times, the illness carried a terrible stigma. I had encountered three cases – two of them in children and one in an adult. They were each kept in bamboo cages like wild animals because relatives were afraid of the spirit that possessed them. I had watched uncomfortably as old-school pentecostal pastors yelled and screamed at children, commanding evil spirits to leave. My mind spun around in a confused, tortured muddle.

When David arrived home from work he found me sitting on the settee, my face red and swollen from crying. The television remote lay next to me, discarded.

"I can't figure out how to switch on the TV," I said, dejectedly.

"No need to get so worked up about it," he joked, pressing the right button.

"No, it's Ana. Mum called. She had another fit," I told him, breaking down again.

"It will be alright. She will be OK. With everything you cope with, I know you can get through this. Relax and watch television; it'll take your mind off it all. I'm going to make a delicious Thai green curry," he told me.

When I arrived back in Seaford, a couple of days later, everyone had calmed down, but I could see Simon had retreated into his shell. The twins were inextricably linked in body, mind, and soul. I phoned Peter and told him what had happened. "Please get them to pray together at church for her," I asked. "And Simon," I added. It always felt better, knowing that people were praying for us.

Soon after we arrived back in the Philippines I took Ana to the hospital for tests. Dr Gundran looked concerned as I told him about the seizures. He told me she would need a CT scan and an EEG to see what was happening in her brain.

"When she was younger, she had a head injury. A boy threw a stone that was sharp like a flint. It sliced into her forehead, cutting right to the bone. We took her to the hospital and had it stitched up. The X-ray was OK," I told him, trying to make sense of it.

"It's unlikely that is connected. We would have seen something earlier," he said, looking into my face. I could see what he was not saying: "This could be serious. Brace yourself, Lesley."

He sent us to the X-ray department for a CT scan. I sat, watching her still body move slowly into the scanner, trying to hold back the tears. She was being brave. I had to try for her sake.

The scan result was normal. We went to another department for the EEG. I felt a deep sadness in my heart, like a weight. The EEG results were also normal. Dr Gundran told me just to observe her, that it was probably linked to the onset of her menstrual cycle.

Perhaps it will be alright now, I told myself. But on the inside I was silently screaming, *God, please heal my little girl!*

Chapter 32

Spring Rain

I'm in His hands, so what have I to fear?
I'm in His hands, I feel Him ever near,
He guides my way, He's in complete control,
I'm in His hands, I'm in His hands.

Roy Turner

Back in the Philippines, a seventeen-year-old Erwin came out of the office at LAMA House with a frown on his face. I waited for him to speak knowing that to push for an explanation would send him scurrying to his room in silence.

"That was my father on the phone. He wants me to come home. He's very sick," he told me after several awkward minutes.

"What are you going to do?" I asked.

"Don't know, don't want to go yet. What about school? We have no money there," he replied sadly.

Peter scheduled the twenty-four-hour trip twice, but each time Erwin refused to go. He wasn't ready. We couldn't alleviate his fears with the usual, "If things get bad you can just get on a bus and come back." That wasn't an option in this case. He wrestled with the decision for three weeks then eventually realized that he couldn't leave his sick father there alone. I watched as he got his things together. In the last month or so he had grown tall and his angular face was losing its childlikeness. His voice, which he had rarely used, was now a few tones lower.

"Perhaps you'll find a girlfriend there," I joked with him.

He smiled, putting very few clothes in his travel bag. I thought how handsome he looked when he smiled, another rarity.

"These are for the boys here," he said, pointing to the pile of clothes lying on the bed.

I had seen this before, when Domingo prepared to go home to a place much poorer than LAMA House. "They don't want to appear proud," Peter told me then.

I went downstairs and gathered everyone together so we could pray for Erwin before he left. When he came down the stairs to join us he was wearing an old black T-shirt, worn trousers, and flip-flops, having also given his shoes away. He had changed into his "poor clothes". Peter asked Cesar to pray. The boys and staff bowed their heads, with their hands on Erwin's shoulders, and we prayed God's blessing on him.

"Make sure you text us. We won't forget you, Erwin," I told him, giving him my cell phone number.

"Thank you, Maam," he said.

My mind was wandering as I tried to listen to Peter's sermon in church. I silently prayed for God to keep Erwin, and to heal Ana. As I opened my Bible to find the text of the sermon another verse caught my attention in Zechariah 10:1: "Ask the Lord for rain in the spring, and he will give it."

It jumped off the page, like a command. But what did it mean?

When I studied it later I found other verses about latter or spring rain in the Old Testament, referring to God's favour and refreshment. In Proverbs 16:15 it said, "When the king smiles, there is life; his favour refreshes like a gentle rain."

How lovely! I thought. I imagined God smiling on us! *Lord, I ask you for favour on LAMA House, my family, and our church.*

Soon after that, my brother and sister, Philip and Esther, came for a short visit. We were enjoying the sunshine, sipping tea, and chatting in the garden. Times together were so few and far between. The scene reminded us of times sitting in the garden of the Old Vicarage in Pollington.

"I wonder how David Nellist is doing these days?" Philip said, reminiscing.

"Yes, remember how he used to play that big accordion and belt out those old gospel songs?" I commented, smiling.

"I'm asking rain, in the time of the latter rain. Let it fall, Lord! Let it fall!" we sang together, mimicking him playing the accordion.

"He used to sing that like an Irish drinking song!" Philip laughed.

"Ask the Lord for rain in the spring," the familiar quiet voice reminded me.

* * *

All too soon, preparations were being made for Philip and Esther to return to England. Determined to have some fun, I booked flights to Hong Kong for Michael and me, with a stop over for Philip and Esther. It was an inexpensive package deal.

We stayed in a hotel in busy Yau Ma Tei, visiting Jackie Pullinger's new place at Shing Mun Springs, and the factory where former addicts worked. We visited what used to be Kowloon Walled City, now transformed into the Walled City Garden where a monument honouring Jackie's work stood. Eager to experience everything, I signed us up to join the tour to Shenzhen City in China for a day. It was fascinating. Michael loved every minute. For some unknown reason he was always very interested in anything Chinese or Korean.

"Shenzhen City was built in the 1970s, replacing a small fishing community. The region was opened up as a special economic zone and quickly grew from a population of 30,000 to over 11 million, now mostly young people," our young tour guide told us on the bus.

We were sitting at the front, so she chatted to us as the bus travelled to a theme park and shopping centre. She told us that many Filipinos joined the tours and that several had tried to give her a Bible. "We have no god in this city. I don't worship God or Buddha. There is a Catholic church in China, somewhere in the mountains, but nobody could tell you how to get there," she said.

I thought about the millions of young people in Shenzhen City with no knowledge of God and no Bible. Her words rang in my ears long after I returned home to the Philippines with Michael, like a call to prayer: "We have no god in this city."

China was still in my thoughts as I sat in the regional jail, back in San Fernando. Next to me sat Solomon, a frail-looking man in his fifties. He had a Bible, which he obviously took great delight in. I could see he had underlined most of it and scribbled notes in the margins. He carefully turned the pages, searching intently for the verses mentioned in Peter's sermon. Having been there for eighteen years, guilty until proven innocent, he was the longest-serving inmate.

"I accepted Christ many years ago. I love reading my Bible," he told me.

He always wore his smart clothes for the chapel service – black faded trousers and a long-sleeved yellowing-white shirt – but they were still old and threadbare. "None of my relatives or friends ever came to visit me here," he said, sadly.

When I went back a couple of weeks later there was an air of excitement in the jail service. As Nestor stood up to lead the singing, I looked around for my seat-mate. Apo Solomon was absent. ("Apo" means "Lord", a title given to respected elderly folk.)

"Apo Solomon is not here today. He had his final hearing last week and the judge sentenced him to eleven to seventeen years. He has already served eighteen, so he was promptly released," Nestor announced.

Everyone applauded as Nestor jumped up and down with glee, clapping his hands like a cheerleader.

"Think of it: eighteen years in this place and all the time God took great care of him," he said, standing still with his hands cupped in front of him.

In that moment I *got* the picture, as I looked at Nestor's hands. I could see Erwin and the boys who had come and gone from LAMA House, each of them precious to God. And I saw each of my children – completely safe in *His* hands! In the situation, yes, but sheltered in His hands. And there was no need to fear.

* * *

Four months had passed since Ana had had the seizures in England. She was back to her normal busy self, spending her free time at church with Michael and Simon and the worship team. After the young people's church one Friday, she stayed at Pastor Fred's house for the night with Simon, Allaika, and Hoven. The following morning, the four friends were playing games on the computer when, without warning, Ana collapsed and slid on to the floor. Her face hit the concrete as she began to have a seizure.

She knocked out a tooth and her lip was torn, with the broken tooth embedded in it. Hearing their shouts for help, Pastor Fred ran inside the house. Simon and Hoven were trying to carry Ana's limp body, with blood all over her shirt! They quickly told him what had happened. He took her to the hospital.

I arrived at LORMA Medical Centre as soon as I could. She had already been taken to the operating room for emergency surgery. Rushing through the hospital, my mind was a blur. I slumped down in one of the seats in the narrow hallway outside the operating room. From inside, Dr Tolentino noticed my arrival and he came outside to reassure me. "Don't worry; I can fix it. Her tooth has broken off and will have to be capped. The lip is repairable," he told me.

He was operating for longer than I expected. I phoned my parents, told them what had happened, and asked them to pray. "Lord! My beautiful Ana," I pleaded. I didn't know what to pray. She was still sleepy when the nurse wheeled her bed out. Dr Tolentino followed close behind.

"It was more difficult than I first thought – which is why we were so long. I had to reattach the muscle to repair her smile. But I think you will agree that it went well. I managed to follow the lip line for most of it and when the swelling has subsided, it will hardly be noticeable," he told me.

Repair her smile… repair her smile… His words resounded in my head. He looked at me, concerned. I wasn't alright.

"Please… don't worry," he said, smiling weakly.

I stayed next to her bed until she opened her eyes. She lifted her hand to feel the bandage covering her upper lip and began to cry.

"The doctor said you won't notice the scar later. You just need your tooth fixed, like Michael did when he fell off his skateboard. Dr Tolentino did a great job. Isn't he lovely?" I said, trying to allay her fears.

She didn't respond.

Anti-convulsive medicine was prescribed. At first it made her sleepy. Ana was always so full of life; now an enemy was trying to steal that away. How dare he!

"He who dwells in the secret place of the most High shall abide under the shadow of the Almighty!" I shouted at the enemy again (from Psalm 91:1). But this time his fleeing was not so obvious. There are no formulas with God.

When we went back to the hospital for her follow-up check-up, Dr Tolentino was pleased with the result. He had indeed done an excellent job. This time Ana managed a tentative, slightly crooked smile. You look like Angelina Jolie, I joked, trying to hide my real feelings. The actress had made it fashionable to have swollen lips! Dr Tolentino agreed. Ana liked him – she looked at me as if to say, "Yes, Mummy, he is lovely!" Suddenly, my eyes filled with tears. I so missed Dr Christian again.

Soon, she was full of life once more, busy preparing weekly Bible studies for school and activities for the children's church on Sunday. We slept together on the floor, praying every night for God to take her illness away. Instead, He helped both of us face the problem head-on and dispel the fear that came with it. We turned to our Bibles for support. In my Amplified Bible, John 14:27 told us not to be "fearful", "intimidated", or "unsettled". That summed up exactly how we felt. It also described my immediate response to the deep-rooted sexual problems that enslaved some of the boys at LAMA. Fearful, Intimidated. Unsettled.

I read from the United Christian Broadcast devotions that my father sent me, "God's finest treasures are hidden, like gold or diamonds. He does not always remove the unpleasant from our lives because often his best rewards are hidden there!"

Ana loved to study her Bible. I could see God was building extraordinary courage in her soul. She only suffered seizures two or three times in a year. Piolo and Carlos had also been having seizures, though more often and more severe. Piolo's self-esteem was shattered because of frequent fits, and the side effects from the medicine made him moody and depressed.

In church, Ana led the youth choir. She quoted Psalm 139:13–18 before they sang their song:

You made all the delicate, inner parts of my body and knit me together in my mother's womb. Thank you for making me so wonderfully complex! Your workmanship is marvellous – how well I know it. You watched me as

I was being formed in utter seclusion, as I was woven
together in the dark of the womb. You saw me before I
was born. Every day of my life was recorded in your
book. Every moment was laid out before a single day had
passed. How precious are your thoughts about me, O
God! They are innumerable! I can't even count them; they
outnumber the grains of sand! And when I wake up in
the morning, you are still with me!

As Ana read the words, the choir sang softly in the background:

You hold the universe!
You hold everyone on earth!
You hold the universe! You hold… and you hold!

I remembered – they were the words that God gave me when I
was pregnant with the twins. Now they were sixteen years old!
I looked at Ana, and Simon accompanying the choir on the
guitar, and I thought my heart would burst.

Sitting at the back of the church with Pastor Fred's wife,
I noticed a man in front of me who didn't usually attend the
service. As usual Pastor Fred asked people to stand if it was their
first time attending. As the smartly dressed man got to his feet to
introduce himself, he began to tremble from head to foot.

"I came here to ask for forgiveness Pastor, because I mocked
you and your church for years. My wife is a Christian, but I
wouldn't allow her to come here. Please forgive me. I am sick,
and may not have long to live. I was running for councillor in
the local elections, but last week I took down all my campaign
posters. I feel like I have been beaten and it is God who has
finally won!" he said.

Pastor Fred told him that there wasn't a problem, that
he was forgiven, but the man continued to weep and tremble
uncontrollably. Ike's mother got out of her seat and joined
Pastor Fred behind the pulpit.

"This is my neighbour, Tony. He came to my home when he was campaigning for the elections. For years he has ridiculed me for being a Christian. When he apologized to me I thought it was only so he could get my vote. I told him he needed to know Jesus. I don't know what happened between then and now, but he is here, praise the Lord!" she explained.

The congregation responded with applause. I could see the man sitting in front of me still couldn't stop crying and shaking.

Pastor Fred invited him to come forward for prayer. Tony repeated the words as Pastor Fred prayed with him: "Heavenly Father, I have been wrong. I ask you to forgive me and make me clean. I believe Jesus died for my sins and I accept Him as my Saviour. I make Him Lord of my life. Thank you for loving me. Thank you for your peace in my heart. Amen."

He could hardly make his legs work to get back to his seat, where he sat with his head bowed, crying quietly. I had never seen the Holy Spirit come over someone with such obvious, bone-rattling conviction. Tony later told us that he was an alcoholic. His doctor had told him that his liver would never recover. He had only a few months to live.

In the days that followed, he introduced his best friend and drinking partner to Jesus. Joker attended the church services drunk at first, dancing with our boys with special needs at the front of the church. Gradually, he stopped drinking altogether; instead he craved more of God. In 2012 he joined our workforce at LAMA House. The boys adopted him as their father.

Sadly, Tony died peacefully in his sleep at the age of forty-six. At the wake I assured his wife that her husband was in heaven. She looked at me sceptically, worried about his alcoholism and the destruction that had resulted from it. "I want to believe you, but how can I be sure?" she asked. I reminded her how Jesus had met with Tony in such a special way, and explained that salvation is a gift that none of us deserve. She sighed a deep sigh of relief. I think she understood.

***

One Sunday, Joker was in church with his wife and daughter. Alejandra's son John Mark led the congregation in worship, with Michael, Ana, Simon, Ammen, Hoven, and Aljhun – our worship team. I could almost hear angels worshipping Jesus with us. John Mark knelt on the ground in adoration. The little children came inside as before – silently, reverently. They knelt at the front of the church, some of them crying and praying, waiting for God to meet with them again. I looked over at Aljun, Ike's ten-year-old son, who was playing the drums. He lifted his head to heaven, with tears running down his face. It looked like he was being drenched in a sudden downpour of rain.

"It's raining," the Holy Spirit whispered to me.

"Oh!" I gasped.

It was the rain in springtime, and it felt as if *nothing* else mattered!

Chapter 33

In Christ is Everlasting Life

I hadn't seen Tatang Sia for months. Mariano told me his father had been very ill with renal failure and was having dialysis three times a week. So when I saw him sitting at his store front I pulled up a plastic stool and sat down next to him for a chat.

"Hi Lesley, how are you? You look good. You have gained a bit of weight! I am getting thinner," he said.

"We have been praying for you," I told him.

"It is difficult being ill like this, especially with all the medical expenses, but I am happy because my family are all settled and doing well, including my grandchildren," he said, smiling contentedly.

I smiled back at him.

"Mariano is doing OK; his family are all fine. Business is good. Betty is enjoying life in America. Anson and his family are in New Zealand. He is pastor of a Chinese church," he told me, summarizing his family news. "All my medical bills are paid. I am ready to leave this life – no need to spend more money on doctors," he concluded.

His doctor had suggested a kidney transplant, but he decided not to have any more procedures done. He seemed so full of peace.

"Can I pray with you, that God will heal you?" I asked.

"No, it's OK. All is well," he assured me.

***

As the school year in 2008 came to a close I booked flights to England for myself and Ana. This time I had arranged an itinerary of twenty-five churches to visit during the six weeks.

I told my listeners the real-life stories: Erwin leading his father to Christ, and how he put on his poor clothes when the time came to go home; Apo Solomon, safe in God's hands for eighteen years inside the jail; and the inmates who understood that they could be washed cleaned. I told them about the rain in springtime that came down on Pastor Fred's church. As I spoke about the wonder of God at work, people began to weep. They longed for God to shower their churches with the same refreshing rain.

Ana and I ate well, slept well, and travelled well on cheap, booked-in-advance train tickets. The English countryside was at its best in springtime. We had a very special time together.

We arrived back in the Philippines on a Saturday.

"Did you know that Tatang Sia died on Friday?" Pastor Jim asked me, when I stepped inside LAMA House on Monday morning.

I felt disappointed. I wasn't sure if he had accepted Jesus for himself. I told Pastor Jim about my conversation with Tatang in his shop, and how peaceful he was as he talked about his family.

Alejandra had recently returned from the Middle East, where she had been working as a nanny. She came with me and Peter that evening to the wake. The highway outside Joces Funeral Home was lined with cars when we arrived. The entire Chinese community had gathered to pay their last respects. Chinese funerals were lavish affairs, steeped in ritual and superstition. We approached the chapel nervously, unsure of what we would find there. But as we entered the building Bella hurried over to us, as if she had been waiting for the most important guests to arrive. "Tatang gave his life to Jesus before he died. We have great peace because we know he is in heaven with Jesus. We are not sad," she told me in hushed, excited tones.

Mariano greeted us as we made our way down the hallway to the chapel where the coffin was laid. We waited outside, not sure if it would be proper for us to enter and unsure of the Chinese customs. The chapel was full of family and friends, all wearing white, and the overflow chapel opposite was also filled to capacity. Mariano's son came to meet us at the door and beckoned us inside.

Hanging from the ceiling were many white banners with Chinese script written on them. Bella told me they represented each Chinese family present at the wake. An elaborate open coffin was positioned at the front, draped in a red banner, surrounded with flowers.

Anson jumped up from his seat when he saw us. All eyes were on him; people were puzzled as to why he was so happy. He could not contain his excitement as he told us of the events leading up to his father's death.

"When Bella told me that Tatang was deteriorating, I arranged to come from New Zealand right away, anxious that he should accept Christ. I arrived on the twenty-first and went directly to his bedside. But before I could say anything he took hold of both of my hands and smiled. 'Anson, in Christ is everlasting life,' he said. I was amazed! I told him I had come to pray with him so I could lead him to Christ, but he already knew Him! He just smiled and held my hands, repeating, 'In Christ is everlasting life.' I asked him if he wanted to be baptized and he told me 'Yes! Yes!', so I contacted the Baptist pastor and we baptized him in the name of Jesus!"

Anson accompanied us to the coffin, where we stood for a few minutes together. I asked about the beautiful red drape inscribed with yellow embroidered Chinese script.

"It says 'In Christ is everlasting life!' " Anson explained, beaming.

"This is so wonderful, Anson," I said, overwhelmed with happiness.

"Everyone is asking me what it means. I don't mind what Chinese rituals the others observe at the funeral. They might think I am crazy but I'm so full of joy because one day I will see him again in heaven!" he said.

As I hugged Nanang Sia, I sensed the same peace radiating from her.

"I'm glad you could be here with me to witness this day," I told Alejandra, as we walked hand in hand back to the jeep.

We both felt like we were walking in the clouds.

Shortly after Tatang Sia's funeral Peter went to Hawaii for two months. While he was away Michael helped me with the driving, waking up early to take the twins to school every morning. It wasn't easy getting everyone up and out of the door before 7 a.m. Before we knew it, it was the beginning of August 2008.

One Sunday morning, the service had started as we came through the back door quietly. We had overslept and were late. As we sat down at the back with the boys from LAMA House, Carlos whispered something to Ana.

"Mummy! Carlos said Cathy has been killed. He said her heart was cut out!" Ana told me, her face white as a sheet.

"What? Don't take any notice of that! That's horrible!" I retorted.

Putting my arm around Ana's shoulders, I frowned at Carlos. Why would he say something like that? It wasn't like him.

Pastor Fred stood up to address the congregation. "I have some very bad news. We have just heard that Cathy, one of our young people from Pugo, has been killed," he said.

I gripped Ana's shoulders tightly. She looked up at me, in dreadful pain, buried her head in my lap, and started to sob.

Everyone was crying as Pastor Fred continued, his voice shaking. "She was getting ready to come to church, and was on her way to her cousin's house to invite her. No one could stop the man; what he did was so brutal we can't believe it. A lot of our children saw what happened. The police came and arrested him, but it was too late for Cathy," he told us.

My mind couldn't process the news. It couldn't possibly be true. It was too evil, too unthinkable. As the service continued, we were only going through the motions, as if in a terrible, distorted nightmare. But at LAMA House afterwards reports of what happened forced us to face up to the gruesome reality. The national media were in Pugo, and police officers were continuing investigations. Even they had never heard of such brutality. Mario, who worked as our carpenter, came to LAMA House in a daze, relating what he had seen. He had witnessed the murder as it took place very close to his house. He blamed himself, and was consumed with guilt because he froze in terror and was unable to rescue Cathy or shield his children from seeing it.

"Why would God save me from alcoholism and give me a new life, then allow something so terrible to happen to Cathy? She was His child... she was perfect," he asked me. There were no answers.

Jose also lived near the crime scene. His children, like Mario's, were exposed to the full horror of it. When the police finally came, Jose's older daughter helped him to lift Cathy's mutilated body into a tricycle to take her to the hospital. The terror was etched on the children's faces.

"How will they recover from this?" Mario's wife Maricel asked me, searching my face for answers. She taught the children's Sunday School at church. I hugged her close to me, silently. I had no idea what to say.

Ana had another seizure in the night, worse than before. I cried as her body stiffened and she struggled to breathe, pleading desperately for God to carry the sorrow for her and spare her any more pain.

Jeanette had to break the awful news to her husband Ben, who was working in the Middle East. Their precious daughter was dead. Our team of pastors held evening services for two weeks at the wake, as we waited for Ben to come home. "The Lord gave Cathy to us, and now He has taken her away. We don't understand, but He is God," Jeanette told everyone one night at the wake.

Though confused and blanketed in grief, it was clear she, and Ana, were being carried in God's strong arms. It was headline news and reporters interviewed Jeanette over and over again. The scenes were replayed on national television every day, every gory detail. Jeanette looked worn out.

There were seemingly endless discussions of what happened, in graphic detail. Autopsy pictures were passed around and people visited the crime scene. Perhaps they felt that by talking about it often, they would eventually become desensitized. I shielded my children from the photos and stories as much as I could. The man was in jail, but fear gripped the village. I could see it in the faces of those who attended the wake, in the boys and staff at LAMA House, and the young people and children at church. Many couldn't eat meat for months afterwards because of the memory of what the man had done to Cathy.

In church, a very dark cloud covered the congregation. It was difficult to sing about God's goodness and love. I could see that Pastor Fred felt he had nothing to give, so I asked him if I could speak. "Thank you," he said, relieved.

From behind the pulpit I looked across at Mario, who was sitting at the back staring blankly ahead. Next to him sat Peter's brother Jerry and his family, who considered Cathy as their own daughter. They were completely weighed down with grief. Jeanette and Ben and their three boys sat next to them, lifelessly.

"God didn't do this!" I said. I could see them grasp the words, like a lifeline. "We have an enemy, and he won't sit back idly when God pours out His blessing on us. But we do have a hope. We have the Holy Spirit to comfort and teach us. It's OK to question Him and, even though we may never understand, He will give us his peace. If we understood everything about God, He would not be God. This is so terrible, we can hardly bear it – but we don't grieve like those who have no hope, because we know that Cathy is alive with Jesus forever!" I told them.

Peter couldn't change his return flight to come home for the funeral. He would be in Hawaii for another month. As we left home for the funeral, I had never felt so alone in all my life. "It's you and me, Lord," I whispered resolutely,

"This will be the hardest part," I warned Michael, Ana, Simon, and the boys. They nodded silently.

The coffin was taken by hearse from Jeanette and Ben's home in Pugo to the big Catholic church in Bauang. Hundreds of people joined the funeral procession through the village, singing Cathy's favourite worship songs that were playing from the car stereo. Everyone was dressed in white. When we came to the church there were hundreds more people already inside. A group of students stood outside, with banners protesting against drug abuse. Television crews were there with their cameras; it would be on the national news again. We took our places inside the church, Ana sitting with Cathy's family. The service was a beautiful tribute to our beautiful girl. All the students and teachers from Cathy's school attended, dressed in their uniforms. For almost one hour after the service people filed reverently past the coffin. It reminded me of the funeral service for Princess Diana.

"She was our princess," Ana told me.

* * *

For some time we had been planning to construct a playground for the younger boys at LAMA House, but it was quite an expensive project and we had put it on hold. Derek and Margaret Martin from England donated money from their ruby wedding anniversary, and then Steve and Joy Pegg's daughter had her class of students raise money for it. So we decided to make the playground a memorial to Cathy.

Mario and the team of builders started work on it right away. It was therapy for them. Ben, Cathy's father, was fashioning the wooden posts for the see-saw when a team of US Marines arrived unexpectedly.

"God has sent the Marines!" I told Karen, our new bookkeeper, as we watched them approaching.

"We have been assigned in the Philippines for a few weeks, working with the coast guard here. We heard about LAMA House and all chipped in with a bit of money to give you," their captain told me.

I introduced them to Ben, Mario, Pastor Jim, and Karen and explained the story behind the playground. I was glad to have someone to talk to in my own language, and told him all about Cathy and the children whose faces displayed the awful trauma.

"We have just come from Afghanistan. All I can tell you Maam is that it takes time. But time does heal," he replied. He seemed so young, and his team even younger.

"How long have you been working in the Philippines?" he asked.

"It is twenty-six years this year," I told him.

He was surprised at my answer.

"What you are doing is very honourable," he said.

I objected. They risked their lives; my efforts paled in comparison. But I thought about the principle of giving your life for others and knew nothing could compare to living that way.

"It is in losing your life that you find it," I thought aloud.

"Yes," he agreed.

We had never had a visit from the US Marines before. I felt God had sent them to us for a higher purpose than just to donate some money. Their dignified manner and powerful presence brought calm perspective, a blessing that was beyond understanding.

Karen and I accompanied the marines to the office, to write a receipt for their donation. I smiled as she nervously attempted to count the money three times.

Receipt in hand, Captain Varda and his men left.

"Are you OK, Karen? You forgot how to count for a while there," I joked.

"Phew! They are *so* handsome!" she laughed.

* * *

Ana arrived home from school at the beginning of October, with a spring in her step. "Mummy, I found a really nice verse, look! Here in Job 19:25–27: "But as for me, I know that my Redeemer lives, and that He will stand upon the earth at last. And after my body has decayed, yet in my body I will see God! I will see him for myself. Yes, I will see Him with my own eyes. I am overwhelmed at the thought!" she read.

Wonderfully, God had spoken to her to put her mind at rest. She knew Cathy was happier with Him, and that she would see her again in heaven.

Later that month, we were shaken with more bad news when a brain aneurism almost took the life of Mama Norma, our cook at LAMA House. She had emergency brain surgery. We expected recovery to be very slow and difficult. The church prayed fervently.

On 15 December, Cathy's birthday, we held a memorial service to dedicate the new playground. As families from the barrio arrived, I could still see the sadness hanging over them. Many had tears in their eyes. Cathy's brothers planted a tree as Peter spoke: "We have to release the pain and anger. You don't have to forget in order to forgive. We can't ever forget. But we hope that this playground will be a reminder of Cathy's love of life. The plaque reads, 'Donated by Derek and Margaret Martin, Class 4D of Longlevens Junior School, and the US Marines – in memory of Cathy, who always made us smile!' That is what we choose to remember, her lovely smile," Peter said, fighting back the tears.

Each child who witnessed Cathy's murder held a balloon. There were twenty or so. Everyone stood in complete silence as the blue and white balloons were released, floated up, grouped together, and disappeared from sight. For a long time afterwards people in the barrio talked about how the balloons joined together to make their journey heavenwards, as usually they fly off in different directions. Someone suggested an angel took hold of them and carried them away.

That Sunday we sang Cathy's favourite song. The words by Reuben Morgan go like this:

Hide me now
Under your wings.
Cover me
Within your mighty hand.

When the oceans rise and thunders roar,
I will soar with You above the storm.
Father, You are king over the flood,
I will be still and know You are God.

Since Cathy's death, Ana and friends had not been able to sing it without breaking down in tears. But this time the meaning did not seem so jumbled up in our minds. We knew that no matter what, He was still God.

Can anything ever separate us from Christ's love?
Does it mean he no longer loves us if we have trouble
or calamity, or are persecuted, or are hungry or cold
or in danger or threatened with death?... No, despite

all these things, overwhelming victory is ours through Christ, who loved us. And I am convinced that nothing can ever separate us from his love. Death can't, and life can't... Our fears for today, our worries about tomorrow, and even the powers of hell can't keep God's love away.

Romans 8:35–38

Chapter 34

Author and Finisher

Mama Norma recovered very quickly from brain surgery. In her place, we asked Jeanette to work as cook and house-mother. Jeanette was an inspiration. She possessed that deeper spiritual capacity that comes from trusting in God's goodness despite having experienced the absolute worst that humankind is capable of. Her faith sustained her as the court case for Cathy's murder dragged on. Whenever I attended a hearing with her I found it gruelling, reliving the details of what happened to Cathy, the man who killed her sitting close to us in the cramped courtroom. It was frustrating and emotionally draining. We longed for it all to be over.

For months the children who witnessed Cathy's murder had terrible nightmares, the trauma stamped on their faces. I was afraid that the damage might be permanent and wished there was some form of professional post-traumatic stress counselling available, as there was in Indonesia after the tsunami. The need for a psychologist had been foremost in my thoughts.

At other times, it seemed psychology was not the answer, but rather God's Word and His holy presence. Time and again we had proved God's Word as a very real antidote to Satan's lies and activity. We taught our boys not to live their lives based on what others had done *to* them, but on what God said *about* them in His Word, and what Jesus had done *for* them. Most of the time we simply watched with amazement as the Holy Spirit painstakingly made them whole again.

Jehu's band and Michael's worship team were often invited to minister in youth gatherings. There was a special anointing and sense of destiny on them. At the beginning of 2010 we revisited the detention centre with them, having arranged a praise concert for the detainees. The band and the worship team were nervous as they looked out at the audience of severe faces. It was not at all what they were used to, but they gradually relaxed as the boys in the audience clapped and swayed in time with their music.

Andy Pegg was visiting and joined the team. He told the boys how accepting Jesus as his Saviour had completely changed his life for the better. He had spent his childhood years in the jungles of Papua New Guinea, where his parents, Steve and Joy, were missionaries. He lived his life on the edge. That had led him into drugs and gangs, but when he recently surrendered to Christ he was miraculously freed. Now he was filled with passion for Jesus, a greater, wilder adventure!

The young detainees could identify with his testimony and listened carefully to every word. When Peter asked if anyone would like to accept Jesus into their life, almost everyone put up their hand.

I sent a text to Pastor Fred suggesting the little children lead worship in church as the worship team were tired after the praise concert. Three little girls had just arrived at Pastor Fred's house – their parents had sent them to deliver some fish for his dinner. After they barbequed the fish and ate together, he asked them to practise some worship songs with him. Pastor Jim brought three of the little boys from LAMA House to join them.

They arrived early on Sunday morning, dressed up in their best Sunday frocks, ribbons in their hair, and their best sandals on. Our LAMA boys were smart in cotton shirts that my mother had sent them. When Pastor Fred asked them to join him at the front to lead worship, the girls took off their sandals. He asked them why they had done that. They didn't answer him, because they didn't really know why.

The presence of God was very real as they sang. I whispered to Peter that everyone should take off their shoes because it seemed we were standing on holy ground. Everyone bent down and took off their shoes with tears in their eyes. Nothing is more effective than God's love and His presence in its power to make us strong in the broken places. Over time, as the children from Pugo worshiped, the nightmares were erased and their faces only reflected His smile.

News reached us in February 2010 that Pastor Abe Duclayan had suffered a serious stroke, the first of several that paralyzed him and left him unable to speak. He cried when Peter and I visited to pray with him. I couldn't help but remember the times he had laid his hands on me and prayed with miracle-working power. It was sad to see him so weak and small. But God is God of our strong places and our weak places. Pastor Abe's wife Stella and son Ray carried their ministry through the long, difficult months that followed. "I'll always be here to help you. Your family are my family," I promised Ray. He knew I meant it.

In March 2012 Ray texted me telling me that Maam Stella was critically ill. I rushed to the hospital right away. When I arrived at the intensive care unit she was on a ventilator as the doctors had suggested her lower leg be amputated due to gangrene in her foot. Her lungs and heart were not functioning.

She was agitated, not wanting any more procedures done. Ray had to make the most difficult decision of his life – whether to stop the ventilator or struggle on with another operation against her will. I held his hand and we prayed together – that was all I could do. The next day she was allowed to go home, to be with Pastor Abe and her friends and family. She died on 16 March at the age of fifty-seven. I felt honoured to have been with her and Ray in her final moments.

Almo and Amado came with us to attend the nightly services before the funeral. Almo's son looked exactly like him when he was little. But whereas Almo conversed in grunts, his son had grown-up conversations with me as soon as he learned to talk. When they came to visit me, he showed me the colouring and writing he was learning in nursery, and proceeded to tell me all the gossip from their barrio, in great detail. I loved to watch father and son together.

People came from all over the region to say goodbye to Maam Stella, many of them old friends from Miracle Bible College from when I was there in 1984. It seemed strange that so much time had passed. I didn't feel that old, but Maam Stella was only a few years older than me.

Then on 30 March we heard the sad news that Pastor Bercero had died, at the age of sixty-five. He had also been ill for several years, following a series of strokes. Peter and I went to Miracle Church that evening to visit the wake. Many of our old friends were there when we arrived. I looked around for Sammy, but couldn't find him. *I've hardly seen him in the past twenty years*, I thought, unhappily.

At the last night of the wake, I found him. He looked so broken. I went to sit next to him as photos of Pastor Bercero were flashed on a screen at the front of the church. One came up on the screen of Sammy and me at his high school graduation, soon after I first arrived in the Philippines. I smiled and commented, and Sammy tried to smile back, but I could see he was completely spent.

At the funeral, Peter and I went over to stand with him. I prayed silently for God to give him the strength he needed. My instinct was to hold on to him and never let him out of my sight again, but Filipino culture didn't allow for such public displays of affection. So I sat down next to Mrs Bercero, and hugged her instead. "I am very tired. It has been a difficult few years," she whispered as I kissed her forehead.

"Can you get Sammy's cell phone number?" I asked Peter before we left the cemetery.

The next day I sent a text to him. "When I arrived in the Philippines in 1983, you became my little brother," I said.

"That's right," he replied. How I had missed him! We were reconnected!

At the beginning of 2011, I entered into the struggle to reaccredit LAMA House with the DSWD for the third time. The standards had become even more stringent under President Ninoy Aquino. That was all very well, but the weight almost crushed me. For the whole year it took all my time and effort to improve on policies, make long-range plans, and provide reports and forms for everything we did at LAMA House. But I knew God was with me to help me as He opened up the way for the right people to come alongside me.

I found two psychologists who were thrilled to join our team. Ester and Pearl were both professors in psychology at a nearby university. God gave us professors! I had no idea how to formulate the many forms needed. Sammy, with his knowledge and experience in business administration, helped me with it all. He was literally a godsend. In the end, LAMA House was one of the few facilities that received accreditation.

Earlier, on 14 September 2010, I had accompanied Jeanette to the courtroom for the final sentencing of the man who had killed her daughter. Two years had passed. She was worried that the judge would accept his insanity plea, allowing him to go free after a few years. She gripped a photo of Cathy in her hand as we waited all morning for our turn. There were still several preceding cases when the judge abruptly decided to read out the sentence. She must have seen the torture that Jeanette was going through, sitting directly behind the accused.

The judge ordered the man to stand to his feet.

"You are found guilty beyond all reasonable doubt. You will be sentenced to life in prison with no opportunity of bail," she told the accused.

Then she looked over at Jeanette, with a faint smile.

It was finished!

But, as we left it all behind and made our way back to LAMA House we felt nothing – not even relief.

It is easy sometimes to understand why bad things happen to bad people. But if we go through life on that assumption, and somehow believe that only good things should happen to good people, it won't help us cope with inevitable pain. Only God's grace is sufficient. Jeanette understood that.

In one of my favourite books, *Personal Revival: God's Way of Setting Our Hearts on Fire*, author S. J. Hill says this: "A life without suffering, a life without the oil of Myrrh, will be a life without the beauty and anointing of Christ. In the Lord, nothing of real spiritual value comes cheap."

He goes on to explain:

> *Each encounter with the pressure of God's "oil press", is not only intended to crush our self-will, with its pride and independence, but also to allow the anointing oil of God's Holy Spirit to be fully released in our lives. How many times have we made attempts in our own strength to grow in the character of Christ only to fail miserably? How many times have we made "spiritual New Year's resolutions" only to never act on them? The only way we can experience the anointing, the beauty and the holiness of Jesus is to allow the Holy Spirit to blend the various ingredients of His grace into our lives. The "Great Perfumer" is the only One who knows this wonderful "art". Therefore, we must be willing to undergo the process… Our Father always leads us this way to prepare us for a richer, purer anointing!*

The Bible speaks of people sometimes having great faith, and sometimes little faith, and says everyone has a measure of faith. When Peter, the disciple, risked everything and dared to walk on water with Jesus he started to sink when he saw the waves. Jesus grabbed him and told him his faith was small. The other disciples were still cowering in the boat, distant observers, who probably had keen advice for the sinking Peter. Surely Jesus was not berating him... with his little faith he had just walked on water.

When little David faced Goliath, a giant and trained killer, he picked up five stones to put in his slingshot. Why five? Some theologians suppose the five represent the name of Jesus; others say Goliath had four brothers. Could it be that he was not sure he could do it with the first shot... that he had just enough faith to stand there, in the name of the Lord of Hosts... with his five stones? I can relate to that.

My friend Grant, who was in the youth group at Brunswick Baptist Church in Gloucester with me, told me what Pastor Charles Price had to say on the subject. At Keswick Convention one year Pastor Price had told a story about the first time he flew on an airplane when he was eighteen years old. He was a bit nervous, knowing that planes sometimes come down when they are not supposed to. He got on the Boeing 747 and was seated with two other people. On his right, a little old lady who had never flown before was terribly nervous, gripping the seat armrests. She told him she was going to visit her grandchildren for the first time; if not for them she would not even consider risking her life. On his left a well-travelled businessman was seated. He was not nervous at all. He simply relaxed and took out a book to read through the journey.

Each had a different measure of faith. But they all arrived at their destination safely. "That's because," he explained, "the all-important issue is not the quantity of faith you have, but the object you put your faith in. If you have mustard seed-sized faith and you put that in God, God will work!

"Of course, the more you *know* the object of your faith, the more utterly trustworthy you know Him to be!"

What do we have to do so that we can know Him like that?

A young man asked Jesus that question. The story is in Luke 18:18–27:

"Good teacher, what should I do to get eternal life?"

"Why do you call me good?" Jesus asked him.
*"Only God is truly good. But as for your question, you
know the commandments: 'Do not commit adultery. Do
not murder. Do not steal. Do not testify falsely. Honour
your father and mother.'"*

*The man replied, "I've obeyed all these
commandments since I was a child."*

*"There is still one thing you lack," Jesus said. "Sell
all you have and give the money to the poor and you will
have treasure in heaven. Then come, follow me."*

*But when the man heard this he became sad, because
he was very rich. Jesus watched him go and then said
to his disciples, "How hard it is for rich people to get
into the Kingdom of God! It is easier for a camel to go
through the eye of a needle than for a rich person to enter
the Kingdom of God!"*

*Those who heard this said, "Then who in the world
can be saved?" He replied, "What is impossible from a
human perspective is possible with God."*

If we think Jesus is only talking about money we miss the point. This good man was also rich morally. They are probably the saddest words in the Bible, I think, having done the same thing myself: "Jesus watched him go." As he sadly walked away, people were thinking, "How then can *anyone* be saved?" Where does that leave us… who have failed so miserably? Was Jesus being unreasonable? The fact is, we can't be good enough. We can only know God because Jesus has covered our sins in His righteousness. When we simply accept that, his Holy Spirit does the unexplainable.

As I prepare this book for the publisher, Sammy prepares to work at LAMA House as my assistant, having resigned from his job as a manager at a large company. Five little street boys have just arrived from San Fernando City – scared, unmanageable, their feet unbelievably dirty.

Editing these pages, I can see the hand of the "Great Perfumer" that S. J. Hill mentioned in his book in each one of my chapters:

12.5 lb pure myrrh – laying down one's life;
6.25 lb cinnamon and sweet calmus – bowed down in true worship, a channel through which life can flow;
12.5 lb cassia – costly, extravagant love for God; our desires, ambitions, wills, all given to Jesus;
1 gallon of olive oil – the work and presence of the Holy Spirit in our lives.

To know God like this, to trust in how huge He is, and to have a little faith in the broken little ones He brings across our path – it's worth leaving everything for.

Peter said, "We have left our homes and followed you."
"Yes," Jesus replied, "and I assure you, everyone who has given up house or wife or brothers or parents or children, for the sake of the Kingdom of God, will be repaid many times over in this life, as well as receiving eternal life in the world to come."

Luke 18:28–30

Further information about
LAMA Ministries

If you would like to contact LAMA Ministries, the address to write to in the Philippines is:

LAMA House
PO Box 19
San Fernando City
La Union. 2500
Philippines

Website: www. lamaministries.org
Email: lesley.gomez@gmail.com

United Kingdom Charity Registration number: 1008940
Life And More Abundant Ministries